ICC GUIDE TO INCOTERMS 2000

Understanding and Practical Use

by Professor Jan Ramberg

International Chamber of Commerce

The world business organization

Published in November 1999 by
ICC Publishing S.A.
International Chamber of Commerce
The World Business Organization
38 Cours Albert, 1er
75008 Paris, France

Published by arrangement with ICC Publishing S.A.

ICC Publishing, Inc.
156 Fifth Avenue
New York, NY 10010

ICC Publication No. 620
ISBN 92-842-1269-3

Foreword

By Maria Livanos Cattaui, Secretary General of ICC

The *Guide to Incoterms 2000* is the authoritative companion work to *Incoterms 2000*, the ICC official rules for the interpretation of trade terms. The guide responds to business needs for a better understanding of these ICC rules that are used in countless commercial transactions every day.

Incoterms have been revised in line with the latest changes in contemporary commercial practice. An understanding of modifications to the 1990 edition of Incoterms is essential to ensuring that Incoterms 2000 are applied in a uniform way worldwide.

The present guide explains in detail each of the 13 terms that constitute Incoterms 2000. It is an expert commentary on the various obligations governed by Incoterms and draws attention to pitfalls in drafting international sales contracts. Diagrams give a graphic presentation of the seller's and buyer's respective transport obligations and, in particular, the distribution of costs and risks. Illustrations make it easier to understand all aspects of the new Incoterms.

I am confident that this guide will be an indispensable tool for all those involved in international commercial transactions. It will be required reading for traders, carriers, freight forwarders, insurers, bankers, lawyers and researchers.

ICC is indebted to Professor Emeritus Jan Ramberg of the University of Stockholm, Chair of the ICC Working Party on Trade Terms, which drafted Incoterms 2000. Author of both the *Guide to Incoterms 1980* and *Guide to Incoterms 1990*, Professor Ramberg has participated in three successive revisions of Incoterms. As an internationally respected writer and lecturer, he was the obvious choice as author of the *Guide to Incoterms 2000*.

Contents

Seller's and buyer's obligations: an overview   51

UNDERSTANDING
INCOTERMS

What are Incoterms, and what can they do for you?

The word "Incoterm" is an abbreviation of International commercial terms, and the chosen Incoterm is a term of the contract of sale (N.B. not of the contract of carriage).

Trade terms are, in fact, key elements of international contracts of sale, since they tell the parties what to do with respect to

■ carriage of the goods from seller to buyer, and

■ export and import clearance.

They also explain the division of costs and risks between the parties.

Merchants tend to use short abbreviations – such as FOB and CIF – to clarify the distribution of functions, costs and risks relating to the transfer of goods from seller to buyer. But misunderstandings frequently arise concerning the proper interpretation of these expressions.

For this reason, it was considered important to develop rules for the interpretation of the trade terms that the parties to a contract of sale could agree to apply. Incoterms, first published by the International Chamber of Commerce in 1936, constitute these rules of interpretation. Their official title is International Rules for the Interpretation of Trade Terms.

Referencing Incoterms in a contract of sale

Although Incoterms, in so far as they reflect generally recognized principles and practices, may become part of the contract of sale without express reference, the parties are strongly advised to

■ include in their contract in conjunction with the trade term the words "Incoterms 2000"; and

■ check whether a standard contract used in their contract of sale contains such a reference, and, if not, superimpose the standardized reference "Incoterms 2000" to avoid the application of any previous version of Incoterms.

In recent years, Incoterms have been revised at 10-year intervals (Incoterms 1980, 1990 and 2000). These revisions are necessary to ensure that Incoterms represent contemporary commercial practice. Nevertheless, a disadvantage is that confusion may arise in the marketplace when merchants either fail to observe there has been a change in the rules of interpretation or fail to clarify which version of Incoterms should apply to their contract. In addition, fundamental changes to the rules, if not properly introduced, could endanger the status of Incoterms as a generally recognized international custom of the trade. Indeed, the reason the 1980 UN Convention on Contracts for the International Sale of Goods (CISG) did not deal with interpretation of trade terms was a belief that this task could be more efficiently taken care of by the International Chamber of Commerce in cooperation with its national committees worldwide.

To avoid confusion and difficulties in applying Incoterms, a reference to the current version should always be made in the contract of sale. When parties negotiate their contract individually, they should take care not only to refer to Incoterms but also to add the year 2000. If they use a standard contract they should check whether it has been updated to include reference to "Incoterms 2000". If not, the previous year should be replaced by the year 2000.

The differences between Incoterms 1990 and Incoterms 2000

The most important differences in substance between the 1990 and 2000 versions concern

- the placing of the export clearance obligation under FAS on the seller (previously on the buyer);

- the specification of the seller's obligation to load the goods on the buyer's collecting vehicle and the buyer's obligation to receive the seller's arriving vehicle unloaded under FCA; and

- the placing of the import clearance obligation under DEQ on the buyer (previously on the seller).

In addition, the terminology in Incoterms 2000 has, in some instances, been changed for consistency and ease of understanding. The revision aimed at generally updating Incoterms and the result may, to some, appear rather meagre. In particular, the strong demand for a change of the traditional "FOB-point" met considerable resistance from the great majority of the ICC national committees.

But the result of the revision should not be underestimated, since it has improved the understanding of FOB, CFR and CIF and contributed to a better use of Incoterms, so that these terms can be avoided when they are no longer appropriate. In other words, rather than removing the notion of "crossing the ship's rail" – the so-called FOB-point in FOB, CFR and CIF – the parties are invited to choose such terms as FCA, CPT and CIP where delivery of the goods is connected to the handing over of the goods to the carrier.

What Incoterms cannot do for you

Incoterms do not deal with

- transfer of property rights in the goods;

- relief from obligations and exemptions from liability in case of unexpected or unforeseeable events; or

- consequences of various breaches of contract, except those relating to the passing of risks and costs when the buyer is in breach of his obligation to accept the goods or to nominate the carrier under an F-term.

Merchants often believe that Incoterms can solve most of the problems which may arise in practice. Indeed, most of the questions put forward to the ICC Panel of Experts on Incoterms concerned matters other than the interpretation of Incoterms themselves. Frequently, the questions referred to contractual relations other than the contract of sale, such as the obligations of the parties under documentary credits, contracts of carriage and storage. Many questions concerned obligations of the parties other than those connected with the delivery of the goods. Therefore, it is necessary to emphasize that Incoterms are only rules for the interpretation of terms of delivery and not of other terms of the contract of sale. This explains why – apart from the seller's fundamental obligation to make the goods available for the buyer or to hand them over for carriage or deliver them at destination, and apart from the buyer's obligation to take delivery – Incoterms deal only with obligations in connection therewith, such as the obligations to give notice, provide documents, procure insurance, and pack the goods properly and clear them for export and import.

Transfer of property rights

In many jurisdictions, the transfer of property rights in the goods requires that the party take possession of the goods either directly or indirectly through the transfer of documents, such as the maritime bill of lading, controlling the disposition of the goods. However, in some jurisdictions, the transfer of property rights in the goods – the so-called transfer of title – may depend solely on the intention of the contracting parties.

Frequently, the contract of sale determines whether the buyer has become the owner of the goods. In some cases, the buyer may not become the owner when the seller, under a so-called retention of title clause, may have decided to retain title to them until he has been paid. The applicable law will decide the extent to which such clauses are effective in protecting the seller when he has surrendered possession of the goods to the buyer. The ICC Model International Sale Contract (hereinafter referred to as ICC Model Contract; see ICC publication N° 556 in the Appendix) underlines that retention of title clauses are not always effective and that the seller should carefully check the relevant law, normally the law of the country where the goods are situated, to determine if and to what extent he may rely on Article 7 of Part B of the Model Contract (see p. 9 of publication No. 556).

Unforeseeable and unavoidable events

Even though, according to Incoterms, the parties undertake obligations to perform various matters to the benefit of the other party – such as procuring carriage and clearing the goods for export and import – they may be relieved from such obligations, or from the consequences of non-performance, if they can benefit from exemptions under the applicable law or terms of their contract other than those concerning Incoterms. Thus, according to the CISG, the parties may be relieved from their obligations if they are prevented from performing due to reasonably unforeseeable and unavoidable "impediments beyond control". Standard contracts frequently contain explicit force majeure, relief or exemption clauses more or less corresponding to the main principle of CISG Article 79. Such a clause appears in the ICC Model Contract, Part B, Article 13.

Consequently, if a seller or a buyer is prevented from exporting or importing the goods due to an unforeseen export or import prohibition, his obligation under the contract of sale may be suspended, or, if the prohibition lasts for a long period of time, avoided altogether. In the aforementioned Article 13, a period of six months is required in these cases before a party is entitled to terminate the contract with notice. Although Incoterms do not deal with the circumstances in which an obligation undertaken in connection with delivery of the goods may be avoided or modified, it is important to remember that any type of obligation – whether covered by Incoterms or not – is subject to the applicable law or other terms of the contract.

Breaches of contract

Incoterms – in the A5, B5 and A6, B6 clauses – deal with the transfer of risks and the division of costs. It follows from the A5 and B5 clauses that the risk may be transferred from the seller to the buyer before the goods have been delivered, if the buyer has failed to fulfil his obligation to take delivery as agreed or to give appropriate notice to the seller when the buyer is to nominate the carrier under the F-terms. In these cases, costs arising because of the buyer's failure to fulfil his obligation would also fall upon him under the B6 clauses of Incoterms.

However, apart from these specific cases involving the buyer's breach, Incoterms do not deal at all with consequences following from breaches of the obligations under the contract of sale. These consequences follow from the applicable law or other terms of the contract. To note a few examples: if the buyer does not pay for the goods in time, he has to pay so-called default interest (see the ICC Model Contract, Part B, Article 6). If the seller does not deliver the goods in time, he has to pay so-called liquidated damages to the buyer. These damages are calculated by charging certain percentages of the price of the goods for each period of delay (according to the ICC Model Contract, Part B, Article 10.1, this would amount to 0.5% of the price for each complete week of delay). When the maximum of liquidated damages has been reached (5% of the price of the delayed goods), the buyer may terminate the contract by notification to the seller after having given notice to the latter allowing him a further five days for the delivery.

If the goods do not conform with the requirements of the contract, the consequences are set forth in Article 11 of the ICC Model Contract. The Article says that the seller should either replace the goods with conforming goods, repair them or reimburse the price to the buyer. If the contract is terminated, the buyer may be entitled to damages not exceeding 10% of the price of the non-conforming goods. If the buyer retains the non-conforming goods, he may obtain a discount not exceeding 15% of the price.

Agreeing on modifications to the standard terms

In Part A of the ICC Model Contract, the parties are asked to consider whether the standardized terms in Part B are suitable, and, if not, to agree on modifications. In some cases, where time is of the essence, it may be appropriate to insert a fixed cancellation date, so that if goods are not delivered by that date the buyer could immediately cancel the contract by notification to the seller (Part A, clause 9 of the Model Contract). In addition, the percentages of the price payable in case of delay according to the standardized terms in Part B may be replaced by higher percentages or a fixed amount, depending on an agreement by the parties.

Summary: limits of Incoterms

In summary, as far as the seller's obligation to deliver conforming goods is concerned, Incoterms determine when the seller has fulfilled his obligation to deliver the goods on time but no more. The consequences following from the seller's non-performance must be found elsewhere. Ideally, the simultaneous use of Incoterms and the ICC Model Contract should provide most of the answers required.

Incoterms and contracting practice

Incoterms standardize contract practice by enabling the parties to

- use generally recognized key words;
- agree on the most common understanding of such key words; and
- avoid misunderstandings in the use of them.

Problems remain because

- commercial practice is inconsistent;
- variations of the basic key word may be not appropriate or sufficiently clear;
- the Incoterm is not sufficiently precise; and/or
- the parties inadvertently choose the wrong term.

The need for interpretation of "key words"

Short abbreviations, such as FCA, FOB and CIF, can be regarded as "key words", which, when used, unlock a number of rights and obligations. But these key words cannot be understood unless they are given a specific meaning through rules of interpretation. It is only through interpretation that Incoterms are indispensable. In the absence of an authoritative interpretation, merchants may suffer from great confusion.

It can be debated whether the key words included in Incoterms represent consistent commercial practice. Ever since the first version of Incoterms in 1936, every effort has been made to ensure that this is the case. But a number of short expressions used by merchants do not correspond to Incoterms. To note a few examples, the term CFR frequently appears in contracts of sale as C&F. In some cases, CFR appears as C+F. One can generally assume that the parties in these cases intended that the abbreviations mean the same as CFR, but it is far better, for the sake of clarity, to use the term as written in the official text.

In other cases, however, the parties may choose an expression which is not consistent with any of the terms represented by Incoterms. One example is FOB+I. Here it is apparent that the parties intended to add an insurance obligation for the seller. But it is not clear whether it is of the same kind of obligation as one finds under CIF and CIP. Consequently, disputes can arise as to the extent of the seller's insurance obligation when it appears in another term.

In the preambles to the various Incoterms, strong warnings have been inserted to the effect that merchants should explain as precisely as possible what they mean when they use a variation or an addition to an Incoterm.

The most common practice

Unfortunately, commercial practice is not the same in all parts of the world. Therefore, Incoterms can do no more than reflect the most common practice. In many cases, it is impossible to reflect in Incoterms what actually happens in connection with the loading and unloading of the goods to and from the means of transport. Nonetheless, as noted, in Incoterms 2000 further efforts have been made to assist the users of Incoterms in this regard. In particular, under the term FCA when the goods are picked up, the revision clarifies the seller's obligation to load the goods on to the buyer's collecting vehicle, and the buyer's obligation to unload the goods when they are delivered for on-carriage on the seller's arriving vehicle.

However, it has not been possible to find such a consistent commercial practice with respect to the loading of ships under FOB and the unloading from ships under CFR and CIF. Here, the type of cargo and the loading and unloading facilities available in the seaports will determine the extent of the seller's obligations under FOB and the type of contract he has to procure to the benefit of the buyer under CFR and CIF.

Before the contract of sale is concluded, therefore, the parties are advised to ascertain if there are any particular customs of the port where the goods are to be loaded under FOB, because these customs are quite different in different ports and may create surprises for the uninformed party. If, for example, the goods are to be loaded on board a ship in the seller's home port, and under FOB the buyer has to nominate a ship, he should ascertain the extent to which costs will be included in the FOB freight and whether there will be some additionals debited to him following the loading of the goods on board.

The traditional FOB point – meaning that risks and costs shift from the seller to the buyer when the goods pass the ship's rail at the named port of shipment – has been criticized for not reflecting what actually takes place in seaports. Nevertheless, ever since the 1700s many customs of the port and commercial practices have been developed around the notion of the FOB point. Even though a different wording would perhaps better reflect contemporary commercial practice, confusion simply could not be avoided if such a fundamental notion as the traditional FOB point were to be changed. For these reasons, it was decided to retain the FOB point in Incoterms 2000.

Under the term EXW, it is a fairly consistent commercial practice that the seller assists the buyer in connection with the loading of the goods on to the buyer's collecting vehicle, either by bringing the goods on to a ramp for loading or by loading the goods on to the vehicle. However, under EXW the seller has no obligation to assist; he only has to make the goods available for the buyer and no more. If the buyer wants to ensure that the seller's obligation is extended, he has to agree with him at the time the contract is concluded. This is sometimes done by adding the word "loaded" after the term EXW ("EXW loaded"). However, such an addition does not clarify whether the seller's risk of loss of or damage to the goods should be extended to include the loading operations. The parties should make clear whether the addition of the word "loaded" means "loaded at seller's risk" or "loaded at buyer's risk".

If it is intended that the seller bear the risk during the loading operations, the parties could preferably contract using the trade term FCA, since in Incoterms 2000 it is now made clear that under FCA the seller has to load the goods on to the buyer's collecting vehicle. The choice of FCA instead of adding "loaded" after EXW would bring the parties entirely within the authoritative interpretation of the trade term, whereas any self-made addition means that they contract at their own peril. However, using FCA instead of EXW also shifts the obligation to clear the goods for export from the buyer to the seller, which may or may not be what the parties intend.

Containerization

Trading patterns are usually difficult to change, even if the reasons for the choice of the trade term have changed and call for quite another choice. As an example, consider the changed routines for cargo handling. Since the late 1960s, particular difficulties have arisen in maritime trade where containerization (which occurs when the goods are prepared and stowed in containers before the arrival of the ship) has made the traditional FOB point wholly inappropriate. It bears repeating that FOB, CFR and CIF are appropriate only when there is delivery to the carrier by handing over the goods to the ship – specifically across the ship's rail – which simply does not take place when the goods are containerized.

When containerization takes place, the goods are either collected at the seller's premises (a common practice when homogenous cargo is stowed by the seller in containers constituting a full load, i.e., so-called FCL-containers) or delivered to a cargo terminal where the goods are stowed in containers for later lifting on board the container vessel (the normal case when heterogeneous goods do not constitute a full load, i.e., so-called LCL-containers).

The parties may think the differences really do not matter and may believe that things will sort themselves out in any case. This is incorrect. The seller should take care not to remain at risk after the goods have been handed over to the carrier that the buyer nominates. This is particularly important when the seller has no possibility to give instructions with respect to the care and custody of the goods, which occurs, for example, when the carrier is obliged only to take instructions from his own contracting party, the buyer.

Insurable interest under FOB (please see page 26)

A Seller's insurable interest	B Buyer's insurable interest

Seller's risk | Buyer's risk

No Insurance | Buyer's warehouse-to-warehouse insurance

Damage occurs here!

Checking how the goods are handed over for carriage

It also happens that the parties may choose a trade term intended for maritime carriage when they contemplate using other modes of transport. They believe, quite wrongly, that if a trade term has served well for maritime carriage it must also be appropriate for other modes of transport.

FCA, FOB, CPT, CFR, CIP and CIF compared

A Seller	C Carrier	B Buyer

Risk/cost transfer point under **FCA CPT CIP**

Risk/cost transfer point under **FOB CFR CIF**

C-terms

Contract of Carriage between Carrier & Seller

F-terms

Contract of Carriage between Carrier & Buyer

However, the parties are always strongly advised to check how the goods are, in fact, handed over for carriage, thereby avoiding the choice of a term which keeps the seller at risk after the goods have left his direct or indirect control. The choice of FOB should be restricted to cases in which the goods are actually intended to be (a) lifted across the ship's rail, or (b) tendered to the ship in hoses for liquid cargo, or (c) filled from silos when the cargo is to be carried loose in bulk. In all other cases, FOB should not be used. Instead FCA, indicating the actual place where the goods are handed over for carriage, is the appropriate term.

Under the C-terms, since the seller makes the contract of carriage, it may seem irrelevant whether the risk passes when the goods cross the ship's rail or earlier when they are received by the carrier in his terminal. Nevertheless, if the seller wishes to avoid being at risk after handing over the goods for carriage until loading on board the ship, he should refrain from using CFR or CIF and instead use CPT or CIP, where the risk passes upon the handing over to the carrier. With regard to container traffic, such handing over will normally take place in the carrier's terminal before the arrival of the ship. If loss of or damage to the goods occurs during the carrier's period of responsibility, it may, in practice, become impossible to ascertain whether it has occurred before or after the passing of the ship's rail. This is another reason for choosing a trade term, such as FCA, CPT or CIP, where the risk of loss of damage to the goods passes from the seller to the buyer when the goods are handed over to the carrier.

The seller's duty to provide substitute goods

It should also be noted that the seller's possibility to recover from his insurer in case of loss of or damage to the goods does not relieve him from his duty to perform the contract; he is still required to provide goods in substitution for the goods which might have been lost or damaged while he was still at risk, for example, during the period from handing over the goods for carriage until they crossed the ship's rail.

Cargo handling costs

Buyers are often concerned that their agreement to accept delivery at an inland point, rather than when the goods pass the ship's rail, could result in an obligation for them to pay additional costs charged by cargo handling facilities, terminals or the carriers themselves (transport handling charges, THC). However, this can easily be taken care of by an agreement between the parties either to split these costs or to place them entirely on the seller (for example, by inserting clauses to read "50% of THC to be paid by the seller" or "THC for seller's account").

Checking availability of documents required under an Incoterm

It happens that the parties fail to take into account that the maritime terms call for particular documents – namely a negotiable bill of lading or a so-called sea waybill – which are simply not available when other modes of transport are used. Negotiable bills of lading are not used for other modes of transport because sale of the goods in transit – which traditionally requires a bill of lading for title of the goods to be transferred to the next buyer – does not occur when the goods are carried by road, rail or air. This means that if a seller in London, for example, undertakes to sell goods CIF Yokohama when the goods are to be carried by air from London to Yokohama, he will find himself in the unfortunate position of not being able to fulfil his obligations under CIF to present an on board bill of lading to his buyer. Moreover, he would be the victim of his indifference or ignorance in that he has given the buyer the possibility of escaping a bad bargain by invoking the seller's breach of contract in not presenting the correct document under CIF Incoterms.

Why are as many as 13 Incoterms required?

The purpose of Incoterms is to reflect contemporary commercial practice and to offer the parties the choice among

■ the seller's minimum obligation only to make the goods available for the buyer at the seller's premises (EXW);

- the seller's extended obligation to hand over the goods for carriage either to a carrier nominated by the buyer (FCA, FAS, FOB), or to a carrier chosen and paid for by the seller (CFR, CPT) together with insurance against risks in transit (CIF, CIP);

- the seller's maximum obligation to deliver the goods at destination (DAF, DES, DEQ, DDU, DDP).

Incoterms are sometimes criticized for offering an abundance of different terms. Would it not be possible to restrict the number of terms so that the parties would be invited either to choose delivery at the seller's place or at the buyer's place? The answer is that commercial practice involves different trading patterns for different types of cargo. With respect to commodities, such as oil, iron, ore and grain, the goods are frequently carried in chartered ships accepting the cargo as a full load. In this type of trade, the ultimate buyer may not be known, since the goods may be sold in transit. This, in turn, explains the need for a negotiable transport document, the bill of lading. Moreover, even if the ultimate buyer is known, he is usually not prepared to accept costs and risks which occur in the seller's country. This explains the need for the maritime terms, which are still used for the largest volume of world trade.

With respect to manufactured cargo, however, maritime terms are seldom appropriate. Here, in most cases, the parties are well advised to use one of the Incoterms appropriate for delivery at the seller's place (EXW or possibly FCA) or delivery at the buyer's place, i.e., the destination terms, DDU and DDP.

With respect to insurance, it is only when the goods are intended to be sold in transit that it is appropriate to let the seller undertake an insurance obligation to the buyer. In other cases, the buyer should preferably arrange his own insurance so that the insurance cover can be adapted to his particular needs.

Which Incoterm should be chosen?

Commercial practice and the type of goods will dictate whether

- the seller should refrain from undertaking any additional obligation;

- the seller is prepared to do more than to make the goods available to the buyer at the seller's premises;

- the buyer's bargaining position allows him to require the seller to undertake extended obligations;

- the seller is able to undertake additional obligations, and, in particular, to quote a more competitive price by extending his obligations;

- it is necessary to use the maritime terms FAS, FOB, CFR or CIF when the goods are intended to be resold by the buyer before they reach the destination.

The ICC Model International Sale Contract

INTERNATIONAL CHAMBER OF COMMERCE

For the guidance of users of this model contract, the following box contains a list of some transport documents in common use, with an indication of the type of transport for which they are appropriate. Some of the documents listed hereunder are documents of title, which give to their holder the right to dispose of the goods, while others are simply documents which evidence the delivery of the products to a carrier or warehouseman.

Type of Document	**Bill of Lading**
Mode of Transport	Sea. Also frequently used for multimodal transport.
Comments	Transferable Document of Title allowing buyer to sell or pledge goods while in transit by transferring the documents at any rate where made out "to order".
Type of Document	**Multimodal Transport Document**
Mode of Transport	Transit involving carriage by at least two different modes of transport.
Comments	Known by many names: Combined Transport Document, Container Bill of Lading, Fiata Multimodal Transport Bill of Lading and other variations.
Type of Document	**Seawaybill**
Mode of Transport	Sea.
Comments	Known by many names: Cargo Quay Receipt, Non-negotiable Bill of Lading, Liner Waybill. Non Transferable. Seller may alter delivery directions until discharge, unless the SWB contains a NO DISP clause preventing such change.
Type of Document	**Mate's Receipt**
Mode of Transport	Sea.
Comments	Document providing proof of delivery to a carrier. Sometimes given to shipper when selling FOB or FCA, to be tendered to buyer instead of Bill of Lading.
Type of Document	**Air Waybill**
Mode of Transport	Air.
Comments	Sometimes also known as air consignment note.
Type of Document	**Consignment Note**
Mode of Transport	Land.
Comments	Also sometimes known as CIM (rail) or CMR (road) consignment note or waybill.
Type of Document	**Warehouse Warrant**
Mode of Transport	Land & Sea.
Comments	Transferable document used when the goods are warehoused for collection by buyer at seller's end or at buyer's end.
Type of Document	**Freight-forwarder's Documents**
Mode of Transport	Sea, Air, Land or multimodal.
Comments	Important to identify whether the forwarder is undertaking responsibility for the carriage of the goods as carrier or as agent of the carrier.
Type of Document	**Packing List**
Mode of Transport	Sea, Land or multimodal.
Comments	A document recording what has been packed into a lorry, package or container. May represent proof of delivery as between seller and buyer, but important to identify who has issued the list and at what stage.

ICC International Sale Contract (Manufactured Goods Intended for Resale)
A. SPECIFIC CONDITIONS

These Specific Conditions have been prepared in order to permit the parties to agree the particular terms of their sale contract by completing the spaces left open or choosing (as the case may be) between the alternatives provided in this document. Obviously this does not prevent the parties from agreeing other terms or further details in box A-16 or in one or more annexes.

SELLER   CONTACT PERSON   BUYER   CONTACT PERSON
NAME AND ADDRESS   NAME AND ADDRESS   NAME AND ADDRESS   NAME AND ADDRESS

A-1 GOODS SOLD
DESCRIPTION OF THE GOODS

IF THERE IS INSUFFICIENT SPACE PARTIES MAY USE AN ANNEX
A-2 CONTRACT PRICE (ART. 4)
CURRENCY:
AMOUNT IN NUMBERS: AMOUNT IN LETTERS:

A-3 DELIVERY TERMS
Recommended terms (according to Incoterms 1990): see Introduction, §5

☐	**EXW**	Ex Works	named place:
☐	**FCA**	Free Carrier	named place:
☐	**CPT**	Carriage Paid To	named place of destination:
☐	**CIP**	Carriage and Insurance Paid To	named place of destination:
☐	**DAF**	Delivered At Frontier	named place:
☐	**DDU**	Delivered Duty Unpaid	named place of destination:
☐	**DDP**	Delivered Duty Paid	named place of destination:

Other terms (according to Incoterms 1990: see Introduction, § 5)

☐	**FAS**	Free Alongside Ship	named port of shipment:
☐	**FOB**	Free On Board	named port of shipment:
☐	**CFR**	Cost and Freight	named port of destination:
☐	**CIF**	Cost Insurance and Freight	named port of destination:
☐	**DES**	Delivered Ex Ship	named port of destination:
☐	**DEQ**	Delivered Ex Quay (duty paid)	named port of destination:

Other delivery terms
☐

CARRIER (where applicable)
NAME AND ADDRESS   CONTACT PERSON

The present contract of sale will be governed by these Specific Conditions (to the extent that the relevant boxes have been completed) and by the ICC General Conditions of Sale (Manufactured Goods Intended for Resale) which constitute part B of this document.
SELLER   BUYER
SIGNATURE   SIGNATURE

PLACE _____ DATE _____   PLACE _____ DATE _____

Extract from ICC publication No.556. © ICC

Extract from ICC publication No.556. © ICC

Terms and business strategies

Sellers and buyers seldom reflect on the choice of an Incoterm for every transaction. Normally, the choice is determined by their business strategy. As noted, the choice of the maritime terms in most cases depends on the type of the cargo and the buyer's intention to sell the goods in transit. Here, the choice between any of the F-terms rather than the C-terms depends on the ability of sellers and buyers to obtain the most favourable contract of carriage.

In countries where the seller has good possibilities of procuring maritime transport, or where he is induced to use a national shipping line, he may prefer to use CFR or CIF. Where the buyer for the same reasons has good possibilities to procure the transport, he is likely to insist on the choice of FAS or FOB. In the same manner, the choice between CFR and CIF depends on the seller's and the buyer's insurance arrangements and their possibilities to arrange insurance at the most competitive rate.

In principle, the same considerations apply with respect to the sale of manufactured goods. In this case, however, sellers, in order to remain competitive, frequently have to sell on extended terms using either DDU or DDP. But when a small exporter sells goods to a sizeable wholesaler or department store, these buyers may find it more advantageous to arrange for transport in order to ensure just-in-time deliveries at the most competitive price. In such cases, the buyer may prefer to use EXW or FCA.

CPT or CIP may be appropriate when the buyer prefers that the seller procure carriage (CPT), or carriage as well as insurance (CIP), but if the buyer would nevertheless accept bearing the risk of loss of or damage to the goods when in transit. It should be added that the term CIP unamended is inappropriate with respect to manufactured goods, since the insurance cover is far too restrictive and additional insurance is therefore required. Normally, the most extended cover available (e.g., Clause A under the Institute Clauses of the London Underwriters) is appropriate.

Recommended terms and other terms

The ICC Model Contract lists all Incoterms in A3 of the specific conditions. In addition, there is a particular box and space for delivery terms other than Incoterms. However, as indicated, the parties should carefully consider whether it is appropriate to use a term other than an Incoterm. If they do so, they should ensure that no misunderstandings could arise with respect to its interpretation.

The ICC Model Contract distinguishes between "recommended terms" and "other terms". It appears that only maritime terms have been listed under "other terms". This has caused some concern in countries (such as Japan) where, in most cases, goods are exported or imported on maritime trade terms.

But in the case of manufactured goods, it is unlikely that the choice of a traditional maritime term will be appropriate, because these goods are usually containerized. If so, FCA, CPT or CIP should be chosen and not FAS, FOB, CFR or CIF.

Manufactured goods will rarely be picked out of the ship by the buyer under the trade term DES or landed on the quay under DEQ. If, under a D-term, the seller is likely to make the goods available to the buyer in a cargo terminal, either DDU or DDP would be appropriate.

The distinction between "recommended terms" and "other terms" in the ICC Model Contract contributes to an appropriate choice of the trade term, so that the agreed point of delivery under the trade term coincides with the point where the goods are actually handed over for carriage.

Incoterms and the contract of carriage

The relation between Incoterms and the contract of carriage creates particular problems, because

■ some Incoterms can be used only when the goods are intended to be carried by sea (FAS, FOB, CFR, CIF, DES and DEQ);

■ the same terms are often used in both contracts of sale and contracts of carriage;

■ commercial practice under contracts of carriage changes from time to time and varies in different places, ports and regions;

■ the contract of sale is sometimes difficult to match with the contract of carriage;

■ the parties may continue to use a traditional Incoterm when it has become inappropriate because of changed commercial practice (for example, they may continue to use FOB instead of FCA when there is delivery not to the ship, but to a carrier's terminal in or outside the port area);

■ the seller under the C-terms enters into the contract of carriage with the buyer as beneficiary; this makes it necessary to give the buyer the possibility of claiming the goods from the carrier, even though the buyer did not make the contract with him;

■ the parties do not understand the exceptions from, and limitations of, the carrier's liability (particularly with respect to carriage of goods by sea).

Charter parties

As noted, the maritime terms FAS, FOB, CFR, CIF, DES and DEQ can be used only when the goods are intended to be carried by sea, and a wrongful use of these terms may cause serious problems. Moreover, even a correct use of the maritime terms may cause problems in practice. As one example, the terms FAS and FOB are used as terms in charter parties as well, but as such they do not necessarily correspond to their use in Incoterms. Instead, the exact terms of the charter party will decide what they mean. This is particularly important with respect to the time under the charter party that is offered the charterer for bringing the goods alongside the ship (FAS) or for loading them onboard (FOB). If that time is exceeded, the charterer will have to pay compensation to the shipowner (so-called demurrage). If the charterer uses less time, thereby saving time for the shipowner, he may be paid for this in the form of so-called dispatch money. The terms of the charter party will not concern the FAS or FOB seller, since he is not a party to the contract with the shipowner. It is therefore necessary to match the conditions of the charter party with the terms of the contract of sale so that the FAS or FOB buyer, in his capacity as charterer in the charter party, does not have to pay demurrage without recourse against the seller when the latter fails to bring the goods to the ship within the time needed for avoiding payment of demurrage to the shipowner.

Under CFR and CIF, the seller will charter the ship, and it will be in his self-interest to speed up the loading operations to avoid demurrage payments to the shipowner and possibly to earn some dispatch money. However, the problem now appears at destination. Under B4 of CFR and CIF, the buyer must not only accept delivery at the point where the goods according to A4 have been loaded on board the vessel at the port of shipment, but he must also "receive them from the carrier at the named port of destination". Here again, the terms of the charter party might not match the terms of the contract of sale.

Therefore, even if according to the charter party the shipowner has no obligation with respect to the discharging operations (as under the charter party term "free out"), this does not necessarily mean the seller has the right under CFR and CIF to procure a contract of carriage which does not include the discharge of the goods from the ship. In order to clarify that discharging costs are included, the parties sometimes add the words "liner terms" to CFR and CIF. Although this normally means that the discharging operations are included, there is no authoritative interpretation of "liner terms". The parties are therefore advised to clarify in the contract of sale to what extent the cost of discharging operations is included.

When the discharging operations are for the buyer's account under the contract of sale, it is necessary to specify how much time he is allowed before he has to pay demurrage for keeping the ship in port. The buyer must be prepared to discharge the ship as soon as so-called notice of readiness has been given. If time starts to run before he is ready to undertake the discharge, he assumes the risk. In addition, he will assume the risk for various hindrances preventing the discharging operations unless the hindrances are excepted under the terms of the contract of sale. Again, it is necessary to match the terms of the contract of sale with the terms of the charter party.

Normally, the buyer does not risk having to pay the seller demurrage when the goods are carried by liner shipping companies. In this case, the goods are normally discharged by these companies and stored in cargo terminals until they are received by the buyers. This is particularly true with respect to containerized cargo. But the problem of matching the terms of the charter party with those of the contract of sale is particularly important with respect to commodities carried in bulk. Because commercial practice differs in different ports and changes from time to time, a failure to match the terms of the contract of sale with the terms of the charter party may result in unpleasant and expensive surprises for the contracting parties.

Usual, normal and suitable carriage

Under the C-terms, it is for the seller to procure carriage "on usual terms – by the usual route in a seagoing vessel – of the type normally used for the transport of goods of the contract description". The reference to what is "usual" and "normal" does not necessarily mean that the seagoing vessel is, in fact, "suitable" or that it minimizes the risk of loss of or damage to the goods. But if the seller knowingly selects a substandard vessel, which is therefore not "normal", the buyer may hold him responsible if there is damage to or loss of the cargo.

Risk distribution under CIF

The maritime carrier's responsibility is usually limited to the exercise of due diligence in ensuring that the vessel is seaworthy when it leaves port. He is exempt from liability for fire or for loss of or damage to the cargo resulting from errors in the navigation and management of the vessel. This limited liability explains the need for sellers and buyers to take out marine insurance to protect themselves against risks they have to bear under the contract of carriage. If the goods are sold under any of the C-terms, the buyer can obtain protection, either by the obligation of the seller to take out insurance under CIF or through his own insurance arrangements.

The bill of lading

The fact that under the C-terms the seller procures the contract of carriage for the benefit of the buyer puts the buyer in a position where he has to exercise rights against someone with whom he has not made the contract. This, indeed, explains the development of the bill of lading used for maritime carriage. Possession of the bill of lading controls the right to claim delivery of the goods from the carrier at destination. It is a fundamental obligation of the seller under CFR and CIF A8 to provide the buyer with such a document, which enables him to claim the goods from the carrier at the port of destination and, unless otherwise agreed, to sell the goods in transit by the transfer of the document to a subsequent buyer.

Traditionally, only the negotiable bill of lading could fulfil both of these functions. But in recent years other maritime documents have also been used. Now, even without a bill of lading, the buyer is entitled to claim the goods from the carrier at destination. So-called sea waybills (liner waybills, cargo quay receipts) contain instructions from the shipper to the carrier to deliver the goods to a named person at destination. These instructions can also be made irrevocable, with the result that the shipper is prevented from giving further instructions to the carrier. The instructions can also be given by an electronic data interchange message, as discussed in later sections.

Sale of goods in transit

Incoterms do not contain a term for sale of goods in transit. In practice, CFR or CIF are frequently used. When the seller has concluded a contract of carriage with the carrier, he will obtain a bill of lading which may be used for the first contract of sale, as foreseen in Incoterms A8. But the buyer may then, in a second contract, appear as seller and hand over the same bill of lading to the second buyer. Subsequent sales may be implemented to transfer the risk from the seller to the buyer at the time the contract is concluded, when the goods may be in mid-ocean and nothing can be ascertained regarding their condition. CISG, in Article 58, therefore provides that it may follow from the transport document that the parties have intended the risk to pass at the time the goods were handed over to the carrier. If so, the buyer is protected by his right of action against the issuer of the transport document. In this manner, CFR and CIF are also appropriate to use for the sale of goods in transit.

Unlawful rejection of Bill of Lading by Buyer under CFR/CIF

The duties under Incoterms to load and unload the goods

When vehicles are used to pick up and deliver the goods, Incoterms in FCA have adopted the main principle that the party in charge of the loading and unloading facilities should be responsible for the operations so that the seller loads the goods on the collecting vehicle sent to him by the buyer, and the buyer unloads the goods from the seller's arriving vehicle sent by him to deliver the goods at a place named by the buyer.

Changes in FCA, DDU and DDP

Incoterms 1990 in FCA A4 gave an account of delivery to the carrier in no fewer than seven different situations, namely with respect to rail, road, inland waterway, sea, air, unnamed and multimodal transport. In spite of these efforts to obtain appropriate guidance on the important point where the FCA-buyer fulfilled his delivery obligation, further precision was required. Thus, Incoterms 2000, instead of describing how delivery can be achieved under the different modes of transport, deals only with the most common situations where difficulties occur. In practice, the seller generally loads the goods whenever the buyer sends a vehicle to collect them, while the buyer unloads the goods from a vehicle sent by the seller to deliver the goods at a place named by the buyer. This frequently occurs also under the D-terms: the seller loads the goods on a collecting vehicle sent by the buyer to pick up the goods, while the buyer generally unloads the goods from the seller's arriving vehicle. But such commercial practice is not sufficiently firm to be reflected also in DDU/DDP A4.

The duties connected with export and import clearance

Incoterms are based on the main principle that the party best positioned to undertake the function to clear the goods and to pay duties and other costs in connection with export and import should do so. Thus,

- under all F-terms the seller should do what is necessary to clear the goods for export;

- under all C-terms the seller assumes the obligation with respect to export, and the buyer assumes the obligations with respect to import;

- under all D-terms except DDP the buyer should do what is necessary to clear the goods for import;

- under EXW the buyer has to assume the obligations with respect to export as well as import (this is an exception from the main principle, following from the nature of EXW to express the seller's minimum obligation); and

- when there are no customs requirements, all Incoterms can be used without variations, since the obligations relating to export and import clearance are relevant only "where applicable".

The obligation to clear the goods for export and import respectively is not only a matter of functions and costs. It is also essential to know whether the seller or the buyer will be at risk when difficulties arise. Normally, difficulties result in delays only as a consequence of inadequate or incorrect information provided to the customs authorities or because of inappropriate customs procedures. But in some cases, wrong information may result in customs fines, or an unforeseen export or import prohibition may prevent the goods from leaving or entering the country and thus prevent the performance of the contract of sale.

Incoterms do not resolve the question whether the party obliged to perform the export or import clearance obligation is liable to the other party for breach of contract, or whether such breach would be excused at law or under the terms of the contract of sale (see Article 79 of the CISG).

Normally, it is appropriate that the party domiciled in the country of export or import undertake to clear the goods for export or import, as the case may be. First, it is easier for him to determine any costs, difficulties or risks connected with the clearance of the goods. Second, customs and tax regulations in a country may have been made on the assumption that the exporter and the importer respectively would assume costs in connection with the clearance; this would permit a tax deduction by a party domiciled in the country without according the same benefits to foreigners. The parties are reminded in the preamble to DDP that it may be appropriate to exclude from the seller's obligations some of the costs, such as VAT, payable upon import of the goods.

Change in FAS

To be consistent in placing the clearance obligation on the party domiciled in the country, a change has been made in the term FAS which, in Incoterms 1990, placed the export clearance obligation on the buyer. This has now been changed so that the clearance obligation is instead placed upon the seller. Since this is an important change, it has been marked with capital letters in the preamble to FAS. It now follows that under all F-terms the clearance for export obligation is placed on the seller.

EXW and export formalities

Whenever the term EXW is used for an intended export sale, in order to be consistent with the policy chosen for the F-terms it might seem appropriate to place the clearance for export obligation on the seller. However, this would have meant a departure from the main principle that the term EXW should represent the seller's minimum obligation only to make the goods available for the buyer at the seller's premises. In cases where no immediate export is intended by the buyer, or perhaps no export at all but a resale to another party in the country is intended, a change of EXW with respect to the clearance obligation would have left the parties without the possibility of choosing an appropriate Incoterm. Therefore, it was decided to leave EXW unamended in this respect, but with a warning in the preamble that the buyer should ensure that he can carry out the export formalities directly or indirectly. If he cannot, he should abstain from using the term EXW unamended.

Since all C-terms, like the F-terms, represent shipment contracts, it follows that the seller must clear the goods for export while the buyer must clear them for import.

Customs-free regions

There has been some confusion with respect to the use of Incoterms in intra-European Union trade. The parties often looked for an Incoterm which did not deal with customs clearance at all, since it was no longer required, at least not in the traditional sense. This problem arises, of course, not only in intra-European Union trade, but also in other regions where customs procedures are not required. Although it goes without saying that an Incoterm may be used even if some of the obligations falling upon the seller or buyer have become redundant, it is now made clear in Incoterms 2000 that stipulations with respect to clearing of the goods for export or import only take effect "where applicable".

Even in customs-free regions, specific requirements may well be stipulated for a certain type of goods, for example, for alcohol and tobacco (so-called bonded cargo).

Responsibility for charges

In practice, charges of different kinds may be levied in connection with the discharge of the goods. To avoid placing the liability on the seller to pay for all these charges, the word "official" was used in some places in Incoterms 1990. This word does not appear in Incoterms 2000, but it should be observed that under clause A2 the seller is obliged only to "carry out all customs formalities" and that under clause A6 he is relieved from paying additional costs after he has fulfilled his delivery obligation under clause A4. Consequently, such additional costs unrelated to "customs formalities" shall not be for his account.

Incoterms and insurance

Incoterms deal only with the seller's obligation to take out insurance to the benefit of the buyer under CIF and CIP. Under all other terms, it is for the parties themselves to arrange insurance as they see fit.

The seller's insurance obligation to the benefit of the buyer

- stems from the nature of the C-term, which requires the seller to contract for carriage – without assuming the risk of loss of or damage to the goods in transit;

- requires the seller only to take out insurance on minimum terms (the C-cover under the Institute Clauses of the London Underwriters); and

- invites the buyer to agree with the seller to arrange additional insurance or to arrange it himself.

Whenever the goods are not intended to be sold in transit, it is natural for the contracting parties to arrange their own insurance in order that the seller can protect himself against risks of loss of or damage to the goods up to the point he is at risk. For the seller, this will require transport insurance up to the point of delivery according to the F-, C- and D-terms, and, conversely, there is no need for transport insurance when the goods are sold EXW.

Insurance when the parties use FOB instead of FCA

Problems arise when the transportation risk is split between the seller and the buyer at some intermediate point. In this case, the seller has no insurable interest after he has reached the point noted in the A4 clauses of Incoterms, while the buyer has no insurable interest before that point. This means that an FOB-buyer has no insurable interest before the goods have crossed the ship's rail, and that, accordingly, the FOB seller remains at risk until that point has been reached.

If the parties use FOB when FCA should have been used instead, the seller remains at risk even after the goods have been handed over to the carrier nominated by the buyer at the carrier's terminal or at a place other than the ship itself. Normally, sellers have general insurance arrangements (so-called open cover) which protects them in such cases. However, a seller who fails to cover himself adequately in these situations will not normally benefit from the buyer's insurance, even if that insurance contains a so-called transit clause to the effect that the insurance protection lasts from warehouse to warehouse, thereby covering the period before loading the goods on board. There are two reasons for this: first, the FOB-seller is not a contracting party to the FOB-buyer's insurance contract; and second, the FOB-buyer has no insurable interest before the goods have passed the ship's rail.

Insurance under CIF and CIP

CIF and CIP are the only two Incoterms dealing with insurance. The former is an addition to the maritime term CFR and the latter to CPT, which relates to all modes of transport. Since goods are normally not resold in transit except when they are carried by sea, CIF is the most common Incoterm containing an insurance obligation for the seller to the benefit of the buyer. This explains why the seller's obligation is limited to take out only minimum insurance, because if the goods are intended to be resold in transit, one does not know beforehand the insurance arrangements of the subsequent buyers.

Nevertheless, minimum cover is often inappropriate even with respect to goods intended for sale in transit. The goods may become damaged because of contamination, breakage or penetration of seawater into the vessel. Such risks are not included in the minimum cover under clause C of the 1982 Cargo Clauses of the London Underwriters. But they are covered with respect to entry of seawater into the vessel under clause B (1.2.3), as well as to all of the risks mentioned in clause A.

When insurance is excluded

Note, however, that there is no insurance protection under any of the A-, B- or C-clauses for loss, damage or expense caused by the nature of the goods, inadequate packing of the goods or such loss or damage or expense which is proximately caused by delay. There is also a general exclusion of coverage for loss, damage or expense arising from insolvency or financial default of the owners, managers, charterers or operators of the vessel. This may expose the buyer to uninsured risks, since the seller under CFR and CIF may escape liability, provided he can prove he has fulfilled his obligation under A3 to "contract on usual terms … for the carriage … by the usual route in a seagoing vessel … of the type normally used …". If loss or damage occurs because of inadequate packing, the seller may be liable under the A9 clauses of Incoterms, but neither of the parties can obtain protection from insurers.

Risks of war and labour disturbances

The standard cover under clauses A, B and C excludes war risks as well as loss, damage or expense caused by strikes, other labour disturbances, riots and other civil commotion. If insurance against such risks is requested, the A3(b) clauses of CIF and CIP require the seller to arrange coverage against them, but only if the coverage is procurable.

Incoterms and documentary credits

The relation between Incoterms and documentary credits concerns the seller's obligation to deliver documents to the buyer in order to prove that the seller has fulfilled his obligations under the Incoterm and the contract of sale and that, consequently, the buyer is obliged to pay him. In this context the parties should ensure that

- the instructions given by the buyer to the bank undertaking the documentary credit (the issuing or opening bank) are fully compatible with the requirements under the contract of sale;

- the seller is offered the opportunity in advance, and well before the handing over of the goods for carriage, to check the terms of the documentary credit;

- inconsistency between the requirements under the documentary credit and the requirements under the contract of sale is avoided, since the buyer may be in breach of his payment obligation if the seller cannot get paid under the documentary credit when his documents conform with the contract of sale; and

- the buyer does not instruct the bank to pay against a transport document which does not control the disposition of the goods and which would therefore not prevent the seller from sending the goods to someone else after he has been paid.

Documentary Credits and the Contract of Sale

Buyer
Instructs the opening
bank that the following
documents are a condition
for payment:
**Invoice
Bill of Lading
Inspection certificate
by N.N.**

**Contract
of
Sale**

The Contract of Sale
stipulates only:
**Invoice
Bill of Lading**

**The buyer fails to perform his obligation to pay if the bank does not pay.
BUT the Seller should check the Buyer's instructions to the bank
and OBJECT to the additional documents**

In practice, problems frequently arise because sellers and buyers fail to ensure that the instructions given to the issuing or opening bank conform with the terms of the contract of sale. To assist sellers and buyers in understanding the documents required in different situations under the contract of sale – and to enable the seller to check that the documents required under the contract conform with the documents he has to present under the documentary credit – the ICC Model Contract in the Introduction, Article 8, lists the most common documents as follows:

Type of Document	**Bill of Lading**
Mode of Transport	Sea. Also frequently used for multimodal transport.
Comments	Transferable Document of Title allowing buyer to sell or pledge goods while in transit by transferring the documents at any rate where made out "to order".

Type of Document	**Multimodal Transport Document**
Mode of Transport	Transit involving carriage by at least two different modes of transport.
Comments	Known by many names: Combined Transport Document, Container Bill of Lading, FIATA Multimodal Transport Bill of Lading and other variations.

Type of Document	**Seawaybill (SWB)**
Mode of Transport	Sea.
Comments	Known by many names: Cargo Quay Receipt, Non-negotiable Bill of Lading, Liner Waybill. Non-Transferable. Seller may alter delivery directions until discharge, unless the SWB contains a NO DISP clause preventing such change.

Type of Document	**Mate's Receipt**
Mode of Transport	Sea.
Comments	Document providing proof of delivery to a carrier. Sometimes given to shipper when selling FOB or FCA, to be tendered to buyer instead of Bill of Lading.

Type of Document	**Air Waybill**
Mode of Transport	Air.
Comments	Sometimes also known as air consignment note.

Type of Document	**Consignment Note**
Mode of Transport	Land.
Comments	Also sometimes known as CIM (rail) or CMR (road) consignment note or waybill.

Type of Document	**Warehouse Warrant**
Mode of Transport	Land and Sea.
Comments	Transferable document used when the goods are warehoused for collection by buyer at seller's end or at buyer's end.

Type of Document	**Freight-forwarder's Documents**
Mode of Transport	Sea, Air, Land or Multimodal.
Comments	Important to identify whether the forwarder is undertaking responsibility for the carriage of the goods as carrier or as agent of the carrier.

Type of Document	**Packing List**
Mode of Transport	Sea, Land or Multimodal.
Comments	A document recording what has been packed into a lorry, package or container.
	May represent proof of delivery as between seller and buyer, but important to identify who has issued the list and at what stage.

In Section A, Specific Conditions Article 7 of the ICC Model Contract, the parties are invited to insert a date on which the documentary credit must be notified to the seller a certain number of days before the date of delivery. The parties should ensure that the time period is sufficient for the seller to check that the documents mentioned in the instructions to the bank conform with the documents required under the contract of sale.

Note that only the bill of lading is a transferable document of title that can be used when the buyer intends to sell or pledge the goods while they are in transit. This sale or pledge is completed by the transfer of the paper document or its electronic equivalent. Note further that the "sea waybill" is not transferable and that the seller can alter the delivery directions unless the document contains a clause preventing this (irrevocable instructions to the carrier to deliver the goods to a named person, or a so-called NO DISP-clause).

The Sea Carrier's release of the goods to the Buyer

Incoterms and electronic commerce

The replacement of paper documentation with electronic data interchange (EDI) was recognized already in Incoterms 1990. It should be observed that

- the buyer may still insist on paper documentation unless there is an agreement to communicate electronically (an EDI agreement);

- any EDI system replacing paper documentation should provide for electronic equivalents to paper documents and must for such purpose be sufficiently secure and well developed;

- an increased replacement of paper documents by EDI is foreseen in the early 2000s through the use of BOLERO and similar systems.

Early attempts to take account of electronic commerce

In the late 1980s, it was already anticipated that electronic commerce would grow to such an extent that traditional requirements with respect to paper documentation under Incoterms would have to be supplemented with options for the parties to provide electronic equivalents to paper documents. Thus, at the end of every A8 clause (except in EXW, where there are no documentary requirements), both Incoterms 1990 and Incoterms 2000 refer to situations where seller and buyer have agreed to communicate electronically. If they have done so, the paper document can be replaced by "an equivalent electronic data interchange (EDI) message".

At the same time that Incoterms 1990 were developed, the Comité Maritime International (CMI) presented its Rules for Electronic Bills of Lading. Under these Rules, the right to control the goods and to transfer that right to someone else required possession of a "Private Key", which was to be made available to the shipper by the carrier upon his receipt of the goods. The Private Key could be construed in any technically appropriate form the parties could agree upon for securing the authenticity and integrity of an electronic transmission. The transfer of the Private Key to a subsequent party was to be effected by a notification to the carrier that the current Holder intended to transfer its right of control and transfer to a proposed new Holder. If the latter accepted to become a new Holder, the carrier was to cancel the current Private Key and issue a new one to him.

EDI agreement

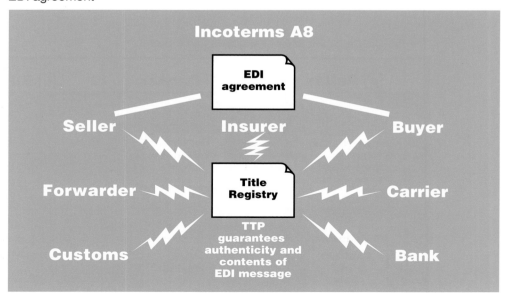

The system was based on the principle that the Private Key was at all times unique to the Holder and could not be transferred to a new Holder. The Private Key was separate and distinct from any means used to identify the contract of carriage and from any security password or identification used to access the computer network. If a proposed new Holder did not wish to participate in the electronic system, the Rules gave the current Holder the option to demand a paper bill of lading from the carrier, which could then be transferred to the new Holder. Such a paper bill of lading would then have to contain a statement to the effect that the paper bill of lading was issued upon the termination of the EDI procedures. Upon issuance of the paper bill of lading, the Private Key would be cancelled and the EDI procedures terminated.

Under the CMI Rules, there were, in effect, three players – the carrier, the shipper (acting as the first Holder) and the consignee (acting as the second or subsequent Holder). Provided they all wanted to participate in the EDI procedures according to the Rules, no major problems were expected. However, the market was not prepared to accept the system. Instead, the CMI Rules inspired further moves by international bodies. UNCITRAL developed the 1996 Model Law for Electronic Commerce, containing two important Articles on transport documents (Articles 16-17). The Model Law was based mainly on the system under the CMI Rules for Electronic Bills of Lading. Generally, the Model Law recognizes that a paper document is no more than a medium representing certain functions, the first to evidence an agreement, and the second to give a party the legal right to claim the goods from the carrier at destination and to transfer rights to the goods in transit. If these functions of a paper document can be obtained by another medium, such as the electronic exchange of messages, this should, according to the Model Law, be recognized worldwide.

Reliability of electronic v. paper systems: BOLERO and others

Rightly or wrongly, the market considers that a paper document still represents the most reliable method of providing evidence and securing the authenticity of the document's contents. To be generally accepted, an electronic system must be equally reliable as paper documentation. Presumably, the slow development of electronic systems for transport results from the erroneous assumption that they are not sufficiently reliable.

Matters are likely to change very quickly, at the start of the millennium. A system called BOLERO, sponsored by the Society for Worldwide Interbank Financial Telecommunication (SWIFT) and the Through Transport Club (TTC), has been developed. BOLERO differs from the system under the CMI Rules in that the electronic messages are received and sent through a Trusted Third Party (TTP). The authenticity and integrity of the electronic message is secured by digital signatures which identify the senders and receivers and exclude the possibility that the parties will change the contents of the message once it has been sent. Consequently, the party managing the system can, as BOLERO does, guarantee the correct delivery of the EDI message.

The BOLERO system offers an added value to all those participating by requiring them to subscribe to a Rule Book that provides the "electronic agreement" referred to in the A8 clauses of Incoterms. The system is not limited to participation by carriers, shippers and consignees, but is also open to other parties, such as freight forwarders, insurers, customs authorities, banks and governmental bodies issuing licenses or certificates of origin.

Variations of Incoterms

Since Incoterms reflect only the commercial practice most commonly used, the parties may wish to either depart from Incoterms or add provisions in order to obtain further precision. It must then be observed that

■ the parties operate outside the scope of Incoterms and contract at their own peril;

■ they should therefore carefully consider whether a departure from Incoterms is appropriate;

■ an amended or added term should be carefully worded to avoid unintended consequences; and

■ an added obligation does not necessarily change the risk distribution under Incoterms; risks do not necessarily follow from functions and costs, as evidenced by the C-terms under which the seller has to pay for the freight up to the indicated destination but does not have to assume the risks of loss of or damage to the goods after dispatch from the country of export.

In the preamble to several terms, the need to adapt an Incoterm has been recognized. In some cases, such as under EXW, commercial practice frequently differs from the rules of interpretation under the rules. As noted, EXW has nevertheless been retained in its traditional wording because of the need to include a term available to the parties when they do not wish to place any obligation on the seller in addition to his simply making the goods available to the buyer at his premises.

Normally, it is not necessary to transform what the seller does into a legal obligation. Consequently, when the seller, for example, assists the buyer in moving the goods on to a ramp for subsequent loading on the buyer's collecting vehicle – or even assists the buyer in loading the goods on to that vehicle – it is rare that the parties see a need to use a contract term to ensure that the seller, if he does not assist the buyer, is held liable for non-performance.

Additions to EXW

If the parties wish to put additional obligations on the seller, they should make clear exactly what these imply. If, for instance, the parties merely add the word "loaded" after EXW, it is reasonable to assume that the seller is obliged to load the goods on the buyer's collecting vehicle. But it is not clear whether they also wish the seller to be at risk until the goods have been so loaded. It is also unclear what would happen to the risk of loss of or damage to the goods if the buyer's collecting vehicle did not arrive in time. Should the seller nevertheless remain at risk?

If the parties do not want any change in the risk allocation under EXW, but only want to add an obligation for the seller to load the goods on the buyer's collecting vehicle, they may add after the word "loaded" the words "at buyer's risk", or, even more precisely, "at buyer's risk subsequent to the seller's notice that the goods are available for the buyer".

Additions to FOB

In some cases, the trade term will not assist the parties in determining exactly how the costs of loading or discharge should be distributed between them. This is the case with the maritime terms FOB, CFR and CIF. Under FOB, the notion that risks and costs are transferred from the seller to the buyer when the goods pass the ship's rail is not very helpful for the distribution of the loading costs. This will depend upon customs of the various ports, which may differ considerably. Therefore, the parties frequently seek further precision by adding after FOB words such as "stowed" or "stowed and trimmed". Here again, it is not clear whether they refer not only to functions and costs, but also to risks, and intend that the latter go along with the former. Clarifications similar to those suggested for EXW would then be appropriate: for example, "stowed but at buyer's risk after the goods have passed the ship's rail".

The danger of unspecified variants of Incoterms

Additions to FCA

When the parties use FCA instead of FOB, the point of delivery is shifted from the ship's rail to an inland point in or outside the port area in the country of shipment. Consequently, a number of costs may arise from the FCA point until the goods have been placed on board the ship. In particular, difficulties arise with respect to various costs debited in connection with the handling and storage of the goods in cargo terminals, so-called Transport Handling Charges (THC). The buyers' reluctance to accept payment of THC may explain why the parties continue to use FOB, even though FOB reflects an incorrect reception point. However, if the parties wish the seller to pay the THC, it would be better to say this explicitly: "FCA Bremen Incoterms 2000, THC for seller's account". Alternatively, the parties can divide the THC into percentages: "50% of THC for seller's account".

Additions to the C-terms

Additions to the C-terms are particularly cumbersome, since these terms represent so-called shipment contracts, under which the seller fulfils his obligations in connection with the shipment of the goods. If obligations referring to the destination are added, this may be interpreted to change the basic nature of the term – from a shipment term to an arrival term – with the result that the seller would be at risk until the goods have actually arrived at the destination.

However, when expressions such as "CIF landed" or "CIF outturn weights" are used, these are normally not interpreted to change the basic nature of the term. The word "landed" is usually understood as referring only to the costs of discharge, and the term "outturn weights" merely signifies that the buyer should pay according to the weight ascertained after discharge, so that, for instance, condensation of the goods during the transport should be disregarded when fixing the price. However, this does not mean that the seller would bear the risk of fortuitous loss of or damage to the goods during the carriage. Nevertheless, if the parties merely intend to clarify the extent to which the seller should pay for the discharge of the goods at the port of destination, it would be preferable to say this explicitly (for example: "discharging costs until placing the goods on the quay for seller's account").

Incoterms and other terms in the contract of sale

Since it has an obvious relation to the price, the reference to Incoterms is usually made in the seller's offer: the more obligations for the seller, the more expensive his offer becomes. If there is a sale contract in writing, or a standard contract such as the 1998 ICC Model Contract, the reference to the chosen Incoterm is in the part of the contract dealing with delivery. It should be noted, in particular, that

■ even in the absence of specific relief clauses, exemptions at law are available to the benefit of both parties (for example under the CISG Article 79);

■ Incoterms do not deal with property rights in the goods; and

■ Incoterms require the seller to deliver goods conforming with the contract of sale but do not deal with the consequences if they are non-conforming.

A quick glance at the ICC Model Contract, Part B General Conditions shows the relative importance of an Incoterm compared with other terms of the contract. Reference is made to EXW in Article 7, but there is a reminder that another term might also be appropriate, signalled by the introductory words "Unless otherwise agreed". No reference is made to the Incoterms version current at the time when the ICC Model Contract was published (1998), since it was already known at that time that a new version was forthcoming. Instead, Article 1.4 states that any reference made to a publication of the ICC is deemed to be made to the version current at the date the contract is concluded.

Delivery terms are indispensable for the implementation of the contract of sale. In the absence of a delivery term, the parties would simply not know what to do. Most of the other terms concern problems arising when the contract is not performed as contemplated (various breaches of contract, such as too-late delivery or delivery with non-conforming goods, late payment, insolvency and resolution of disputes).

Increase of costs after the contract is concluded

As noted, Incoterms contain specific provisions for the transfer of costs and risks from seller to buyer, but the risks referred to are limited to the risk of loss of or damage to the goods. Thus, Incoterms do not deal with the problems caused by an increase of costs between the time of the conclusion of the contract and the performance. For example, consider the case in which a seller in Sudan quoted a CIF price for delivery of the goods in Hamburg, but because of the war between Egypt and Israel, the Suez Canal was closed. The seller, at the time, had not yet arranged contracts of carriage and insurance. He had to make a contract for the carriage of the goods around the Cape of Good Hope, and, apart from the cost increase resulting from the considerably longer distance, the freight rates rose sharply as a result of the war. The seller sought unsuccessfully to avoid the contract because of the considerable cost increase, but the UK House of Lords, in an oft-quoted decision, ruled against him. If the seller had quoted an FOB price, the risk of the cost increase would have been borne by the buyer instead.

Risk of performance if goods are lost or damaged

Another important question concerns the risk of performance in case the goods become lost or damaged. Incoterms can resolve who has to bear the risk of the loss of or damage to the goods, but they do not determine whether the affected party is relieved from his obligation to perform. Consequently, if the seller has undertaken to deliver the goods under any of the D-terms and the goods are lost in transit, he is still obliged to perform by finding substitute goods as quickly as possible. If unforeseen and fortuitous events have caused the loss or damage, he may avoid having to pay damages caused to his buyer by the delay. But he cannot avoid the duty to perform the contract, unless he can be relieved under a term of the contract or, exceptionally, under the applicable law.

Non-conforming goods

When non-conforming goods are delivered to the buyer, the non-conformity may or may not be cured by the seller. If the seller fails to cure the non-conformity or to provide substitute goods in time, the buyer may be entitled to avoid the contract. Here again, the conclusions which may be drawn from Incoterms are limited to the question of whether or not the goods have been delivered and whether any non-conformity has resulted after the time the risk of loss of or damage to the goods has been transferred from the seller to the buyer.

Transfer of risk v. transfer of property rights

In practice, merchants often confuse the transfer of the risk with the transfer of property rights in the goods. This is understandable, since a change of possession of the goods often also implies a change of ownership. However, a transfer of the risk may well occur before the change of possession or ownership – namely, if the buyer fails to take delivery as agreed or if the seller has agreed with the buyer that the former will remain the owner until he has been paid ("retention of title").

Unfortunately, the method of determining whether title to the goods has passed differs among jurisdictions, and the matter is outside the scope of the CISG. Whether some international unification of the law will be reached in the future remains to be seen. In the meantime, the parties are advised to take appropriate measures to protect themselves whenever there is a risk the other party may become insolvent or incapable of fulfilling his obligations. The ICC publication *Transfer of Ownership in International Trade* (N°546) is indispensable in providing first-hand information. In practice, parties often protect themselves by contractual guarantees, for example, in the form of demand guarantees, or by documentary credits, whereby the seller may be paid in connection with the shipment of the goods provided he is able to present the proper documents to the bank.

Incoterms and dispute resolution

International contracts of sale usually contain terms dealing with resolution of disputes which determine

- where disputes, in the absence of amicable settlement, should be litigated;
- how disputes should be resolved (by courts of law or by arbitration); and
- which law or rules of law should be applied.

The choice of arbitration

Contracting parties seldom reckon with the risk that conflicts between them will arise and that they will fail to settle their differences amicably in case something unexpected occurs. However, when they contract by incorporating standardized terms, these terms frequently contain clauses dealing with the resolution of disputes. In some cases, the clauses stipulate that the parties should first try to settle their disputes amicably. This, of course, goes without saying. Fortunately, the parties can usually settle either between themselves or with the assistance of lawyers. But there may be situations where, for one reason or another, they will require the assistance of a neutral, third person in their settlement negotiations (so-called conciliation). If this does not result in a settlement, the parties may have no other alternative than to have their dispute resolved by arbitration or by litigation before courts of law. The ICC Rules of Conciliation and the ICC Rules of Arbitration offer well-designed rules, and, in case of arbitration, the procedure is supervised by the ICC International Court of Arbitration, ensuring equality and fairness and resulting in an enforceable arbitration award (see ICC publication N° 581).

Jurisdiction of the arbitral tribunal

When negotiating a contract, parties with equal bargaining positions normally prefer not to give the other party any advantage by agreeing to a dispute resolution in the latter's country, which entails the application of the law of that country. When the parties choose arbitration they can avoid such choices simply by allowing disputes to be resolved under rules of various arbitration institutions, such as the ICC Court of Arbitration. If the parties have not stipulated the place of arbitration, it will be fixed by the ICC Court (Article 14 of the ICC Rules), and if the parties have not chosen the applicable law, the arbitral tribunal will apply the rules of law which it determines to be appropriate (Article 17.1). Although Part B Article 14 of the General Conditions in the ICC Model Contract refers to ICC Arbitration, Part A of the Specific Conditions Article 15 also offers the parties the opportunity to specify another kind of arbitration, or, alternatively, litigation before a named court of law.

Alternatives to arbitration and litigation

Arbitration and litigation before courts of law should be regarded as methods to resolve disputes when all other efforts have failed. Even though arbitration provides a smoother system by offering secrecy during the proceedings and a quicker, and sometimes more reliable, way to obtain an award than litigation – where a decision by a lower court may be appealed to higher courts – arbitration can be a costly and cumbersome exercise. In recent years, alternative methods for dispute resolution have expanded (so-called ADR procedures), enabling the parties to obtain an award in a simpler way at a reduced cost.

It is true that any simplification of the dispute resolution process which limits a party's opportunity to present his case in full, using all appropriate evidence, may create uncertainty regarding the correctness of the award. But in practice a losing party seldom understands why he lost in any event, so the choice between maximum certainty and optimal simplification frequently results in opting for the latter.

Need for specificity in referencing arbitration

An arbitration agreement should be in writing and a reference to arbitration rules must be clear and specific. The following arbitration clause is recommended by ICC: "All disputes arising out of or in connection with the present contract shall be finally settled under the Rules of Arbitration of the International Chamber of Commerce by one or more arbitrators appointed in accordance with the said Rules."

THE FOUR GROUPS OF INCOTERMS

Main Components

Important differences between shipment and arrival contracts

There is an important distinction between the delivered-terms ("D-terms") and the other trade terms with respect to determining the critical point when the seller has performed his delivery obligation. Only with the D-terms (DAF, DES, DEQ, DDU and DDP) is the seller's delivery obligation extended to the country of destination. Under the other trade terms he fulfils the delivery obligation in his own country, either by placing the goods at the disposal of the buyer at his (the seller's) premises (EXW), or by handing over the goods to the carrier for shipment (FCA, FAS, FOB, CFR, CIF, CPT and CIP).

To make the important distinction between this fundamentally different nature of the "groups" of trade terms, contracts of sale are often classified accordingly, as, for example, when the D-terms would turn the contract of sale into arrival contracts. Contracts using F-terms or C-terms would fall into the category of shipment contracts.

It is important to note that the seller's obligation to arrange and pay for the carriage does not in itself extend his delivery obligation up to the point of destination. On the contrary, the risk of loss of or damage to the goods will pass at the point of delivery, and the insurance which the seller has to take out under the trade terms CIF and CIP will be for the benefit of the buyer, who has to assume the risk after the delivery point.

The C-terms, by extending the seller's obligation with respect to costs of carriage and insurance respectively to the destination, make it necessary to consider not one but two critical points: one for the division of risks and another for the division of costs. Because this is not always easily understood, the C-terms are frequently misunderstood by merchants, who believe them to be more or less equivalent to D-terms. This, of course, is completely incorrect.

A seller having sold his goods on C-terms is considered to have fulfilled his delivery obligation even if something happens to the goods after the point of shipment, while a seller having sold the goods on D-terms has not fulfilled his obligation in similar circumstances.

Consequently, if the goods are lost or accidentally become damaged after shipment but before the goods have arrived at the agreed destination point, a seller having sold the goods upon D-terms has not fulfilled his contract and can therefore be held liable for breach of contract. He will normally have to provide substitute goods in place of those lost or damaged, or make other agreed restitution.

In this respect, the interrelation between the trade term and the other terms of the contract of sale is vital, since the risk falling upon the seller may be eliminated, or at least modified, by various so-called relief clauses or force majeure clauses in the contract of sale.

The basic distinction between C- and D-terms becomes crucial when goods are damaged in transit. With C-terms, the seller has already fulfilled his delivery obligations, while with D-terms the seller may be liable for breach of contract.

It follows that the parties must always observe the fundamental difference between the C-terms and the D-terms and that a seller having sold the goods under D-terms should carefully consider the need to protect himself against breach of contract and non-fulfilment risks by adequate force majeure clauses or other relief clauses in the contract of sale.

The abbreviations: E-, F-, C- and D-terms

The different nature of the trade terms can be evidenced by the grouping of the terms in four categories, using the first letter as an indication of the group to which the term belongs. The first group has only one trade term, namely EXW. But in the other three groups there are three F-terms (FCA, FAS and FOB), four C-terms (CFR, CIF, CPT and CIP) and five D-terms (DAF, DES, DEQ, DDU and DDP).

- ■ The letter F signifies that the seller must hand over the goods to a nominated carrier Free of risk and expense to the buyer.

- ■ The letter C signifies that the seller must bear certain Costs even after the critical point for the division of the risk of loss of or damage to the goods has been reached.

- ■ The letter D signifies that the goods must arrive at a stated Destination.

This grouping and identification of the various trade terms should enable merchants to understand the different fundamental meanings of the terms and guide them to the most suitable option.

Incoterms 2000

Group E Departure	**EXW**	Ex Works
Group F Main carriage Unpaid	**FCA** **FAS** **FOB**	Free Carrier Free Alongside Ship Free On Board
Group C Main carriage Paid	**CFR** **CIF** **CPT** **CIP**	Cost and Freight Cost, Insurance and Freight Carriage Paid To Carriage and Insurance Paid To
Group D Arrival	**DAF** **DES** **DEQ** **DDU** **DDP**	Delivered At Frontier Delivered Ex Ship Delivered Ex Quay Delivered Duty Unpaid Delivered Duty Paid

The term EXW: placing the goods at the disposal of the buyer

EXW represents the seller's minimum obligation, since he only has to place the goods at the disposal of the buyer. Although it may appear from the contract itself or from the surrounding circumstances that the buyer intends to export the goods, it is entirely up to him whether he wishes to do so. According to the trade term, there is no obligation for either party to do anything with respect to export.

Nevertheless, it follows from B2 that the buyer must carry out all tasks of export and import clearance, and, as stipulated in A2, the seller merely has to render his assistance in connection with these tasks. The buyer has to reimburse the seller for all costs and charges incurred in rendering this assistance (B6).

Neither of the parties has any obligation to the other with respect to contracts of carriage and insurance. However, if the buyer wishes to have the goods carried from the seller's place he should, for his own benefit, arrange for carriage and cargo insurance.

F-terms and C-terms: the carriage-related terms

F-terms: main carriage not paid by seller

F-terms and pre-carriage

While under the F-terms the seller has to arrange any necessary pre-carriage to reach the agreed point for handing over the goods to the carrier, it is the buyer's function to arrange and pay for the main carriage. Section A3 of the F-terms does not mention anything with respect to pre-carriage, since there is no need to explain how the seller is able to reach the point for the handing over of the goods to the carrier.

FCA and handing over goods for carriage

As noted, FCA is the main F-term which can be used irrespective of the mode of transport and should be used whenever handing over to the carrier is not completed alongside a ship or over a ship's rail. In the two latter cases, the terms FAS and FOB should be used instead of FCA.

The circumstances defining the handing over of the goods to the carrier differ according to the mode of transport and the nature of the goods. Practices also vary from place to place. Since the buyer has to arrange for the transport, it is vital that he instruct the seller precisely regarding how the goods should be handed over for carriage. He should also ensure that the precise point where this will occur is mentioned in the contract of sale. This is not always possible to do when making the contract, since the exact point may be decided subsequently. In this event, it is important that the seller, when quoting his price, consider the various options available to the buyer for requiring the seller to hand over the goods for carriage. The seller, of course, should know how the goods are to be packed, whether they are to be containerized and whether they should be delivered to a terminal in his vicinity or elsewhere.

Full loads and less-than-full loads

The quantity of the goods will determine whether they are suitable to constitute so-called full loads (railway wagon loads or container loads), or whether they must be delivered to the carrier as break bulk cargo to be stowed by him, usually at his terminal. In the container trade, the important distinction is made between full loads and less-than-full loads (FCL for full container load and LCL for less than full container load).

In practice, the seller often contracts for carriage

Although all of the F-terms clearly place the obligation to contract for carriage on the buyer, in practice the seller frequently performs it when the choice is more or less immaterial to the buyer. This is particularly common when there is only one option available, taking into account the place and the nature of the goods, or when the freight would be the same even though there are several options for carriage.

When there is a "liner service" from the seller's country, the seller frequently contracts for carriage under FOB. This practice is called "FOB additional service". In many cases the practice with respect to road transport is less firm; indeed, it may vary from forwarder to forwarder and from carrier to carrier. Nevertheless, the seller frequently contracts for the road carriage, though it is intended that the buyer should pay for it.

Current commercial practice makes it difficult to set down in a legal text what the parties are obliged to do. But though from a strictly legal point of view the seller is not concerned with the main contract of carriage, his duties according to commercial practice are reflected under the heading A3. If there is such a practice, the seller may contract for carriage on usual terms at the buyer's risk and expense.

When the seller declines or the buyer wants to contract for carriage

The seller may decline to contract for carriage and may notify the buyer accordingly. The buyer may also specifically ask the seller to assist him or tell the seller that he intends to contract for carriage himself.

It is important for the buyer to notify the seller of his intentions if, for instance, he has a special relationship with a carrier making it important for him to exercise his right according to B3 to arrange the contract of carriage.

Buyer's risk if transport is unavailable

Even though the seller under an F-term is requested or intends to perform the contracting for carriage according to commercial practice, the buyer always will bear the risk if, because of unforeseen circumstances, transport facilities fail to be available as contemplated.

Division of loading costs under FOB

When the cargo is delivered containerized or in less-than-full loads to the carrier's terminal, the division of loading costs seldom presents any particular problems. However, the situation is quite different when under FOB the cargo is to be delivered in the traditional manner over the ship's rail.

If the ship's rail is used for the division of loading costs, it would seem that one would have to count the costs of labour, hiring of cranes, etc. by counting the work hours and the time used before and after the passing of the ship's rail. This, however, is not done in practice. Instead, the custom of the port will decide the extent to which loading costs under FOB should be distributed between seller and buyer. If this is known to both parties, no difficulties should arise. But frequently the buyer may not know the custom of the port in the seller's country and indeed may find out later that the custom works to his disadvantage.

For this reason, it is important that the FOB buyer consider this problem when negotiating the contract of sale and the price for the goods.

Seller's export clearance under FAS

Incoterms 1990, as well as the previous versions of Incoterms, placed the export clearance obligation on the buyer, since delivering alongside the ship was deemed to constitute delivery in the seller's country (the ship's rail constituted a kind of imaginary customs border). However, this no longer reflects commercial practice, which requires the party domiciled in the country to be in charge of the clearance obligation (except under EXW, which represents the seller's minimum obligation). Consequently, FAS has been changed so that, in Incoterms 2000, the export clearance obligation is placed upon the seller. Conversely, the import clearance obligation under DEQ has also been changed in Incoterms 2000 so that it is now placed upon the buyer (see p.159).

C-terms: main carriage paid by seller

Two groups of C-terms

There are two groups of C-terms. One is intended to be used only when the goods are carried by sea (CFR and CIF). The other group (CPT and CIP) can be used for any mode of transport, including sea and multimodal transport.

Do not use CFR or CIF for anything other than sea transport

Sometimes the parties fail to observe the important distinction in the previous paragraph, and use CFR and CIF for modes of transport other than carriage by sea. The seller then puts himself in the unfortunate position of being unable to fulfil his fundamental obligation to present a bill of lading, or to present a sea waybill or similar document as required under CFR or CIF A8.

Note, however, that if the buyer intends to sell the goods in transit, he may lose this option if he receives the incorrect transport document. In such a case, he would be able to cancel the contract because of the seller's breach in not providing the correct document. Also, when the market for the goods falls after the contract of sale has been entered into, a buyer could, in certain circumstances, use the seller's breach as a means of avoiding the market loss by cancelling the contract of sale.

Wrongful use of CFR/CIF

C-terms are not equivalent to D-terms

The C-terms may present some difficulties, since only the point of destination is mentioned after the respective term: for example, in a contract of sale concluded between a buyer in New York and a seller in London, only New York is likely to be mentioned after the C-term, with nothing usually being said about shipment from London. Obviously, this can give rise to the false impression that the goods are to be delivered in New York and that the seller has not fulfilled his obligation until they have in fact been delivered.

Consequently, it is not uncommon that the contract will indicate, for example, "Delivery New York not later than..." (with a particular date being given). But this notation would demonstrate that the contracting parties failed to understand the fundamental nature of the C-term, since under it the seller fulfils his obligation by shipping the goods from his country.

This confusion arises because the seller undertakes to arrange and pay for the main carriage up to destination. This payment obligation, however, is only in addition to the fundamental obligation to ship the goods from the seller's place.

Two "critical points" under C-terms

Since the C-term must show the extent to which the seller undertakes to arrange and pay for the main contract of carriage – with the addition of insurance under CIF and CIP – indicating the point of destination under C-terms is inevitable. The C-term also establishes that the seller fulfils his delivery obligation by handing over the goods for shipment in his country, and that this has to be accepted as delivery by the buyer (A4 and B4 respectively).

Thus, under the C-terms there will be not only one relevant point as under the F-terms – the point of shipment – but two critical points, one coinciding with the point of shipment under the F-terms, the other indicating the point up to which the seller would have to pay for carriage and insurance. It would be easier for traders to understand the fundamental nature of the C-terms if both of these critical points were indicated. However, this is usually not done, since the seller at the time of entering into the contract of sale may prefer to retain a certain liberty with regard to the exact point or port of shipment. A seller in Stockholm, for example, having sold the goods under CFR or CIF to a buyer in New York, may wish to delay deciding whether he wishes to ship the goods directly from Stockholm, or have them carried by road to Gothenburg or perhaps even to Rotterdam for carriage by sea to New York.

Do not stipulate date of arrival under C-terms

If the contract of sale refers to a C-term, but also indicates arrival at destination on a particular date, the contract becomes ambiguous. One would then not know if it was the intention of the contracting parties that the seller will have breached the contract if the goods do not actually arrive at destination on the agreed date, or whether the fundamental nature of the C-term should supersede this interpretation.

In the latter case, the seller's obligation is limited to shipping the goods so that they could arrive at the destination on the agreed date, unless something happens after shipment, which, according to the C-term, would be at the risk of the buyer.

Seller's insurance obligation under CIF and CIP

In Incoterms the C-term exists in two forms: CFR and CPT when there is no insurance obligation for the seller, and CIF and CIP when, according to A3b, the seller must obtain and pay for the insurance.

Otherwise, CFR and CPT are identical to CIF and CIP respectively.

Cost of insurance depends on intended transport

Under CFR and CPT, where the seller has no insurance obligation, the buyer should be aware of the relation between the cost of insurance and the intended carriage of the goods. If the goods are deemed to be exposed to greater risks during the transport (for example, during the shipment of goods on deck or in older ships), the insurance premium will become more expensive – if insurance is available at all.

The "minimum cover" principle of CIF and CIP

The obligation of the seller to obtain and pay for cargo insurance under CIF and CIP A3b is based on the principle of "minimum cover" as set out in the Institute Cargo Clauses drafted by the Institute of London Underwriters. But such minimum cover could also follow any other similar set of clauses.

In practice, however, "all risk-insurance" (Institute Clause A) is preferred to less extended cover (Institute Clauses B or C), since the minimum cover is appropriate only when the risk of loss of or damage to the goods in transit is more or less confined to casualties affecting both the means of conveyance and the cargo, such as those resulting from collisions, strandings and fire. In such cases, even the minimum cover would protect the buyer against the risk of having to pay compensation to a shipowner for his expenses in salvaging the ship and cargo, according to the rules relating to general average (the York/Antwerp Rules of 1994).

Unsuitability of minimum cover for manufactured goods

Minimum cover is not suitable for manufactured goods (particularly not for goods of high value) because of the risk of theft, pilferage or improper handling or custody of the goods. Therefore, extended insurance coverage is usually taken out as protection against such risks (Institute Clause A is then advisable). A buyer of manufactured goods should stipulate in the contract of sale that the insurance according to CIF or CIP should be extended as indicated. If he does not, the seller can fulfil his insurance obligation by providing only minimum cover (Institute Clause C).

The buyer may also wish to obtain additional coverage not included in Institute Clause A – for example, insurance against war, riots, other civil commotions, or strikes or other labour disturbances. This would normally be accomplished by specific instructions to the seller. Alternatively, the buyer may himself arrange for appropriate additional insurance. This can be done either case by case or through general arrangements with his insurer.

The question of whether it is correct to follow the principle of minimum insurance coverage has been much debated. While it may appear appropriate to use the extended coverage (Institute Clause A) as a "point of departure" and then deduct from this extent of the coverage in cases where the contract of sale concerns only rough cargoes exposed to major casualties, the choice to retain the traditional "minimum principle" has prevailed. This may constitute a serious trap for the unwary buyer.

Guarding against fraud under CFR and CPT

Statistical evidence indicates that fraud occurs more frequently under the CFR and CPT terms than under other terms, largely because the buyer does not normally have sufficient control over the particular method and the type of transport involved. Therefore, the CFR or CPT buyer is advised to consider specific stipulations in the contract of sale restricting the seller's option to arrange for carriage as he pleases (for example, the buyer can mention a particular shipping line or identify the carrier).

How to prevent delivery until payment has been made

Sellers uncertain about the buyer's ability or willingness to pay the price can take measures to prevent delivery of the goods before payment has been made. There are two ways to do this: (1) instructions to prevent the buyer from obtaining the goods before payment can be given to a carrier, a freight forwarder or a bank; and (2) instructions to require cash from the buyer on delivery (COD instructions) can be given to the carrier or a freight forwarder, and the bank can be instructed not to release the original(s) of the bill of lading until payment has been made. This would probably best be achieved by means of a documentary collection arranged through the international banking system.

Payment by using the irrevocable documentary credit

Payment can also be arranged by requiring the buyer to open an irrevocable documentary credit (also called a letter of credit, L/C) with the seller as beneficiary. This alternative gives the seller the additional advantage of receiving payment earlier, when the goods are shipped from his own country. He then avoids having to transport the goods to destination before payment, where he could run the risk of the buyer's failing to collect the goods.

As beneficiary under a documentary credit, the seller will be paid provided he presents the stipulated documents to the bank completely in order with the requirements of the L/C and within the period allowed. The bank which is to pay under the documentary credit can also be requested to add its confirmation to the irrevocable undertaking of the bank which opened the credit (the so-called opening or issuing bank). In this case the seller obtains a promise to receive payment, not only from the issuing bank, but separately from the confirming bank as well.

Documentary credits are often used with C-terms, and in these cases they are fully consistent with the basic nature of the terms. This is because the seller fulfils his shipment obligation with shipment in his own country and only has to provide evidence with the documents stipulated in the documentary credit that will satisfy the paying bank and the buyer that he has fulfilled that obligation.

Nevertheless, buyers should be aware that with documentary credits banks

■ are not concerned with the contract of sale or the contract of carriage;

■ limit their service to the contract of finance as such;

■ do not undertake to check whether the goods in fact correspond to the contract description;

■ only check that the documents "on their face" appear to be in order; and

■ do not assume any responsibility for the solvency or standing of parties having issued the documents.

Thus, the buyer does not receive comprehensive protection merely by using the documentary credit process.

It follows from the previous paragraphs that, with respect to the C-terms

■ **CFR and CIF should never be used when carriage other than carriage by sea is intended;**

■ **the buyer should always consider the need to restrict the seller's options with respect to arranging the carriage and should require additional insurance coverage from the seller;**

■ **under no circumstances should a stipulation as to time for delivery be mentioned in connection with arrival at destination: it should be mentioned only in connection with the shipment of the goods; and**

■ **if buyers wish to make sellers responsible for the arrival of the goods at destination at a particular time, D-terms should be used instead of C-terms.**

D-terms: delivered terms

Factors determining use of different D-terms

When choosing among the different D-terms, three factors have to be taken into consideration:

■   the mode of transport;

■   the distribution of costs and risks connected with discharging the goods at destination; and

■   the distribution of functions in connection with the clearance of the goods for import.

The trend toward choice of delivered terms

A seller of manufactured goods, whose products have to compete in the country of destination and who has to extend his obligation to the buyer by contract guarantees, often finds it inappropriate to limit his obligation under the contract of sale by fulfilling the contract at some earlier point, for example before the goods are dispatched or before they have reached destination. As one car manufacturer reportedly said: "Although I may be relieved of the risk of damage to my cars sold under an FOB contract, I am not pleased to see how they are being damaged when hopeless efforts are made to squeeze them into a cargo hold of a wholly inappropriate ship."

The seller's need to plan and control cargo movements

Practical problems with respect to arranging the carriage often make terms under which the seller fulfils his obligation by handing over the goods to a carrier inappropriate and less economical. An exporter of goods with a constant flow of cargo in various directions often finds that transport economy (so-called logistics planning) requires him to totally control carriage as well as the delivery at destination. In addition, the seller is often in a better position to obtain competitive freight rates than his buyers.

DES and DEQ for sea transport

The terms DES and DEQ are traditional for carriage of goods by sea. The former means that the buyer must take the cargo out of the ship, whereas the latter places the burden on the seller to ensure that the goods are discharged on to the quay. When the goods are to be carried on liner terms, discharging expenses are usually included in the freight, in which case the term DES is out of place. If, on the other hand, the goods are commodities carried in ships to be chartered by the seller, the distinction between DES and DEQ is particularly important.

DES and "Free out" stipulation in charter parties

If the contract of sale is concluded on DES, the seller charters the ship on terms relieving the shipowner from the discharging operation. Thus, the charter party will be concluded between the seller and the shipowner on terms "Free out", when the word "Free" means that discharging operations are not included in the charter party hire. In such cases, the charter party may make clear that the loading operation is also "free" to the shipowner. If so, the loading expenses have to be borne by the seller, since loading and carrying the goods to the agreed destination under delivered terms would fall upon him. The charter party term in such a case would read "Free in and out" (FIO).

FIO stipulations in charter parties and contracts of sale

There are also variants of FIO used when further distinctions are made: for example, "Free in and out stowed and trimmed" (FIOST) and similar expressions in the charter party. These and similar terms can also appear in the contract of sale. But a contract of sale on delivered terms has to deal only with discharging functions and expenses, since it is unnecessary to deal with expenses which inevitably must fall upon the seller before the goods arrive at the agreed destination.

However, the term FIOST is sometimes used in FOB contracts of sale when the seller's obligation is limited to placing the goods on board the ship in the port of shipment. But such a charter party term is out of place in the contract of sale, since the FOB seller is not concerned with discharging operations in the port of destination. Here, if the seller agrees to do more than merely lift the goods over the ship's rail, the correct term in the contract of sale to specify what the seller has to do in connection with the loading of the ship would read "FOB stowed and trimmed".

Buyer needs to know time of arrival

Under the terms DES and DEQ it is vital that the buyer know the time of the ship's arrival so that the ship is not detained in the port of discharge waiting for the cargo to be removed. It is also important that the goods, when they have been discharged, be removed from the quay as quickly as possible. It is common practice for the seller in the contract of sale to give the buyer notice of the estimated time of the arrival of the ship (ETA), and also for the contract to require the buyer to discharge the ship and remove the cargo from the quay within an agreed time.

Demurrage and dispatch money

If the buyer fails to discharge the ship and remove the cargo from the quay, he may have to reimburse the seller for expenses incurred, "demurrage". Alternatively, the buyer may have to pay port authorities or stevedoring companies for additional storage expenses. To induce the buyer to discharge the cargo, the seller may be prepared to give him an extra bonus for saving time. Corresponding stipulations may also be found in charter parties to the benefit of the seller in his capacity as charterer (so-called dispatch money).

Demurrage can also be charged by the owners or lessors of containers, when the containers have not been unloaded within an agreed period and are unavailable for re-use.

Consistency required between charter party and contract of sale

It is important to make the terms of the charter party and the contract of sale compatible on questions of demurrage and dispatch money. Terms relating to the time the vessel is available for loading and discharge (so-called laytime) and terms relating to demurrage and dispatch are often complicated, since some events – for example, circumstances which could be attributed to the carrier or events beyond the control of either party, such as labour disturbances, government directions or adverse weather conditions – can extend the time available. For these reasons as well, it is necessary that the provisions of the charter party and the contract of sale be consistent.

DAF, DDU and DDP – for all modes of transport

The other D-terms (DAF, DDU and DDP) can be used regardless of the mode of transport. In practice, however, DAF is primarily used for through rail transport, where it signifies that the seller's obligations extend up to the border of the country mentioned after the term. This is usually the border of the buyer's country, but it could also be some third country through which the goods are to be carried in transit.

Avoid "free border" or "franco border"

Terms such as "free border" or "franco border" are even more common in practice than DAF. Nevertheless, these terms are not to be used, since misunderstandings frequently arise with respect to the extent of the seller's obligations. It is clear that the seller has to bear the costs up to the agreed point, but it is not clear whether that point is a "tariff point" or whether a real "delivery point" is intended. If the latter is the case, the seller is also responsible for what may happen to the goods from the time of dispatch until the agreed point is reached.

As noted in the explanation of C-terms, the mere fact that the seller undertakes to pay costs does not necessarily mean that he also has to assume the risks connected with the carriage. For this reason, terms using only the words "free" or "franco" are to be avoided. The term "delivered" should be used instead, if it is intended that the seller bear the risks as well as the costs for loss of or damage to the cargo or for failure to reach the delivery point. If this is not intended, one of the C-terms, for example CPT or CIP, should be used instead of DAF.

The through railway consignment note under DAF

In railway traffic a physical delivery of the goods to the buyer seldom takes place precisely at the border of the buyer's country. The seller often obtains a through consignment note from the railway, covering the whole transit up to the final destination, and also assists the buyer to do whatever is necessary to clear customs and to pass the goods through third countries before they reach the destination. But the seller in these cases can perform these "additional" services at the risk and expense of the buyer in the same way he would under FCA and FOB terms (see the discussion of FCA and FOB above). Then if something goes wrong after the goods have reached the agreed point mentioned after DAF, this would be at the risk and expense of the buyer. Conversely, if something happens which delays the cargo or prevents it from reaching that point, it would be at the seller's risk and expense.

Railway cargo consolidation by freight forwarders

Break bulk cargo is usually handed over to freight forwarders for so-called railway cargo consolidation. In these cases, the freight forwarder unitizes the cargo in full wagon loads and enters into contractual arrangements with the railways on terms which differ from the terms which the seller or buyer could have negotiated with the railway for each individual parcel. Freight forwarders have their own tariffs, and they debit sellers and buyers accordingly.

DAF – a risk division point as well as a tariff point

The point mentioned after DAF, as discussed earlier, would then serve as the "tariff point", so that the costs relating to the carriage before the point will be debited to the seller and the costs thereafter to the buyer. In most cases, the cargo is not discharged from one railway wagon and re-loaded on another at the point mentioned after DAF. Nevertheless, if something happens to the cargo or if the traffic is interrupted, the point mentioned after DAF would also serve as a point for the division of the risks between seller and buyer.

Presumably, sellers and buyers contracting on the term DAF will not consider more than the division of costs. It was therefore debated whether DAF should be retained in Incoterms 2000. As noted, the terms CPT and CIP are quite sufficient if only a division of costs between the parties is intended. But since DAF is still used in some areas, it was decided to retain the term.

EXW, DDU and DDP do not specify loading and discharging

When cargo is to be collected or delivered at destination, difficulties arise in determining exactly what should be done by the seller and the buyer and how the costs should be distributed between them for loading and discharging.

Is it sufficient that the goods arrive on the vehicle provided by the seller? Or do they have to be removed from that vehicle at the risk and expense of the seller? If the latter, can the buyer debit the seller for the work performed by his own personnel in receiving the goods at a ramp in his warehouse? And should the seller load the goods on to a vehicle sent by the buyer to collect the goods from the seller's terminal? Answers to these questions normally follow from commercial practice or from previous dealings between the same contracting parties. Since, in most countries, the seller normally loads the goods on to the buyer's collecting vehicle, while the buyer unloads the goods from the seller's vehicle arriving at his premises or some other place named by the buyer, it was debated whether this could be the general rule in Incoterms 2000. However, the practice with respect to the seller's loading of the goods on to the buyer's collecting vehicle was not considered to be sufficiently firm to do this.

Import clearance under D-terms

As has been said with respect to FAS, it is common practice that the party domiciled in the country arranges export and import clearance. Consequently, in Incoterms 2000, not only FAS but also DEQ has been changed so that under DEQ the buyer must clear the goods for import and pay duty, VAT and other taxes and charges levied upon import of the goods. Thus, only DDP places these obligations on the seller.

Seller should avoid DDP if difficulties expected

If any difficulties seem likely to arise in relation to the import of the goods into the buyer's country, the seller should try to avoid using the term DDP.

Even if no difficulties are expected, each party is usually better suited to assess the possible risks in his own country. Therefore, it is normally better that the seller take upon himself the task of clearing the goods for export, while the buyer procures the import formalities and bears any extra costs and risks incurred in that connection.

Also, it may be that the applicable statutory provisions relating to duties, VAT and similar charges require payment from a party domiciled in the country concerned. A party from abroad, having undertaken to pay these charges, cannot then benefit from advantages accorded to parties domiciled in the country of export or import. Moreover, if the costs are paid by a non-resident, difficulties may arise in deducting the expenditure in the VAT forms submitted to the authorities.

Choice of DDP with exclusion of duty and/or other charges

The seller or his freight forwarder may be prepared to clear the goods for import, without paying duty, VAT and other official charges connected with the import clearance. If so, DDP may still be used but with the addition of the phrase "exclusive of duty, VAT and other import charges".

DDP with such an exclusion is not equivalent to DDU, since the obligation to clear the goods for import still falls on the DDP seller. It is also possible to use DDU, then to add that some costs connected with import should be borne by the seller.

DDU and difficulties of reaching the final destination

Serious difficulties could arise in using the term DDU when the goods have to pass through customs at an earlier point than the agreed point of destination. If so, the goods may be prevented from reaching the destination point as contemplated if they are held up at the customs station, either because of the failure of the buyer to do whatever is required by the authorities or for other reasons.

Since under DDU it is the buyer's task to clear the goods for import, all of the above events are at his risk and expense. This may be cold comfort for a seller who has his transport arrangements interrupted at the customs station but who has the remaining obligation to deliver the goods at the agreed final point of destination. Consequently, sellers are advised to be cautious and to avoid the term DDU when difficulties of this kind cannot be excluded.

By adding the term "cleared for import", it is possible to use DDU and still place the obligation to clear the goods for import on the seller. This means that the seller's obligation is limited to the clearance as such and that the duty, as well as other charges levied upon import, will be unpaid and have to be paid by the buyer.

Charges and the DDP seller

It should be underlined that the "charges" to be paid by the DDP-seller concern only such charges as are a necessary consequence of the import as such and thus have to be paid according to the applicable import regulations. Thus, additional charges resulting from warehousing or services obtained from private parties in connection with the import are not included in the charges payable by the seller under DDP. In Incoterms 1990, this was indicated by the word "official" before the word "charges". However, in some cases the word "official" was misunderstood by merchants; it has therefore been deleted in Incoterms 2000. But, as noted, no change of substance is intended by this deletion.

SELLER'S AND BUYER'S OBLIGATIONS

An Overview

The basic nature of the various trade terms having already been briefly explained, the following section-by-section examination will make it easier for the user of this guide to determine the risks and responsibilities of the parties.

Sections A1, B1: the obligation to exchange goods for money

The essence of any contract of sale is the exchange of goods for money. Incoterms, in sections A1 and B1, simply contain a reminder of this. Needless to say, the contract of sale must specify which goods the seller has to provide and what the buyer must pay for them. In A1 there is also a reminder that the seller should provide the "commercial invoice" and any "evidence of conformity" the contract may stipulate.

Section A9: the seller's packaging obligations

Any particular requirement with respect to checking and marking which the buyer desires solely for his own purposes must be stipulated in the contract of sale. Section A9 makes clear that the costs required solely to place the goods at the buyer's disposal are for the seller's account. In this respect, government agencies in some countries may request that the goods be checked before they are admitted for import or export. Some goods may have to be marked, measured, weighed or counted as a condition for the carrier's acceptance of the goods for carriage. When the contract of sale does not contain detailed provisions on packaging of the goods, or when these cannot be ascertained from previous dealings between the parties, the seller may be uncertain as to what he should do. Under normal circumstances, the seller has to provide some packaging.

However, how the goods should be packed and prepared for the intended voyage may be unclear. A long sea voyage could require strong packaging and special preparations to protect against rusting caused by condensation and humidity. This same degree of protection is unlikely to be required for air carriage of the same cargo.

The seller must pack the goods as required for the mode of transport, but only to the extent that the circumstances of the transport are known to him before the contract of sale is concluded. If these are known, he can take them into consideration when he quotes his price. Therefore, it is important that the buyer duly inform the seller of his intentions, particularly when the contract has been concluded on EXW or under F-terms, when the seller may not otherwise know the buyer's intentions with respect to the carriage.

Section B9: pre-shipment inspection

Pre-shipment inspection (PSI) may be required when the buyer requires a licence or permit from the authorities to ensure that the goods conform with the contract. In these circumstances, the authorities order an inspection and generally engage an independent inspection agency to perform it. Legislation in the country of import will determine whether and to what extent the authorities can require reimbursement of costs paid by them for the inspection; but if reimbursement is required from one of the parties, the buyer will normally bear the cost.

Contractual stipulations relating to inspection usually require the buyer to pay for it. However, there are other variants which require the seller to pay, wholly or partly, for the inspection; in others, the seller has to pay for it to the extent that the inspection shows that the goods were not in condition to satisfy the contract.

PSI should be distinguished from an inspection required by the buyer himself without the involvement of his authorities. Such an inspection may be important for the buyer if he has any reason to doubt that the seller will hand over goods for shipment in conformity with the contract. Using such an inspection can ascertain whether a commodity – such as oil, ore, foodstuffs, or timber – conforms with the contract of sale.

An inspection can also be arranged when the contract of sale is concluded between parties who are not familiar with one another from previous dealings and who may not intend to establish future commercial relations (as in "one-off" contracts on the spot market).

Finally, an inspection can be a means of avoiding maritime fraud. In some notorious cases it has been possible for a fraudulent seller to obtain payment under a documentary credit by presenting documents relating to a cargo and a ship even though neither the cargo nor the ship existed. Had an inspection been performed in these cases, the outcome could have been quite different. Since the inspection is normally performed in the buyer's interest, section B9 of Incoterms requires the buyer to pay the costs unless otherwise agreed. There is an exception to this principle when the inspection has been mandated by the authorities of the country of export.

Sections A2, B2: the obligation to clear the goods for export and import

A reference to Incoterms may sometimes be made in domestic contracts of sale, although this is not usually necessary or appropriate. The overwhelming usage concerns international contracts of sale when the cargo must be carried from country to country. There it is necessary to decide what the seller and the buyer are required to do to clear the goods for export and import, and in Incoterms this is dealt with under the heading "Licences, authorizations and formalities" (A2, B2).

The division of functions with respect to export and import clearance is important in several ways. First, the parties must know who is responsible for doing what is necessary to obtain any required licences or official authorizations and to submit official forms and requests in the country concerned. Second, the obligation to clear the goods – particularly for import – frequently results in the obligation to pay duty, VAT and other official charges. Third, the parties must resolve who bears the risk if it is not possible to clear the goods within the agreed time or at all (for example, if there are export or import prohibitions).

Take precautions against the risk of export and import prohibitions

A seller who has undertaken to clear the goods for export – and particularly for import – is well advised to negotiate with his buyer an extension of the time for delivery or the right to terminate the contract in case of unforeseen restrictions or prohibitions relating to export or import. More than this, it is important that the seller not undertake any activity that he or his agent either cannot do or are expressly forbidden to do by the receiving country.

Obtaining assistance to clear customs

A party having undertaken to clear the goods for export or import or to move them through a third country may often need the assistance of the other party to obtain various documents, for example documents showing the origin or ultimate destination of the goods. Therefore, sections A2 or B2 set out the extent to which the seller or the buyer, as the case may be, has to render this assistance to the other party.

Sections A10 and B10 stipulate that the seller and the buyer respectively have to reimburse any costs incurred by the other party for rendering the requested assistance, which is always provided at the risk and expense of the requesting party.

Sections A3, B3, A4: division of functions, costs and risks between the parties

While it may often be more practical for either the buyer or the seller to be responsible for the whole transport from point of origin to the agreed destination – as is the case under EXW or D-terms – the majority of international sales still use terms under which the obligations of carriage are divided between the parties. Under the F-terms pre-carriage is arranged by the seller; under the C-terms the seller undertakes only to arrange for the carriage and pay the costs, but the risk is transferred from him to the buyer when the goods are shipped. Presumably, this commercial practice is based to a large extent on the tradition in commodity trading which frequently requires the chartering of ships. In this case, the F-and C-terms are still appropriate.

For economy of transport, do not divide functions

A large number of sales transactions now using F- or C-terms involve manufactured goods. In these cases, the optimal transport economy may depend on either the buyer or the seller arranging and paying for the whole of the carriage. This is particularly true when the transport facilities available make it possible for the buyer or the seller to integrate the whole of the transport in one contract of carriage with the operator, even if this involves a contract using more than one mode of transport (so-called multimodal transport).

In such circumstances, the use of F- and C- terms may well diminish. However, in practice the term FCA can come very close to EXW, particularly if the words "cleared for export" are added after EXW. This is because under both FCA and EXW the buyer may be required to let the carrier pick up the goods at the seller's premises. The buyer is then in the same position under both EXW and FCA, since he is responsible for arranging and paying for the whole transport. But under EXW the seller is obliged only to make the goods available at his premises. The loading on to the carrier's vehicle is at the risk and expense of the buyer unless otherwise agreed.

Additional service to the buyer under F-terms

Although there is a fundamental difference between F-terms (FCA, FAS, FOB) and C-terms (CFR, CIF, CPT and CIP), this distinction is blurred in practice because sellers using F-terms still, as an additional service to the buyer, normally arrange the carriage (but at the buyer's risk and expense).

From a strictly legal viewpoint, parties using the F-terms should not find it necessary to specify how the seller should hand over the goods for carriage, since he simply has to follow (1) what the contract of sale specifically provides, or (2) the buyer's instructions. But the seller – though he has no duty under an F-term to do so – frequently takes care of the interests of the "absent" buyer.

While, in FCA A4 of Incoterms 1990, the handing over of the goods was explained with respect to different modes of transport, Incoterms 2000 distinguish only between two different situations – namely (1) when the goods are handed over at the seller's premises and (2) other cases. In the former case, it is for the seller to load the goods on to the buyer's collecting vehicle, and in other cases, it is sufficient that the seller make the goods available unloaded from the arriving vehicle.

While FCA can be used regardless of the mode of transport, FAS and FOB can be used only when the goods are carried by sea or inland waterway transport.

The distinction between FAS and FOB is well established on the question of handing over the goods for carriage. FAS means that the goods should be placed alongside the ship and FOB that they should be placed on board. Nevertheless, difficulties have always been connected with the use of FOB, since the ship's rail as a point for the division of functions, costs and risks between seller and buyer is seldom practicable.

The reference to the ship's rail may have been appropriate in earlier times when the cargo was lifted parcel by parcel (i.e., break bulk) on board the ship by the ship's own crew and equipment. Then "land costs" would fall upon the seller, "ship's costs" upon the buyer.

The custom of the port

Today stevedoring companies usually perform the whole of the loading operation, using either their own cranes or those belonging to the port authorities. Problems then arise as how to divide the bill for their services between the seller and the buyer, since the reference in FOB to the ship's rail does not give sufficient guidance. Instead, it is necessary to follow the custom of the port, which unfortunately may vary considerably from one port to another and which can range from

■ having the buyer pay for the whole of the loading operation (as if FOB in this respect were equivalent to FAS);

■ splitting the costs according to various customs and methods; or

■ having the seller pay all costs of the loading.

Caution when using FOB if custom of port not known

A buyer who does not know the custom of the port in the seller's country should be cautious when using FOB and should require a precise stipulation concerning the loading costs. Short expressions are sometimes used for this purpose (for example "FOB stowed" or "FOB stowed and trimmed").

While it may be clear that the seller's obligation to pay the loading costs is extended by these additions, it is not immediately clear to what extent the seller must also bear the risk of loss of or damage to the cargo which could occur subsequent to the passing of the ship's rail. The parties are therefore advised to clarify their intentions in this respect (for example, by adding a phrase such as "FOB stowed, costs and risks in connection with loading on the seller").

Handing over to the carrier under C-terms

When under the C-terms the seller has to arrange and pay for the carriage, handing over of the goods for carriage should not present any particular problem for seller or buyer. This is because the seller has to perform his duties according to the contract of carriage, which he has himself concluded with the carrier.

Dividing the costs of discharge at destination

Difficulties could arise at the other end of the transport, however, when the goods have to be discharged from the ship or from another means of conveyance. While delivery from a road, rail or air carrier should normally pose no problem, considerable problems may arise when the goods are carried by sea. Liner shipping companies usually include costs of loading and discharge in their freight rates, but in charter party operations there may be provisions stipulating that the discharging operations should be wholly or partly "free" to the carrier ("free out" stipulations). In these cases the buyer must know the ship's time of arrival and the time available for the discharging operations (the "laytime"). He must also ascertain the extent to which he is exposed to the risk of having to pay compensation (demurrage) to the seller if the laytime is exceeded.

Because of these variations, the rules of interpretation in Incoterms cannot specify how discharging costs should be divided between seller and buyer under the different C-terms. The parties are therefore advised to deal specifically with the relevant points in the contract of sale.

Failing such specific arrangements, guidance must be sought from any custom which the parties have developed between themselves in previous dealings, or from the custom of the port.

Section A8: the seller's duty to provide proof of delivery and the transport document

All terms except EXW require the seller to submit to the buyer formal proof that he has fulfilled his delivery obligation (A8). (The difference in EXW, of course, is that the buyer picks up the goods at the seller's premises.)

Under the C-terms, when the seller has to arrange and pay for the carriage, the transport document becomes very important, since it must show not only that the goods have been handed over to the carrier by the date agreed, but also that the buyer has an independent right to claim the goods from the carrier at destination.

CFR, CIF and on board documents

A further problem occurs with CFR or CIF, both of which require the seller to provide more than just a bill of lading. Specifically, he must provide an on board bill of lading, since the document must evidence shipment on board. Not surprisingly, container lines prefer to issue the transport document as a receipt for the goods when they are received for carriage, not at some later stage when the container with the cargo is lifted on board the ship.

It is common for the container line, upon the request of the shipper, to convert the "received-for-shipment" bill of lading with an "on board notation". This, however, causes further paperwork and frequently delay for sellers when payment is to be collected under documentary credits requiring an on board bill of lading rather than a received-for-shipment bill of lading to be presented within a prescribed period after the date on which the goods are loaded on board the ship.

Here again, it would be better to avoid the trade terms CFR and CIF and use CPT or CIP instead, as these terms do not refer to a bill of lading but rather to the "usual transport document", which may or may not be a bill of lading. But this is appropriate only when the buyer really has no need for a bill of lading for the sale of the goods in transit.

Surrender of original bill of lading essential

In some trades, there is a further problem connected with the use of bills of lading. This is caused by the need to present and surrender one original document to the carrier in order to obtain delivery of the goods. Ships frequently arrive at destination before an original bill of lading is available there. In such cases, the goods are often delivered to the buyer against a bill of lading guarantee issued by a bank. This is to protect the carrier if some person other than the person to whom the goods were delivered is the rightful holder of the original bill of lading.

This practice – or rather malpractice – defeats the whole bill of lading system, which depends for its validity on the firm principle that under no circumstances should the goods be delivered except in return for an original bill of lading. If that principle is not strictly followed, one can no longer say that the "bill of lading represents the goods".

Non-negotiable transport documents

In recent years, transport documents other than bills of lading for carriage of goods by sea have been increasingly used. These documents in the "waybill system" are similar to those used for modes of transport other than carriage by sea and when no original document is required to obtain the goods from the carrier at destination. It is sufficient that the consignee be named and that he can properly identify himself, as in the widespread use of air waybills (AWBs) and waybills for international road and rail carriage.

Such documents cannot be used, however, for transferring rights to the goods by the transfer of the document; they are therefore called non-negotiable. They bear various names such as "liner waybills", "ocean waybills", "data freight receipts", "cargo quay receipts" or "sea waybills". Although in such transport documents a buyer or a bank has been named as consignee, the seller and the seller alone enters into a contractual relationship with the carrier when the seller has contracted for carriage. The carrier takes instructions from his contracting party – the seller – and from no one else.

Payment against sea waybills requires caution

If the buyer has paid for the goods in advance, or a bank wishes to use the goods as security for a loan extended to the buyer, it is not sufficient that the buyer or the bank be named as consignee in a non-negotiable document. This is the case because the seller, by new instructions to the carrier, could replace the named consignee with someone else. To protect the buyer or the bank it is therefore necessary that the original instructions from the seller to the carrier to deliver the goods to the named consignee be irrevocable.

It follows that a seller should avoid trade terms such as CFR and CIF obliging him to present an on board bill of lading whenever practical difficulties are involved in obtaining and using such documents. It also follows that the buyer should not pay for the goods, and the bank should not rely on security in the goods, merely by accepting transport documents naming the buyer and the bank respectively as consignees, unless such instructions to the carrier are made irrevocable.

The problems of replacing bills of lading by EDI

Apart from the need to agree on a method for using EDI and adopting international message standards, there should be no particular problems when replacing transport documents by electronic messages. However, it is difficult to replace the bill of lading because it is not only proof of the delivery of the goods to the carrier but also a legal symbol often expressed by the principle that "the bill of lading represents the goods".

As noted, the fundamental principle behind the "negotiable" status of the bill of lading stems from the carrier's obligation to deliver the goods to the holder of one original bill of lading and to no one else. Consequently, the possession of the bill of lading has controlled the rightful delivery of the goods to the entitled party at destination.

How can this be replaced by an electronic message? The solution is to obtain the agreement of all parties concerned. First, they must agree to communicate electronically. Second, the agreement must take a particular form with respect to the replacement of bills of lading. The carrier must agree to deliver the goods only as instructed by the party having the right to give him delivery instructions. While, as noted above, this right has traditionally been tied to the possession of the original bill of lading, it can now be vested instead in the person whom the carrier has authorized to give him electronic instructions.

Incoterms CFR and CIF A8 and EDI

Incoterms 1990, in the trade terms CFR and CIF, section A8, already took the development of EDI into consideration. They did this first by maintaining the traditional principle that, unless otherwise agreed, the transport document must enable the buyer to sell the goods in transit by the transfer of the document to a subsequent buyer. But they also indicated that the transfer could be made by notification to the carrier. In the former case, the negotiable bill of lading is expressly referred to. In the latter, reference is made to a system of notification. In any event, a mere notification to the carrier is not sufficient to replace a bill of lading.

Therefore, parties wishing to replace the bill of lading by electronic messages must necessarily refer to a system, such as BOLERO or similar systems, to enable the buyer to obtain the goods from the carrier at destination and to transfer the rights to the goods to a subsequent buyer while the goods are still being carried.

It follows that the use of EDI requires a particular agreement and a well-developed system following internationally agreed standards (UN/EDIFACT and UNCID), and that the replacement of bills of lading by electronic messages can be implemented only by reference to a notification system such as BOLERO, which is available not only to shippers, carriers and consignees, but also to other parties.

The on board bill of lading under CFR and CIF

In the CFR and CIF terms, reference is made to the on board bill of lading, since under those terms the seller has not fulfilled his delivery obligation until the goods have been placed on board the ship. The bill of lading is critical for the buyer if he intends to sell the goods to another buyer while they are still being carried (sale "afloat"). In these circumstances, transferring the original or the set of originals of the bill of lading can be used to transfer title of the goods to the other party.

Transport document as proof of delivery

Although under the F-terms the buyer must arrange and pay for the carriage – meaning that he enters into a direct contractual relationship with the carrier – the transport document can still be given by the carrier to the seller as proof that the seller has delivered the goods to him. If it is, the transport document will constitute not only evidence of the contract of carriage, but also proof of delivery of the goods to the carrier.

Indeed the seller – in his capacity as a shipper in the contract of carriage – frequently receives the bill of lading from the carrier as proof of delivery of the goods. This often happens, even though from a strictly legal viewpoint it is the buyer who should have received the bill of lading as evidence of the contract made with the carrier, so that the buyer can take delivery of the goods at destination in return for it.

This is further clarified in A8 of the F-terms, which stipulates that the seller must render the buyer, at the buyer's risk and expense, every assistance in obtaining the transport document if the document is not identical with the document proving delivery of the goods to the carrier. Since the possession of the bill of lading is required for the right to give instructions to the carrier and to obtain the cargo from him at destination, it is extremely important that the buyer receive this document from the seller, unless it has been given directly to him by the carrier.

Documents required to obtain delivery under D-terms

Under the D-terms the situation is different from that described in the preceding paragraphs, since the seller has not fulfilled his delivery obligation until the goods have actually arrived in the country of destination. Nevertheless, the buyer may still require a document to enable him to obtain the goods from the carrier at the agreed point of delivery. This may well be the case, for example, if the goods have been sold DES, in which event the buyer takes delivery from the ship and is normally required to surrender an original bill of lading.

The terms DEQ, DDU and DDP may be different in this respect, since the goods under these terms would have been placed on the quay or taken to an interior point in the country of destination. But this does not necessarily mean that they have left the custody of the carrier, and a bill of lading may still be required to obtain them.

Transport documents for carriage by sea

Note the difference between the waybill and the bill of lading:

Waybill

■ The goods are delivered to the party named as consignee.

■ Other than proof of identity, the consignee does not have to produce documents to claim the goods, and the waybill itself is not a document of title.

Bill of lading

■ The goods should be released only in return for an original bill of lading.

■ The bill of lading itself represents title to the goods, and is appropriate when the goods may be sold in transit.

Incoterms accept electronic equivalents for transport documents.

Delivery orders

Sometimes the goods may have been discharged in bulk, and the buyer has to remove his goods from a larger consignment. One bill of lading could then cover the whole consignment, even though the consignment is intended for several buyers. In these cases, it is customary to split the bill of lading into parts by issuing individual so-called delivery orders; these are specifically referred to in section A8 of all D-terms except DAF. (Normally under DAF there is no physical delivery of the goods to the buyer at the "D point", but the carriage continues without interruption to the final destination. This is evidenced by the stipulation in DAF A8 that the seller must provide the buyer at his request, risk and expense with a through document of transport, normally obtainable in the country of dispatch.)

Sections A4 and B4: the seller's obligation to deliver and the buyer's obligation to take delivery

Delivery at the seller's premises

As noted, contracts requiring the buyer to take delivery of the goods at the seller's premises do not normally cause any particular problems in practice. The facilities at the seller's place will determine whether the cargo will be delivered at a ramp where a driver could place his lorry and where forklift trucks can be used by the seller's personnel to place the goods on the lorry. However, it may not be easy to determine how much stowing of the goods on the lorry should be performed by the driver and how much by the seller's personnel. This necessarily depends on the circumstances and is not resolved by the rule of interpretation in EXW A4, which simply states that the goods should be placed "at the disposal of the buyer". However, in Incoterms 2000 it is now clarified that, under FCA A4, the seller has to load the goods on the buyer's collecting vehicle.

Delivery at the buyer's premises

The same problem could arise under DDU and DDP, when it can be very difficult to determine exactly how the seller should arrange to hand over the goods to the buyer. In Incoterms 2000, it is clarified that the seller only has to make the goods available to the buyer not unloaded from the arriving vehicle.

Delivery at the border under DAF A4

Under DAF A4, there will usually not be a "physical" delivery of the goods at the frontier of the buyer's country, unless it is necessary for some reason to have them stored in a warehouse for customs or other purposes pending the loading of the goods on a railway wagon or other means of conveyance for on-carriage.

Delivery at the waterfront under DES and DEQ

Under the terms DES and DEQ the cargo will be made available to the buyer in the ship and on the quay respectively. How the cargo should be received at these points (pumping installations, silos, adjoining railway tracks, cargo terminals, etc.) will depend on the circumstances.

The buyer's acceptance of the seller's handing over for carriage

As noted, there are different customs for handing over the cargo to the carrier. Under the C-terms, when the seller arranges and pays for the carriage, he will deliver the cargo to the carrier in the absence of the buyer. Consequently, there will be no physical delivery of the cargo directly to the buyer.

But the buyer must accept that the cargo is handed over to the carrier as stipulated in A4 of the C-terms and be content with the proof of the delivery which the seller must give him according to A8. This is because the C-terms evidence shipment contracts under which, in principle, the seller fulfils his delivery obligation at the place of dispatch or shipment. What happens to the cargo after the seller has fulfilled his delivery obligation is at the risk and expense of the buyer.

The buyer's obligation to receive the goods from the carrier

Nevertheless, it is also important to note that the buyer has an obligation to the seller to receive the goods from the carrier at the named place or port of destination (B4). If a buyer refuses to honour his obligation to pay for the goods in return for a bill of lading, where applicable, and thereby fails to collect the goods from the carrier, the seller may incur expenses due under the contract of carriage he has concluded with the carrier. These costs will then be included in the seller's claim for damages as a result of the buyer's breach of his contractual obligation.

Sections A5 and B5: the transfer from seller to buyer of the risk of loss of or damage to the goods

Whenever "transfer of risks" is referred to in Incoterms A5 and B5, the expression "loss of or damage to the goods" is used. This means physical loss of or damage to the cargo and does not include other risks such as the risk of delay or non-fulfilment of the contract for other reasons.

The "price risk"

If the risk referred to in Incoterms materializes, the buyer has to pay the price even though he does not receive the goods in contractual condition or at all.

This is the so-called "price risk". Nonetheless, damage to the goods may depend upon circumstances attributable to the seller. For example, the seller may have inadequately packaged the goods. If so, the damage will not have resulted from a transportation risk, and the buyer is then entitled not only to avoid paying for the goods but also to hold the seller responsible for breach of contract.

Incoterms do not specifically deal with other consequences if the seller has not fulfilled his delivery obligation. Such questions are left to the applicable law or to the stipulations in the contract of sale. But in the absence of any provisions in the contract, fulfilment of the seller's delivery obligation also means that any further risks or expenses are for the account of the buyer.

Consequently, while under the C-terms the seller has to pay the normal costs of carriage to the carrier, the buyer has to bear any additional costs resulting from circumstances occurring after the seller has fulfilled his delivery obligation. These may include, for example, extra costs for an unexpected transhipment caused by political events or adverse weather conditions which render the previously agreed routing inaccessible.

However, if such events occur before the seller has fulfilled his delivery obligation but after he has entered into the contract of sale, the extent to which he can escape (if at all) his duty to perform the contract will depend on the other terms of the contract or on the applicable law. Thus, the "price risk" should not be confused with the risk of breach of the contract of sale (caused by delay, non-fulfilment, etc.). The remedies available to the affected party for these breaches are not dealt with in Incoterms.

Premature transfer of risk

In some cases, the risk can be transferred from the seller to the buyer even before the seller has fulfilled his delivery obligation. This could happen as a result of (1) the buyer's failure to do what is required of him to enable the seller to deliver the goods to him, or (2) the buyer's failure to take delivery of the goods (B5).

Therefore, the buyer must give such notice to the seller as the latter requires to prepare the delivery (B7), or the buyer must nominate the carrier under F-terms and accept the goods from the carrier as agreed. Moreover, a buyer having undertaken under DDU to clear the goods for import must fulfil his obligation to do this within the agreed time so the seller can proceed with the on-carriage of the goods to destination as intended. If the buyer fails to do this, he must bear all additional risks of loss of or damage to the goods resulting from his failure (B5).

Appropriation of the goods to the contract

The premature passing of the risk noted in the above paragraphs cannot occur unless it can be ascertained that the goods are intended for the buyer and appropriated to the contract of sale made with him. Or, as expressed in the Incoterms B5 clauses, the goods must have been "clearly set aside or otherwise identified as the contract goods". This appropriation is normally achieved as soon as the goods have been prepared for carriage, since it would then have been necessary to mark them and/or to name the consignee. But it may be that the goods are to be carried in bulk without such marking or naming of the consignee as would amount to appropriation. Then the risk will not pass until effective appropriation has been made, for example, until the issuance of separate bills of lading or delivery orders for parts of the bulk consignment.

Using force majeure clauses to protect the seller from the "breach of contract risk"

A seller who has undertaken to deliver the goods at a point outside of his control – for example, when the goods are to be delivered under D-terms – should consider the need to protect himself (usually by force majeure or other relief clauses) against the risk of having to provide substitute goods instead of those lost or damaged, or to make other agreed restitution. Otherwise, he could face damages for breach of contract if he fails to do this in time or at all.

Section A3b: the seller's insurance obligation

CIF and CIP are the only Incoterms related directly to insurance coverage. This is because it is important for the buyer to obtain insurance when he has left the responsibility of arranging the contract of carriage and paying the freight to the seller. The seller is then presumed to be in a better position to arrange insurance than the buyer. This could still be the case if the goods are to be carried in chartered ships or if they consist of larger consignments of commodities.

But with manufactured goods, sellers and buyers usually have lasting arrangements with their insurers for exports and imports. Therefore, separate insurance arrangements for each shipment would be unnecessary. This being so, there is no reason to impose an insurance obligation on one party to the benefit of the other, since the better solution is to leave the question of insurance to the parties themselves.

Freedom of insurance restricted

In many countries sellers or buyers may be compelled to take out insurance in their own country – either to minimize expenditure in foreign currencies and/or to support the domestic insurance industry. In these cases, a buyer may be ordered to contract for imports on CFR or CPT terms instead of letting the seller arrange the insurance according to CIF or CIP. Conversely, a seller in these countries may be obliged to sell the goods on CIF or CIP terms for the same reasons.

Sections A7, B7 and A10, B10: notices

Conditions for the buyer's giving notice

If there is no specified date or place agreed in the contract and the buyer is entitled to determine

■ the time and/or place when and where he should take delivery under EXW or D-terms;

■ the nomination of the carrier and delivery time under F-terms; or

■ the time for shipping the goods and/or the destination under C-terms, then the buyer has to give the seller sufficient and timely notice (B7).

Conditions for the seller's giving notice

Conversely, the seller must give the buyer sufficient notice of

■ when and where the goods will be placed at the buyer's disposal under EXW;

■ when and where the goods have been delivered to the carrier under F- and C-terms; and

■ when and where the goods are expected to arrive under D-terms so that the buyer can take appropriate measures in time to receive them (A7).

Information relating to insurance

When under CIF and CIP the seller has to take out insurance for the benefit of the buyer, the seller may require information about particulars of the goods which do not appear in the contract of sale. He may also need to be informed about the buyer's wishes for extended or additional insurance. The buyer must then inform the seller accordingly (B10). When the buyer intends to take out insurance himself, or is obliged to do so under his country's regulations, he may also require additional information from the seller, who must then give such information to the buyer upon request (A10).

Sufficient notice

There are no special requirements in Incoterms that notice be given in a particular form (by letter, telex or telefax). Incoterms state only that notice must be "sufficient". If the parties have agreed to communicate electronically, notice may be given by EDI.

Failure to give sufficient notice

Failure to give sufficient notice constitutes a breach of contract which could lead to serious consequences. It could, for example, give the other party the right to cancel the contract. Incoterms deal only with two particular aspects of late or insufficient notice, namely

■ the premature passing of the risk (B5); and

■ the buyer's liability to pay additional costs (B6).

For the premature passing of the risk as well as for the liability to pay additional costs, the parties must be able to ascertain the goods to which the risk or the additional costs relate. This can only be done if the goods can be appropriated to the contract of sale, i.e., if they are clearly set aside for the buyer or otherwise identified as being intended for him

Sections A6, B6, A3b, A10 and B10: division of costs between the parties

Division of costs is a most important element in every contract of sale. The parties must know not only who does what but also how costs resulting therefrom should be divided between them. In most cases the fact that a party must do something means that he must also bear the resulting costs, unless otherwise agreed. But there are many exceptions to this principle and uncertainties arise, particularly with respect to services performed by other parties (for example, stevedores engaged for loading and discharge or costs which cannot clearly be attributed to either the buyer's or the seller's functions, such as (a) "semi-official" charges debited on the export or import of the goods, or (b) charges for their storage pending shipment or delivery). Also, difficulties arise with respect to the division of costs whenever additional costs are caused by unexpected events, such as hindrances causing a ship to deviate or to remain in a seaport longer than expected.

Main principle of distribution of costs

The main principle of the division of costs is clear enough: the seller has to pay costs necessary for the goods to reach the agreed point of delivery, and the buyer has to pay any further costs after that point. But as noted, it is not always easy to implement this principle in practice, since the detailed distribution of functions under the various trade terms is not and cannot be fully defined in Incoterms. Instead, failing precise stipulations in the contract of sale, guidance must be sought from other criteria such as commercial practices used earlier by the same parties or the custom of the trade.

The four main categories of costs

The costs referred to in Incoterms can be grouped in four main categories. These include elements relating to

- dispatch, carriage and delivery;
- customs clearance for export and import;
- services or assistance rendered by one party to the other in addition to what the assisting party is required to do under the relevant trade term; and
- insurance.

Costs related to dispatch, carriage and delivery

This category is by far the most important, since it includes costs relating to

- loading at the seller's premises;
- pre-carriage in the country of export;
- making of the contract (booking the cargo for shipment and issuing the relevant transport documents);
- warehousing, storage and handling charges pending dispatch of the cargo from the country of export;
- hire of transportation equipment and appliances in the country of export;
- the main international carriage;
- warehousing, storage and handling charges subsequent to discharge in the country of import;
- hire of transportation equipment and appliances in the country of import;
- on-carriage in the country of import; and
- unloading at the buyer's premises.

Costs for export and import clearance

With respect to costs for export and import clearance, a firm distinction should be made between duties, VAT and other official charges and the cost for the clearance itself, which is frequently performed by freight forwarders in their capacity as customs brokers. Clearing of the goods will also include costs to obtain licences, certificates, consular invoices, permits, authorizations, and legalization as well as costs for inspection, customs warehouse charges, customs declarations and freight forwarders' service charges.

Costs for services and assistance

This category relates only to costs which one party may be entitled to claim from the other for services or assistance rendered upon request for the clearing of the goods. These include the seller's assistance for the buyer's export clearance under EXW (A2) and the buyer's assistance for the seller's clearing of the goods under DDP (B2). They may also include costs incurred in obtaining documents which the other party could require for the clearance (A10 and B10 respectively).

Costs of insurance

This category is relevant only when the seller has contracted on CIF or CIP terms requiring that he take out insurance for the benefit of the buyer and also that he pay the premium. Any additional insurance (extended coverage or protection against added risks such as war, riots, or civil commotions, or strikes or other labour disturbances) taken out by the seller at the buyer's request has to be paid for by the buyer, unless otherwise agreed in the contract of sale.

Cost distribution systems

In certain cases – for example, freight forwarding services using a pre-arranged cost distribution system such as Combiterms (see annexes) – it may be possible to obtain the more detailed breakdown needed to avoid uncertainty and disputes between the parties over costs. These disputes often concern minor costs, but the time, effort and money spent in resolving the disputes can be out of all proportion.

The parties are therefore advised either to specify the division of such costs not clearly following from the trade term itself, or to agree to apply a pre-arranged cost distribution system. An agreement to use a cost distribution system should be clearly mentioned in conjunction with the trade term by adding the phrase "Incoterms 2000 with cost distribution according to ...".

GOING THROUGH THE 13 INCOTERMS

"Ex works" means that the seller delivers when he places the goods at the disposal of the buyer at the seller's premises or another named place (i.e. works, factory, warehouse, etc.) not cleared for export and not loaded on any collecting vehicle.

This term thus represents the minimum obligation for the seller, and the buyer has to bear all costs and risks involved in taking the goods from the seller's premises.

However, if the parties wish the seller to be responsible for the loading of the goods on departure and to bear the risks and all the costs of such loading, this should be made clear by adding explicit wording to this effect in the contract of sale.[1] This term should not be used when the buyer cannot carry out the export formalities directly or indirectly. In such circumstances, the FCA term should be used, provided the seller agrees that he will load at his cost and risk.

1 Refer to the introduction of *Incoterms 2000*, ICC publication N°560, paragraph 11. (See reproduced pages 184-185 in this text.)

EXW

EX Works
(...named place)

Group **E**
departure

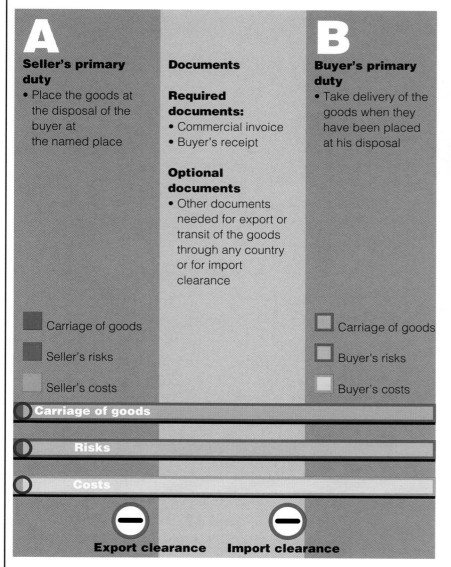

A

Seller's primary duty
• Place the goods at the disposal of the buyer at the named place

Documents

Required documents:
• Commercial invoice
• Buyer's receipt

Optional documents
• Other documents needed for export or transit of the goods through any country or for import clearance

B

Buyer's primary duty
• Take delivery of the goods when they have been placed at his disposal

■ Carriage of goods

■ Seller's risks

■ Seller's costs

□ Carriage of goods

□ Buyer's risks

□ Buyer's costs

Carriage of goods

Risks

Costs

Export clearance   Import clearance

Critical points
◐ Carriage to be arranged by the buyer

◐ Risk transfer from the seller to the buyer when the goods are at the disposal of the buyer

◐ Cost transfer from the seller to the buyer when the goods are at the disposal of the buyer

EXW

A   THE SELLER'S OBLIGATIONS

A1   Provision of goods in conformity with the contract

The seller must provide the goods and the commercial invoice, or its equivalent electronic message, in conformity with the contract of sale and any other evidence of conformity which may be required by the contract.

Comments   The seller must provide the goods in conformity with the contract. It is also usual practice that the seller, in order to be paid, has to invoice the buyer. In addition, the seller must submit any other evidence stipulated in the contract itself that the goods conform with the contract.

This text only serves as a reminder of the seller's main obligation under the contract of sale.

A2   Licences, authorizations and formalities

The seller must render the buyer, at the latter's request, risk and expense, every assistance in obtaining, where applicable[2], any export licence or other official authorization necessary for the export of the goods.

Comments   Under EXW it is the buyer's obligation to obtain export as well as import licences or other official authorizations. It is therefore the seller under this term who should render the necessary assistance and the buyer who should bear any cost involved.

A3   Contracts of carriage and insurance

a)   Contract of carriage: no obligation[3].

b)   Contract of insurance: no obligation[4].

Comments   Since the goods are made available to the buyer at the seller's premises, the seller has no obligation to contract for carriage or insurance.

A4   Delivery

The seller must place the goods at the disposal of the buyer at the named place of delivery, not loaded on any collecting vehicle, on the date or within the period agreed or, if no such time is agreed, at the usual time for delivery of such goods. If no specific point has been agreed within the named place, and if there are several points available, the seller may select the point at the place of delivery which best suits his purpose.

Comments   Under EXW the seller only has to make the goods available to the buyer at the named place of delivery in the seller's own country, which is usually at the seller's premises. Therefore, this term represents the seller's minimum obligation; delivery at the buyer's premises in the buyer's country would represent the seller's maximum obligation, for example DDU, DDP. Exactly how delivery should be performed is not specified, but this normally follows what has been done in previous dealings between the same parties or from the custom of the trade.

Frequently, the seller assists the buyer by bringing the goods onto a ramp from which they can be loaded on an arriving vehicle. The seller may also assist the buyer with the loading of the goods on to the vehicle, for example by using a fork-lift truck. If it is intended that the seller should be obliged to assist the buyer as above, this could be made clear by the parties' adding the words "loaded upon departing vehicle" after EXW in the contract of sale.

2 Refer to Introduction of *Incoterms 2000* paragraph 14. (See reproduced pages 184-185 in this text.)
3 Refer to Introduction of *Incoterms 2000* paragraph 10. (See reproduced pages 184-185 in this text.)
4 Refer to Introduction of *Incoterms 2000* paragraph 10. (See reproduced pages 184-185 in this text.)

A5   Transfer of risks

The seller must, subject to the provisions of B5, bear all risks of loss of or damage to the goods until such time as they have been delivered in accordance with A4.

Comments All Incoterms are based on the same principle that the risk of loss of or damage to the goods is transferred from the seller to the buyer when the seller has fulfilled his delivery obligation according to A4.

All Incoterms, in conformity with the general principle of the 1980 CISG (Convention on Contracts for the International Sale of Goods), connect the transfer of the risk with the delivery of the goods and not with other circumstances, such as the passing of ownership or the time of the conclusion of the contract. Neither Incoterms nor CISG deal with transfer of title to the goods or other property rights with respect to the goods.

The passing of risk of loss of or damage to the goods concerns the risk of fortuitous events (accidents) and does not include loss or damage caused by the seller or the buyer, for example through inadequate packing or marking of the goods. Therefore, even if damage occurs subsequent to the transfer of the risk, the seller may still be responsible if the damage could be attributed to the fact that the goods were not delivered in conformity with the contract (see A1 and the comments to A9).

A5 of all Incoterms contain the phrase "subject to the provisions of B5". This means that there are exceptions to the main rule in the circumstances described in B5 which may result in a premature passing of the risk because of the buyer's failure properly to fulfil his obligations (see the comments to B5).

A6   Division of costs

The seller must, subject to the provisions of B6, pay all costs relating to the goods until such time as they have been delivered in accordance with A4.

Comments As is the case with the transfer of the risk of loss of or damage to the goods, all Incoterms follow the same rule, that the division of costs occurs at the delivery point. All costs occurring before the seller has fulfilled his obligation to deliver according to A4 are for his account, while further costs are for the account of the buyer (see the comments to B6). This rule is made subject to the provisions of B6, which indicates that the buyer may have to bear additional costs incurred by his failure to give appropriate notice to the seller.

Since under EXW the seller's obligation is limited to placing the goods at the disposal of the buyer, all further costs have to be borne by the buyer once the goods have been placed at his disposal. The seller has no duty to bear any costs incurred for export clearance, since under B2 this is the buyer's obligation.

A7   Notice to the buyer

The seller must give the buyer sufficient notice as to when and where the goods will be placed at his disposal.

Comments The seller must give the buyer sufficient notice as to when the goods will be available at the agreed or chosen delivery point, so that the buyer can make preparations in time to take delivery according to B4. There is no stipulation in Incoterms spelling out the consequences of the seller's failure to give such notice. But it follows from Incoterms that the seller's failure constitutes a breach of contract. This means that the seller could be held responsible for such a breach, according to the law applicable to the contract of sale.

EXW

A8 Proof of delivery, transport document or equivalent electronic message

▪ No obligation[5].

Comments Since the seller makes the goods available at his premises, or a named place of delivery in his own country, no particular proof of delivery is required.

A9 Checking – packaging – marking

The seller must pay the costs of those checking operations (such as checking quality, measuring, weighing, counting) which are necessary for the purpose of placing the goods at the buyer's disposal.

The seller must provide at his own expense packaging (unless it is usual for the particular trade to make the goods of the contract description available unpacked) which is required for the transport of the goods, to the extent that the circumstances relating to the transport (for example modalities, destination) are made known to the seller before the contract of sale is concluded. Packaging is to be marked appropriately.

Comments It is necessary for the buyer to ensure that the seller has duly fulfilled his obligation with respect to the condition of the goods. This is particularly important if the buyer is called upon to pay for the goods before he has received and checked them. However, the seller has no duty to arrange and pay for inspection of the goods before shipment, unless this has been specifically agreed in the contract of sale.

The goods must also be adequately packed. But the seller may not know the buyer's intentions concerning the mode of transport and the ultimate destination. There is a considerable difference between a short journey to an adjoining country and an intercontinental carriage by sea, which may expose the goods to the risk of breakage or corrosion from humidity and condensation.

The seller is obliged to pack the goods for a long and difficult carriage only if he knows that this will actually occur. Therefore, it is advisable for the buyer to inform the seller accordingly, or, better still, to specify the required packaging in the contract of sale.

A10 Other obligations

The seller must render the buyer at the latter's request, risk and expense, every assistance in obtaining any documents or equivalent electronic messages issued or transmitted in the country of delivery and/or of origin which the buyer may require for the export and/or import of the goods and, where necessary, for their transit through any country.

The seller must provide the buyer, upon request, with the necessary information for procuring insurance.

Comments Since it is for the buyer to do whatever is necessary with respect to export, transit and import clearance, he may well need the seller's assistance to obtain documents (for example, a certificate of origin, health certificate, clean report of finding, import licence) or equivalent electronic data interchange (EDI) messages issued or transmitted in the country of delivery or import. But any cost incurred by the seller in rendering this assistance must be reimbursed to him by the buyer, according to B10.

Also, the seller may be requested to provide the buyer with information relating to the goods which the buyer may require for insurance purposes, if this information does not follow from the description of the goods in the contract of sale.

---

5 Refer to Introduction of *Incoterms 2000* paragraph 10. (See reproduced pages 184-185 in this text.)

B   THE BUYER'S OBLIGATIONS

B1   Payment of the price

■ The buyer must pay the price as provided in the contract of sale.

Comments   The buyer must pay the price agreed in the contract of sale. B1 constitutes a reminder of this main obligation, which corresponds with the seller's obligation to provide the goods in conformity with the contract of sale, as stipulated in A1.

B2   Licences, authorizations and formalities

 The buyer must obtain at his own risk and expense any export and import licence or other official authorization and carry out, where applicable[6], all customs formalities for the export of the goods.

Comments   Since the seller only makes the goods available to the buyer in the country of export, it is for the buyer to do whatever is necessary with respect to the clearance of the goods for export, transit and import. A prohibition of export or import will not relieve the buyer from his obligation under the contract of sale. However, contracts of sale frequently contain "relief clauses" to the benefit of both parties in such cases. These clauses may stipulate that the affected party will be given the benefit of an extension of time to fulfil his obligation, or, under the worst circumstances, the right to avoid the contract. It may also be possible to obtain such relief under the law applicable to the contract of sale.

Before accepting the obligation to clear the goods for export, the buyer should ascertain that the regulations of the seller's country do not prevent him as a non-resident from applying for an export licence or from performing whatever tasks are necessary to clear the goods for export. Normally, no such difficulties will be encountered, since measures in this regard can be taken by freight forwarders (customs brokers) on the buyer's behalf. If the buyer wishes to avoid the obligation to clear the goods for export, the words "cleared for export" could be added after EXW.

B3   Contracts of carriage and insurance

 a) Contract of carriage: no obligation[7].

b) Contract of insurance: no obligation[8].

Comments   The buyer has no obligation to the seller under the contract of sale to contract for carriage, except as required in order to take delivery according to B4. This is made clear by the words "no obligation" in B3. He would, of course, nevertheless arrange for carriage in his own interest.

B4   Taking delivery

The buyer must take delivery of the goods when they have been delivered in accordance with A4 and A7/B7.

Comments   The buyer must take delivery of the goods when they have been placed at his disposal at the agreed time and place as stipulated in A4. His failure to do so will not relieve him from his obligation to pay the price and could result in a premature passing of the risk of loss of or damage to the goods or make him liable to pay additional costs according to B5 and B6.

---

6 Refer to Introduction of *Incoterms 2000* paragraph 14. (See reproduced pages 184-185 in this text.)
7 Refer to Introduction of *Incoterms 2000* paragraph 10. (See reproduced pages 184-185 in this text.)
8 Refer to Introduction of *Incoterms 2000* paragraph 10. (See reproduced pages 184-185 in this text.)

B5 **Transfer of risks**

The buyer must bear all risks of loss of or damage to the goods

- from the time they have been delivered in accordance with A4; and

- from the agreed date or the expiry date of any period fixed for taking delivery which arise because he fails to give notice in accordance with B7, provided, however, that the goods have been duly appropriated to the contract, that is to say clearly set aside or otherwise identified as the contract goods.

Comments According to the main rule, while the seller under A5 bears the risk of loss of or damage to the goods until the delivery point, the buyer has to bear the risk thereafter. The delivery point is different under the different terms. In EXW and all D-terms, the goods are simply placed "at the disposal of the buyer" at the relevant point, while under the F- and C-terms the delivery point is related to the handing over of the goods to the carrier in the country of dispatch or shipment (see the comments to A4 of these terms). In the terms used for goods intended to be carried by sea, reference is made to delivery alongside the named vessel (FAS A4) or delivery onboard the vessel (FOB, CFR, CIF).

Consequences of buyer's failure to give notice

While the seller under EXW and all D-terms can transfer the risk by his own act of placing the goods at the buyer's disposal, he may be prevented from doing so by the buyer's failure to give notice according to B7. This can occur when it is the buyer's responsibility to determine (1) the time within a stipulated period when the goods are to be made available or (2) the place of delivery (see the comments to B7). The failure to perform these tasks results in a premature passing of the risk: it is not acceptable that the buyer should be able to delay the delivery and the passing of the risk longer than contemplated when the contract of sale was made. Therefore, his failure to notify according to B7 will cause the risk to pass "from the agreed date or the expiry date of any period fixed for taking delivery".

Appropriation and the passing of risk

The risk, however, cannot pass until the goods "have been duly appropriated to the contract'. If the goods are unascertained, i.e., goods of a certain kind which the seller will deliver to his various buyers, appropriation occurs only when the goods are "clearly set aside or otherwise identified as the contract goods".

B6 **Division of costs**

The buyer must pay

- all costs relating to the goods from the time they have been delivered in accordance with A4; and

- any additional costs incurred by failing either to take delivery of the goods when they have been placed at his disposal, or to give appropriate notice in accordance with B7 provided, however, that the goods have been duly appropriated to the contract, that is to say, clearly set aside or otherwise identified as the contract goods; and

- where applicable[9], all duties, taxes and other charges as well as the costs of carrying out customs formalities payable upon export.

The buyer must reimburse all costs and charges incurred by the seller in rendering assistance in accordance with A2.

Comments Although the seller's obligation is limited to placing the goods at the disposal of the buyer at the seller's own premises, EXW A4 does not indicate exactly how this should be done. In practice, the seller will often assist the buyer by bringing the goods onto a ramp from

9 Refer to Introduction of *Incoterms 2000* paragraph 14. (See reproduced pages 184-185 in this text.)

which they can be loaded on to a vehicle for carriage from the seller's place. Or the seller may assist the buyer with the loading of the goods on to this vehicle, for example by placing them on to the vehicle by the use of a fork-lift truck. In these cases, sellers will not usually debit their buyers with costs for work performed by the seller's own personnel and/or for the use of the seller's own equipment. However, if the goods are to be taken from an independent warehouse and the seller stands to incur external costs, he would, according to the main principle of B6, be entitled to debit such costs to the buyer.

Normally, the extent to which the seller will assist the buyer free of charge in removing the goods from the seller's premises will be determined from previous dealings between the same parties or from the custom of the trade. If, however, the parties agree that the seller should be obliged to perform the loading of the goods, the words "loaded upon departing vehicle" may be added after EXW in the contract of sale.

Notice and appropriation

Whenever the buyer is entitled to determine the time or place of taking delivery, his failure to notify the seller according to B7 will not only cause the risk of loss of or damage to the goods to pass prematurely but also make him liable to pay any additional costs caused thereby, for example extra costs for storage and insurance. However, this liability occurs only if the goods have been identified as the contractual goods (see the comments concerning "appropriation" under B5).

Buyer clears goods for export

Under EXW the buyer has to clear the goods for export. Consequently, he will have to pay "where applicable, all duties, taxes and other charges as well as the costs of carrying out customs formalities payable upon export" and reimburse the seller for any assistance the seller provides in performing these tasks.

B7 Notice to the seller

The buyer must, whenever he is entitled to determine the time within an agreed period and/or the place of taking delivery, give the seller sufficient notice thereof.

Comments As discussed in the comments to B5 and B6, the failure of the buyer to notify the seller of the time for shipping the goods or the destination – when the buyer in the contract of sale has been given the option to determine these matters – may cause the risk of the loss of or damage to the goods to pass before the goods have been delivered according to A4. In addition, it can make the buyer liable to pay any additional costs incurred by the seller as a result of the buyer's failure.

B8 Proof of delivery, transport document or equivalent electronic message

The buyer must provide the seller with appropriate evidence of having taken delivery.

Comments The buyer should provide the seller with a customary receipt for the goods. This receipt could be indicated on a packing list or provided by some other document which could constitute "appropriate evidence".

B9 Inspection of goods

The buyer must pay the costs of any pre-shipment inspection, including inspection mandated by the authorities of the country of export.

Comments As noted in the comments to A9, the buyer has to pay for any costs of checking the goods, unless the contract determines that these costs should be wholly or partly borne by the seller. In some cases, the contract may provide that the costs should be borne by the seller if the inspection reveals that the goods do not conform with the contract.

Pre-shipment inspection

In some countries, where import licences or permission to obtain foreign currency for the payment of the price may be required, the authorities may demand an inspection of the goods before shipment, to ensure that the goods conform with the contract. (This is usually called pre-shipment inspection, PSI.) If this is the case, the inspection is normally arranged by instructions from the authorities to an inspection company, which they appoint. The costs following from this inspection have to be paid by the authorities. Any reimbursement to the authorities for the inspection costs, however, must be made by the buyer, unless otherwise specifically agreed between the buyer and the seller.

EXW

B10   Other obligations

The buyer must pay all costs and charges incurred in obtaining the documents or equivalent electronic messages mentioned in A10 and reimburse those incurred by the seller in rendering his assistance in accordance therewith.

Comments   As discussed in the comments to A10, the seller has to render the buyer assistance in obtaining the documents or electronic messages which may be required for the transit and import of the goods. However, this assistance is rendered at the buyer's risk and expense. Therefore, B10 stipulates that the buyer must pay all costs and charges incurred in obtaining these documents or electronic messages. He will also have to reimburse the seller for the seller's costs in rendering his assistance in these matters.

"Free Carrier" means that the seller delivers the goods, cleared for export, to the carrier nominated by the buyer at the named place. It should be noted that the chosen place of delivery has an impact on the obligations of loading and unloading the goods at that place. If delivery occurs at the seller's premises, the seller is responsible for loading. If delivery occurs at any other place, the seller is not responsible for unloading.

This term may be used irrespective of the mode of transport, including multimodal transport.

"Carrier" means any person who, in a contract of carriage, undertakes to perform or to procure the performance of transport by rail, road, air, sea, inland waterway or by a combination of such modes.

If the buyer nominates a person other than a carrier to receive the goods, the seller is deemed to have fulfilled his obligation to deliver the goods when they are delivered to that person.

FCA
Free CArrier
(...named place)

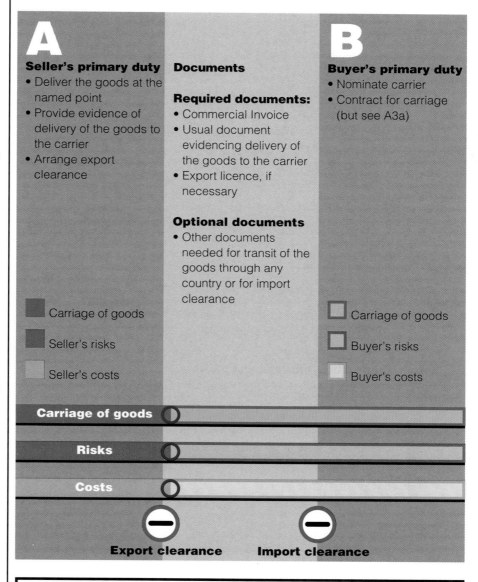

A

Seller's primary duty
- Deliver the goods at the named point
- Provide evidence of delivery of the goods to the carrier
- Arrange export clearance

Documents

Required documents:
- Commercial Invoice
- Usual document evidencing delivery of the goods to the carrier
- Export licence, if necessary

Optional documents
- Other documents needed for transit of the goods through any country or for import clearance

B

Buyer's primary duty
- Nominate carrier
- Contract for carriage (but see A3a)

■ Carriage of goods

■ Seller's risks

□ Seller's costs

□ Carriage of goods

□ Buyer's risks

□ Buyer's costs

Carriage of goods

Risks

Costs

Export clearance   Import clearance

Critical points

◑ Carriage to be arranged by the buyer or by the seller on the buyer's behalf

◑ Risk transfer from the seller to the buyer when the goods have been delivered to the carrier at the named place

◑ Cost transfer from the seller to the buyer when the goods have been delivered to the carrier at the named place

FCA

A THE SELLER'S OBLIGATIONS

A1 Provision of goods in conformity with the contract

The seller must provide the goods and the commercial invoice, or its equivalent electronic message, in conformity with the contract of sale and any other evidence of conformity which may be required by the contract.

Comments   The seller must provide the goods in conformity with the contract. It is also usual practice that the seller, in order to be paid, has to invoice the buyer. In addition, the seller must submit any other evidence stipulated in the contract itself that the goods conform with the contract.

This text only serves as a reminder of the seller's main obligation under the contract of sale.

A2 Licences, authorizations and formalities

The seller must obtain at his own risk and expense any export licence or other official authorization and carry out, where applicable[1], all customs formalities necessary for the export of the goods.

Comments   The seller has to clear the goods for export and assume any risk or expense which this involves. Consequently, if there is an export prohibition or if there are particular taxes on the export of the goods – and if there are other government-imposed requirements which may render the export of the goods more expensive than contemplated – all of these risks and costs must be borne by the seller. However, contracts of sale usually contain particular provisions which the seller may invoke to protect himself in the event of these contingencies. Under CISG and corresponding provisions in various national Sale of Goods Acts, unforeseen or reasonably unforeseeable export prohibitions may relieve the seller from his obligations under the contract of sale.

A3 Contracts of carriage and insurance

a) Contract of carriage

No obligation[2]. However, if requested by the buyer or if it is commercial practice and the buyer does not give an instruction to the contrary in due time, the seller may contract for carriage on usual terms at the buyer's risk and expense. In either case, the seller may decline to make the contract and, if he does, shall promptly notify the buyer accordingly.

b) Contract of insurance

No obligation[3].

Comments   The F-terms all mean that the seller's obligation is limited to handing over the goods to the carrier nominated by the buyer. Consequently, the seller has no obligation to contract for carriage. Nevertheless, if arranging for the carriage is not difficult and if the freight rate would be more or less the same regardless of whether the seller or the buyer contracts with the carrier, it is often more practical for the seller to contract for carriage at the buyer's risk and expense. This explains why, in many cases, a commercial practice has developed to this effect.

It should be stressed, however, that the seller has no obligation to contract for carriage as noted above and that the buyer does not have to let him do so. If there is a commercial practice between the parties, then under F-terms the seller may contract for carriage as an additional service to the buyer, unless the buyer in due time has instructed the seller not to do so.

1 Refer to Introduction of *Incoterms 2000* paragraph 14. (See reproduced pages 184-185 in this text.)
2 Refer to Introduction of *Incoterms 2000* paragraph 10. (See reproduced pages 184-185 in this text.)
3 Refer to Introduction of *Incoterms 2000* paragraph 10. (See reproduced pages 184-185 in this text.)

Therefore, if it is possible for the buyer to obtain a better freight rate than the seller, or if there are other reasons for him to exercise his right to contract for carriage (for example, government directions), he must inform the seller accordingly, preferably when the contract of sale is made. Otherwise, problems and additional expenses may follow if both parties contract for carriage assuming that the other party did not.

Conversely, the seller must promptly inform the buyer if for some reason he does not wish to follow the buyer's request to contract for carriage or to adhere to commercial practice. Otherwise, additional expenses and risks may occur as a result of the failure to arrange for carriage in due time. In any event, the seller does not incur any risk in complying with the buyer's request or with commercial practice, since whatever he does or intends to do is at the buyer's risk and expense.

If transport becomes temporarily unavailable or more expensive, the buyer under all F-terms has to bear these risks.

The seller, even under F-terms, has to contract for any carriage required to reach the place where the parties have agreed that the goods should be handed over for carriage, as, for example, when the goods are to be carried from an inland point to an ocean carrier to be named by the buyer. Such pre-carriage would then be for the seller's account.

A4   Delivery

The seller must deliver the goods to the carrier or another person nominated by the buyer, or chosen by the seller in accordance with A3 a), at the named place on the date or within the period agreed for delivery.

Delivery is completed;

a) If the named place is the seller's premises, when the goods have been loaded on the means of transport provided by the carrier nominated by the buyer or another person acting on his behalf.

b) If the named place is anywhere other than a), when the goods are placed at the disposal of the carrier or another person nominated by the buyer, or chosen by the seller in accordance with A3 a) on the seller's means of transport not unloaded.

If no specific point has been agreed within the named place, and if there are several points available, the seller may select the point at the place of delivery which best suits his purpose.

Failing precise instructions from the buyer, the seller may deliver the goods for carriage in such a manner as the transport mode and/or the quantity and/or nature of the goods may require.

Comments   FCA, as first presented in Incoterms 1980 (where it was referred to as FRC), was originally intended to solve the particular problems arising from changed cargo handling techniques, such as containerization or other means of assembling parcel cargo in transportation units before the vehicle of transport arrived. In such cases, FCA should be used instead of FOB, the latter of which is intended to be used in cases where the seller tenders the goods over the ship's rail. By using FCA instead of FOB, the point of delivery is moved from the ship's rail to the prior point where the goods are delivered to the carrier, either at his cargo terminal or to a vehicle sent to pick up the goods after they have been containerized or otherwise assembled in transportation units at the seller's premises.

FCA

Stipulations on handing over and delivery advisable in contract of sale

It is vital for the seller to know at the time he makes his offer what he may be required to do according to the contract of sale, since this may well affect his costs and should therefore be reflected in the price. Ideally, in the contract of sale the parties should agree on a precise point for the delivery of the goods to the carrier and make clear how the goods should be handed over to him, for example by naming the carrier's cargo terminal and specifying if the goods should be delivered containerized or not.

Also, it is necessary to clarify who should be responsible for loading the goods on to the buyer's collecting vehicle and unloading them from the seller's vehicle used to bring the goods to the place where they should be handed over to the carrier.

In Incoterms 2000 it is the seller who has the duty to load the goods on to the buyer's collecting vehicle, and the seller only has to bring the goods for on-carriage unloaded.

If at the time the contract of sale is concluded, the buyer wishes later to have the option to decide (1) the point where the goods should be handed over for carriage or (2) the mode of transport, it is important to determine the extent of the buyer's options concerning these matters and the time within which he must exercise them. If the buyer is not given options but the contract mentions a place where the carrier has several receiving points, the seller "may select the point at the place of delivery which best suits his purpose".

Normally, it would follow from the mode of transport and the carrier's receiving point exactly how the goods should be handed over for carriage. But, as noted in the preceding paragraph, there may be different alternatives for the handing over, and failing precise stipulations or instructions in the contract of sale, the goods may be handed over to the carrier "in such manner as the transport mode and/or the quantity and/or nature of the goods may require".

The quantity and nature of the goods will determine whether the goods should be containerized by the seller as homogeneous cargo in one full load in a so-called FCL-container, or by the carrier at his cargo terminal as parcel cargo together with cargo from other shippers in a so-called LCL-container.

Who is a carrier ?

Since the carrier under FCA is named by the buyer, it is normally not necessary to decide whether the entity named can be regarded as a "carrier" according to the law applicable to the contract of sale and the contract of carriage. The seller merely has to accept the buyer's nomination. Therefore, the buyer is not compelled to name someone who has the status of a carrier in a legal sense; he could also name "another person" (for example, a freight forwarder).

However, the problem of deciding whether the person engaged for the carriage is a "carrier" in the legal sense may arise whenever the seller chooses this person in accordance with A3. The seller must then "contract for carriage on usual terms at the buyer's risk and expense", and unless otherwise agreed, arrange a contract of carriage and not merely a contract of forwarding agency.

A contract of carriage may be entered into with operators which do not physically perform the carriage as long as they assume liability as carriers for the carriage, see Article 30 of the ICC Uniform Customs and Practice for Documentary Credits (UCP 500).

A5   Transfer of risks

The seller must, subject to the provisions of B5, bear all risks of loss of or damage to the goods until such time as they have been delivered in accordance with A4.

Comments   All Incoterms are based on the same principle, that the risk of loss of or damage to the goods is transferred from the seller to the buyer when the seller has fulfilled his delivery obligation according to A4. A5 of FOB, CFR and CIF further specifies that the risk is transferred when the goods "have passed the ship's rail at the named port of shipment".

All Incoterms, in conformity with the general principle of CISG, connect the transfer of the risk with the delivery of the goods and not with other circumstances, such as the passing of ownership or the time of the conclusion of the contract. Neither Incoterms nor CISG deals with transfer of title to the goods or other property rights with respect to the goods.

The passing of risk for loss of or damage to the goods concerns the risk of fortuitous events (accidents) and does not include loss or damage caused by the seller or the buyer, for example through inadequate packing or marking of the goods. Therefore, even if damage occurs subsequent to the transfer of the risk, the seller may still be responsible if the damage could be attributed to the fact that the goods were not delivered in conformity with the contract (see A1 and the comments to A9).

A5 of all Incoterms contain the phrase "subject to the provisions of B5". This means that there are exceptions to the main rule in the circumstances described in B5 which may result in a premature passing of the risk because of the buyer's failure properly to fulfil his obligations (see the comments to B5).

A6   Division of costs

The seller must, subject to the provisions of B6, pay

- all costs relating to the goods until such time as they have been delivered in accordance with A4; and

- where applicable[4], the costs of customs formalities as well as all duties, taxes, and other charges payable upon export.

Comments   As is the case with the transfer of the risk of loss of or damage to the goods, all Incoterms follow the same rule, that the division of costs occurs at the delivery point. All costs occurring before the seller has fulfilled his obligation to deliver according to A4 are for his account, while further costs are for the account of the buyer (see the comments to B6). This rule is made subject to the provisions of B6, which indicates that the buyer may have to bear additional costs incurred by his failure to give appropriate notice to the seller.

Since the seller's obligation is limited to handing over the goods to the carrier named by the buyer, all further costs have to be borne by the buyer once the goods have been delivered in this way. The seller must, however, pay the costs of customs formalities as well as all duties, taxes and other official charges payable upon export.

A7   Notice to the buyer

The seller must give the buyer sufficient notice that the goods have been delivered in accordance with A4. Should the carrier fail to take delivery in accordance with A4 at the time agreed, the seller must notify the buyer accordingly.

---

4 Refer to Introduction of *Incoterms 2000* paragraph 14. (See reproduced pages 184-185 in this text.)

FCA

Comments The seller must give the buyer sufficient notice as to when the goods will be available at the agreed or chosen delivery point, so that the buyer can make preparations in time to take delivery according to B4. There is no stipulation in Incoterms spelling out the consequences of the seller's failure to give such notice. But it follows from Incoterms that the seller's failure constitutes a breach of contract. This means that the seller could be held responsible for such a breach, according to the law applicable to the contract of sale.

The seller must also inform the buyer if the carrier fails to take the goods into his charge at the time agreed. There is no similar stipulation in the other Incoterms, since under all C- and D- terms, the consequences of any failure of the carrier to take the goods into his charge have to be borne by the seller. Under EXW and other F-terms, the buyer is assumed to have full control of the carrier he names. The duty to notify according to FCA follows from FCA A3a), according to which the seller may contract for carriage at the buyer's risk and expense. Consequently, he has to notify the buyer if something goes wrong.

A8   Proof of delivery, transport document or equivalent electronic message

The seller must provide the buyer at the seller's expense with the usual proof of delivery of the goods in accordance with A4.

Unless the document referred to in the preceding paragraph is the transport document, the seller must render the buyer at the latter's request, risk and expense, every assistance in obtaining a transport document for the contract of carriage (for example a negotiable bill of lading, a non-negotiable sea waybill, an inland waterway document, an air waybill, a railway consignment note, a road consignment note, or a multimodal transport document).

When the seller and the buyer have agreed to communicate electronically, the document referred to in the preceding paragraph may be replaced by an equivalent electronic data interchange (EDI) message.

Comments Since the seller has to hand over the goods for carriage, the carrier normally gives him a receipt which is usually identical to the transport document. If so, that document serves as evidence not only of the contract of carriage – which under F-terms is made by or on behalf of the buyer – but also of the delivery of the goods to the carrier.

If, however, the seller receives a document other than the transport document – for example, a so-called mate's receipt when the goods have been loaded onboard a ship chartered by the buyer – he should, upon the buyer's request, assist the buyer to obtain the transport document. This assistance is rendered at the buyer's risk and expense.

Whenever the parties have agreed to communicate electronically, documents may be replaced by EDI messages.

A9   Checking – packaging – marking

The seller must pay the costs of those checking operations (such as checking quality, measuring, weighing, counting) which are necessary for the purpose of delivering the goods in accordance with A4.

The seller must provide at his own expense packaging (unless it is usual for the particular trade to send the goods of the contract description unpacked) which is required for the transport of the goods, to the extent that the circumstances relating to the transport (for example modalities, destination) are made known to the seller before the contract of sale is concluded. Packaging is to be marked appropriately.

Comments   It is necessary for the buyer to ensure that the seller has duly fulfilled his obligation with respect to the condition of the goods. This is particularly important if the buyer is called upon to pay for the goods before he has received and checked them. However, the seller has no duty to arrange and pay for inspection of the goods before shipment, unless this has been specifically agreed in the contract of sale.

The goods must also be adequately packed. But the seller may not know the buyer's intentions concerning the mode of transport and the ultimate destination. There is a considerable difference between a short journey to an adjoining country and an intercontinental carriage by sea, which may expose the goods to the risk of breakage or corrosion from humidity and condensation.

The seller is obliged only to pack the goods for a long and difficult carriage if he knows that this will actually occur. Therefore, it is advisable for the buyer to inform the seller accordingly, or, better still, to specify the required packaging in the contract of sale.

A10   Other obligations

The seller must render the buyer at the latter's request, risk and expense, every assistance in obtaining any documents or equivalent electronic messages (other than those mentioned in A8) issued or transmitted in the country of delivery and/or of origin which the buyer may require for the import of the goods and, where necessary, for their transit through any country.

The seller must provide the buyer, upon request, with the necessary information for procuring insurance.

Comments   Since it is for the buyer to do whatever is necessary with respect to transit and import clearance, he may well need the seller's assistance to obtain documents (for example, a certificate of origin, health certificate, clean report of finding, import licence) or equivalent EDI messages issued or transmitted in the country of delivery and/or origin. But any cost incurred by the seller in rendering this assistance must be reimbursed to him by the buyer, according to B10.

Also, the seller may be requested to provide the buyer with information relating to the goods which the buyer may require for insurance purposes, if this information does not follow from the description of the goods in the contract of sale.

FCA

B THE BUYER'S OBLIGATIONS

B1 Payment of the price

The buyer must pay the price as provided in the contract of sale.

Comments The buyer must pay the price agreed in the contract of sale. B1 constitutes a reminder of this main obligation, which corresponds with the seller's obligation to provide the goods in conformity with the contract of sale, as stipulated in A1.

B2 Licences, authorizations and formalities

The buyer must obtain at his own risk and expense any import licence or other official authorization and carry out, where applicable[5], all customs formalities for the import of the goods and for their transit through any country.

Comments Since the seller fulfils his obligations by handing over the goods for carriage and clearing the goods for export, the buyer has to take care of any necessary transit formalities and clear the goods for import. These obligations of the buyer are specifically mentioned in B2.

B3 Contracts of carriage and insurance

a) Contract of carriage

The buyer must contract at his own expense for the carriage of the goods from the named place, except when the contract of carriage is made by the seller as provided for in A3 a).

b) Contract of insurance

No obligation[6].

Comments Under all F-terms the buyer has the obligation to contract for carriage, though the seller may, as an additional service, arrange for carriage at the buyer's risk and expense. However, the contract for carriage starts "from the named place", and any prior carriage (pre-carriage) would have to be arranged by the seller (see A3).

B4 Taking delivery

The buyer must take delivery of the goods when they have been delivered in accordance with A4.

Comments The buyer must take delivery of the goods when they have been placed at his disposal at the agreed time and place as stipulated in A4. His failure to do so will not relieve him of his obligation to pay the price and could result in a premature passing of the risk of loss of or damage to the goods, or make him liable to pay additional costs according to B5 and B6.

---

5 Refer to Introduction of *Incoterms 2000* paragraph 14. (See reproduced pages 184-185 in this text.)
6 Refer to Introduction of *Incoterms 2000* paragraph 10. (See reproduced pages 184-185 in this text.)

B5   Transfer of risks

The buyer must bear all risks of loss of or damage to the goods

- from the time they have been delivered in accordance with A4; and

- from the agreed date or the expiry date of any agreed period for delivery which arise either because he fails to nominate the carrier or another person in accordance with A4, or because the carrier or the party nominated by the buyer fails to take the goods into his charge at the agreed time, or because the buyer fails to give appropriate notice in accordance with B7, provided, however, that the goods have been duly appropriated to the contract, that is to say, clearly set aside or otherwise identified as the contract goods.

FCA

Comments   According to the main rule, while the seller under A5 bears the risk of loss of or damage to the goods until the delivery point, the buyer has to bear the risk thereafter. The delivery point is different under the different terms. In EXW and all D-terms the goods are simply placed "at the disposal of the buyer" at the relevant point, while under the F- and C-terms the delivery point is related to the handing over of the goods to the carrier in the country of dispatch or shipment (see the comments to A4 of these terms). In the terms used for goods intended to be carried by sea, reference is made to delivery alongside the named vessel (FAS) or delivery onboard the vessel (FOB, CFR, CIF).

The seller cannot – as under EXW and the D-terms – cause the goods to be delivered and the risk to pass unless he receives instructions or contracts for carriage under the C-terms or on behalf of the buyer (see the comments to FCA A3a). When the buyer is responsible for making the contract of carriage and nominating the carrier and that carrier fails to take the goods into his charge, the buyer incurs the same liability as he would had he failed properly to nominate the carrier or to notify the seller of matters required for handing over the goods for carriage.

Appropriation and premature passing of risk

For risk to pass prematurely, it is required that the goods be identified as the contract goods (they have to be "appropriated to the contract"). When the goods have been prepared for dispatch they have also normally been appropriated to the contract. But a failure of the buyer to give sufficient notice of the date or period of shipment according to B7 causes the seller to defer his preparations. If so, it may not be possible to identify some goods stored at the seller's premises or in an independent cargo terminal as the contract goods on the "agreed date or the expiry date of any period stipulated for delivery". The risk would then not pass until the appropriation has been made.

B6   Division of costs

The buyer must pay

- all costs relating to the goods from the time they have been delivered in accordance with A4; and

- any additional costs incurred, either because he fails to nominate the carrier or another person in accordance with A4 or because the party nominated by the buyer fails to take the goods into his charge at the agreed time, or because he has failed to give appropriate notice in accordance with B7, provided, however, that the goods have been duly appropriated to the contract, that is to say, clearly set aside or otherwise identified as the contract goods; and

- where applicable[7], all duties, taxes and other charges as well as the costs of carrying out customs formalities payable upon import of the goods and for their transit through any country.

7 Refer to Introduction of *Incoterms 2000* paragraph 14. (See reproduced pages 184-185 in this text.)

FCA

Comments   Under FCA the seller fulfils his delivery obligation according to A4 by handing over the goods to the carrier. The buyer must pay the freight and other costs occurring subsequent to the delivery of the goods to the carrier.

Since the buyer has to contract for carriage, he would also have to pay any additional costs incurred because "the carrier named by him fails to take the goods into his charge".

Whenever the buyer is entitled to determine the time or place of taking delivery, his failure to notify the seller according to B7 will not only cause the risk of loss of or damage to the goods to pass prematurely but also make him liable to pay any additional costs caused thereby, for example, extra costs for storage and insurance.

The liability to pay additional costs as noted above occurs only if the goods have been identified as the contract goods (see the comments on "appropriation" in B5).

B7   Notice to the seller

The buyer must give the seller sufficient notice of the name of the party designated in A4 and, where necessary, specify the mode of transport, as well as the date or period for delivering the goods to him and, as the case may be, the point within the place where the goods should be delivered to that party.

Comments   As discussed in the comments to B5 and B6, the failure of the buyer to notify the seller of the time for shipping the goods or the destination – when the buyer in the contract of sale has been given the option to determine these matters – may cause the risk of the loss of or damage to the goods to pass before the goods have been delivered according to A4. In addition, it can make the buyer liable to pay any additional costs incurred by the seller as a result of the buyer's failure.

The buyer's notice should inform the seller of the name of the carrier as well as of any further particulars relating to the delivery of the goods for carriage (such as the mode of transport and the exact point and time for the delivery) unless, of course, the carrier has been chosen by the seller according to A3.

B8   Proof of delivery, transport document or equivalent electronic message

The buyer must accept the proof of delivery in accordance with A8.

Comments   The seller has to provide proof of delivery, and the buyer must accept that proof if it conforms with the contract and with the requirements of A8 (see comments to A8). If the buyer rejects the document giving proof (for example, by instructions to a bank not to pay the seller under a documentary credit), he commits a breach of contract which would give the seller remedies available for the breach under the contract of sale (for example, a right to cancel the contract or to claim damages for breach). However, the buyer is not obliged to accept a document which does not provide adequate proof of delivery, for example, if there are notations on the document showing that the goods are defective or if the document indicates that the goods have been provided in less than the agreed quantity. The document is then considered to be "unclean".

B9   Inspection of goods

 The buyer must pay the costs of any pre-shipment inspection except when such inspection is mandated by the authorities of the country of export.

Comments As noted in the comments to A9, the buyer has to pay for any costs of checking the goods, unless the contract determines that these costs should be wholly or partly borne by the seller. In some cases, the contract may provide that the costs should be borne by the seller if the inspection reveals that the goods do not conform with the contract.

In some countries, where import licences or permission to obtain foreign currency for the payment of the price may be required, the authorities may demand an inspection of the goods before shipment, to ensure that the goods are in conformity with the contract. (This is usually called pre-shipment inspection, PSI.) If this is the case, the inspection is normally arranged by instructions from the authorities to an inspection company, which they appoint. The costs following from this inspection have to be paid by the authorities. Any reimbursement to the authorities for the inspection costs, however, must be made by the buyer, unless otherwise specifically agreed between the buyer and the seller.

B10   Other obligations

The buyer must pay all costs and charges incurred in obtaining the documents or equivalent electronic messages mentioned in A10 and reimburse those incurred by the seller in rendering his assistance in accordance therewith and in contracting for carriage in accordance with A3 a). The buyer must give the seller appropriate instructions whenever the seller's assistance in contracting for carriage is required in accordance with A3 a).

Comments As discussed in the comments to A10, the seller has to assist the buyer in obtaining the documents or electronic messages which may be required for the transit and import of the goods. However, this assistance is rendered at the buyer's risk and expense. Therefore, B10 stipulates that the buyer must pay all costs and charges incurred in obtaining these documents or electronic messages. He will also have to reimburse the seller for the seller's costs in rendering his assistance in connection with these matters or in contracting for carriage in accordance with A3.

"Free Alongside Ship" means that the seller delivers when the goods are placed alongside the vessel at the named port of shipment. This means that the buyer has to bear all costs and risks of loss of or damage to the goods from that moment.

The FAS term requires the seller to clear the goods for export.

THIS IS A REVERSAL FROM PREVIOUS INCOTERMS VERSIONS, WHICH REQUIRED THE BUYER TO ARRANGE FOR EXPORT CLEARANCE.

However, if the parties wish the buyer to clear the goods for export, this should be made clear by adding explicit wording to this effect in the contract of sale.[1]

This term can be used only for sea or inland waterway transport.

1   Refer to the introduction of *Incoterms 2000*, ICC publication Nº560, paragraph 11. (See reproduced pages 184-185 in this text.)

FAS

Free AlongSide Ship
(…named port of shipment)

Group Ⓕ
main carriage
not paid by the seller

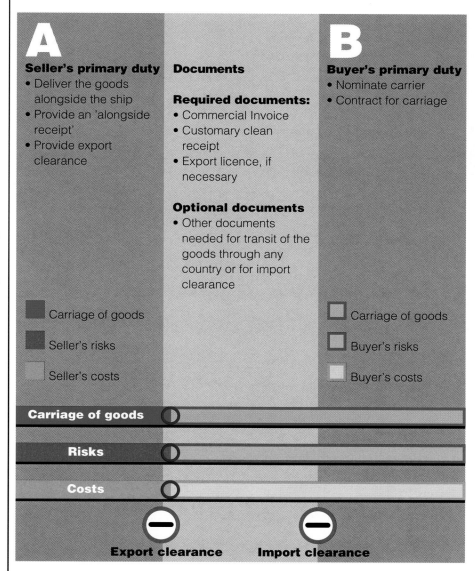

A
Seller's primary duty
- Deliver the goods alongside the ship
- Provide an 'alongside receipt'
- Provide export clearance

Documents

Required documents:
- Commercial Invoice
- Customary clean receipt
- Export licence, if necessary

Optional documents
- Other documents needed for transit of the goods through any country or for import clearance

B
Buyer's primary duty
- Nominate carrier
- Contract for carriage

☐ Carriage of goods

☐ Seller's risks

☐ Seller's costs

☐ Carriage of goods

☐ Buyer's risks

☐ Buyer's costs

Carriage of goods

Risks

Costs

Export clearance   **Import clearance**

Critical points

◐ Carriage to be arranged by the buyer

◐ Risk transfer from the seller to the buyer when the goods have been placed alongside the ship

◐ Cost transfer from the seller to the buyer when the goods have been placed alongside the ship

FAS

A   THE SELLER'S OBLIGATIONS

A1   Provision of goods in conformity with the contract

The seller must provide the goods and the commercial invoice, or its equivalent electronic message, in conformity with the contract of sale and any other evidence of conformity which may be required by the contract.

Comments   The seller must provide the goods in conformity with the contract. It is also usual practice that the seller, in order to be paid, has to invoice the buyer. In addition, the seller must submit any other evidence stipulated in the contract itself that the goods conform with the contract.

This text only serves as a reminder of the seller's main obligation under the contract of sale.

A2   Licences, authorizations and formalities

The seller must obtain at his own risk and expense any export licence or other official authorization and carry out, where applicable[2], all customs formalities necessary for the export of the goods.

Comments   Under FAS it is the seller's obligation to clear the goods for export and to obtain any export licence or other official authorization. This is a change compared with FAS as interpreted in earlier versions of Incoterms. The seller's obligation to clear the goods for export is now the same as under FOB (see the comments to FOB A2).

A3   Contracts of carriage and insurance

a) Contract of carriage

No obligation[3].

b) Contract of insurance

No obligation[4].

Comments   Since in A4 the goods should only be placed alongside the vessel named by the buyer, the seller has no obligation to contract for carriage or insurance.

A4   Delivery

The seller must place the goods alongside the vessel nominated by the buyer at the loading place named by the buyer at the named port of shipment on the date or within the agreed period and in the manner customary at the port.

Comments   The seller fulfils his obligation to deliver the goods by placing them alongside the named vessel in the port of shipment, either on the quay or in lighters. Once this has been done, any further risks and costs in loading the goods onboard are for the account of the buyer.

A5   Transfer of risks

The seller must, subject to the provisions of B5, bear all risks of loss of or damage to the goods until such time as they have been delivered in accordance with A4.

Comments   All Incoterms are based on the same principle, that the risk of loss of or damage to the goods is transferred from the seller to the buyer when the seller has fulfilled his delivery obligation according to A4. A5 of FOB, CFR and CIF further specifies that the risk is transferred when the goods "have passed the ship's rail at the named port of shipment".

---

2 Refer to Introduction to *Incoterms 2000* paragraph 14. (See reproduced pages 184-185 in this text.)
3 Refer to Introduction to *Incoterms 2000* paragraph 10. (See reproduced pages 184-185 in this text.)
4 Refer to Introduction to *Incoterms 2000* paragraph 10. (See reproduced pages 184-185 in this text.)

All Incoterms, in conformity with the general principle of CISG, connect the transfer of the risk with the delivery of the goods and not with other circumstances, such as the passing of ownership or the time of the conclusion of the contract. Neither Incoterms nor CISG deals with transfer of title to the goods or other property rights with respect to the goods.

The passing of risk for loss of or damage to the goods concerns the risk of fortuitous events (accidents) and does not include loss or damage caused by the seller or the buyer, for example through inadequate packing or marking of the goods. Therefore, even if damage occurs subsequent to the transfer of the risk, the seller may still be responsible if the damage could be attributed to the fact that the goods were not delivered in conformity with the contract (see A1 and the comments to A9).

A5 of all Incoterms contain the phrase "subject to the provisions of B5". This means that there are exceptions to the main rule in the circumstances described in B5 which may result in a premature passing of the risk because of the buyer's failure properly to fulfil his obligations (see the comments to B5).

FAS

A6 Division of costs

The seller must, subject to the provisions of B6, pay

- all costs relating to the goods until such time as they have been delivered in accordance with A4; and

- where applicable[5], the costs of customs formalities as well as all duties, taxes, and other charges payable upon export.

Comments As is the case with the transfer of the risk for loss of or damage to the goods, all Incoterms follow the same rule, that the division of costs occurs at the delivery point. All costs occurring before the seller has fulfilled his obligation to deliver according to A4 are for his account, while further costs are for the account of the buyer (see the comments to B6). This rule is made subject to the provisions of B6, which indicates that the buyer may have to bear additional costs incurred by his failure to give appropriate notice to the seller.

Since under FAS the seller's obligation is limited to delivering the goods alongside the vessel named by the buyer, all further costs have to be borne by the buyer once the goods have been made available in this manner.

A7 Notice to the buyer

The seller must give the buyer sufficient notice that the goods have been delivered alongside the nominated vessel.

Comments The seller must give the buyer sufficient notice concerning when the goods have been placed alongside the named vessel. There is no stipulation in Incoterms spelling out the consequences of the seller's failure to give this notice. But it follows from Incoterms that the seller's failure constitutes a breach of contract. This means that the seller could be held responsible for the breach according to the law applicable to the contract of sale.

---

5 Refer to Introduction to *Incoterms 2000* paragraph 14. (See reproduced pages 184-185 in this text.)

FAS

A8 Proof of delivery, transport document or equivalent electronic message

The seller must provide the buyer at the seller's expense with the usual proof of delivery of the goods in accordance with A4.

Unless the document referred to in the preceding paragraph is the transport document, the seller must render the buyer at the latter's request, risk and expense, every assistance in obtaining a transport document (for example a negotiable bill of lading, a non-negotiable sea waybill, an inland waterway document).

When the seller and the buyer have agreed to communicate electronically, the document referred to in the preceding paragraphs may be replaced by an equivalent electronic data interchange (EDI) message.

Comments Since the seller's obligation is limited to placing the goods alongside the named vessel, he may not always receive a receipt or a transport document from the carrier. The seller must then provide some other document to prove that the goods have been delivered. When requested by the buyer, the seller must assist the buyer to obtain the transport document or the equivalent EDI message. This assistance is at the buyer's risk and expense.

A9 Checking – packaging – marking

The seller must pay the costs of those checking operations (such as checking quality, measuring, weighing, counting) which are necessary for the purpose of delivering the goods in accordance with A4.

The seller must provide at his own expense packaging (unless it is usual for the particular trade to ship the goods of the contract description unpacked) which is required for the transport of the goods, to the extent that the circumstances relating to the transport (for example modalities, destination) are made known to the seller before the contract of sale is concluded. Packaging is to be marked appropriately.

Comments The goods must also be adequately packed. But the seller may not know the buyer's intentions with respect to the ultimate destination. There is a considerable difference between a short journey to an adjoining country and an intercontinental carriage by sea, which may expose the goods to the risk of breakage or corrosion from humidity and condensation.

A10 Other obligations

The seller must render the buyer at the latter's request, risk and expense, every assistance in obtaining any documents or equivalent electronic messages (other than those mentioned in A8) issued or transmitted in the country of shipment and/or of origin which the buyer may require for the import of the goods and, where necessary, for their transit through any country.

The seller must provide the buyer, upon request, with the necessary information for procuring insurance.

Comments Since it is for the buyer to do whatever is necessary with respect to transit and import clearance, he may well need the seller's assistance to obtain documents (for example, a certificate of origin, a health certificate, a clean report of finding, import licence) or equivalent EDI messages issued or transmitted in the country of delivery or import. But any cost incurred by the seller in rendering this assistance must be reimbursed to him by the buyer, according to B10.

Also, the seller may be requested to provide the buyer with information relating to the goods which the buyer may require for insurance purposes, if this information does not follow from the description of the goods in the contract of sale.

B   THE BUYER'S OBLIGATIONS

B1   Payment of the price

▩   The buyer must pay the price as provided in the contract of sale.

Comments   The buyer must pay the price agreed in the contract of sale. B1 constitutes a reminder of this main obligation, which corresponds with the seller's obligation to provide the goods in conformity with the contract of sale, as stipulated in A1.

B2   Licences, authorizations and formalities

The buyer must obtain at his own risk and expense any import licence or other official authorization and carry out, where applicable[6], all customs formalities for the import of the goods and for their transit through any country.

Comments   The seller, according to A2, makes the goods available to the buyer in the country of shipment cleared for export, but it is for the buyer to do whatever is necessary with respect to the clearance of the goods for transit and import. A prohibition of import, governmental or otherwise, will not relieve the buyer from his obligation under the contract of sale. However, contracts of sale frequently contain "relief clauses" to the benefit of both parties in such cases. These clauses may stipulate that the affected party will be given the benefit of an extension of time to fulfil his obligation or, under the worst circumstances, the right to avoid the contract. It may also be possible to obtain such relief under the law applicable to the contract of sale.

B3   Contracts of carriage and insurance

a) Contract of carriage

The buyer must contract at his own expense for the carriage of the goods from the named port of shipment.

b) Contract of insurance

No obligation[7].

Comments   In a strictly legal sense, the buyer under FAS has no obligation to the seller to contract for carriage except as required for the buyer to take delivery according to B4. This, however, still obliges the buyer to name and arrange for a vessel, so that the seller can deliver the goods alongside. Indeed, in practice the buyer normally arranges for carriage in his own interest and does not let the ship remain in the port of loading. In this regard, FAS stipulates that the buyer must "contract at his own expense for the carriage of the goods from the named port of shipment".

B4   Taking delivery

The buyer must take delivery of the goods when they have been delivered in accordance with A4.

Comments   The buyer must take delivery of the goods when they have been placed alongside the vessel as stipulated in A4. His failure to do so would not relieve him from his obligation to pay the price and could further result in a premature passing of the risk of loss of or damage to the goods or make him liable to pay additional costs according to B5 and B6.

FAS

---

6 Refer to Introduction to *Incoterms 2000* paragraph 14. (See reproduced pages 184-185 in this text.)
7 Refer to Introduction to *Incoterms 2000* paragraph 10. (See reproduced pages 184-185 in this text.)

FAS

B5   Transfer of risks

The buyer must bear all risks of loss of or damage to the goods

- ■ from the time they have been delivered in accordance with A4; and

- ■ from the agreed date or the expiry date of the agreed period for delivery which arise because he fails to give notice in accordance with B7, or because the vessel nominated by him fails to arrive on time, or is unable to take the goods, or closes for cargo earlier than the time notified in accordance with B7, provided, however, that the goods have been duly appropriated to the contract, that is to say, clearly set aside or otherwise identified as the contract goods.

Comments   According to the main rule, while the seller under A5 bears the risk of loss of or damage to the goods until the delivery point, the buyer has to bear the risk thereafter. The delivery point is different under the different terms. In EXW and all D-terms the goods are simply placed "at the disposal of the buyer" at the relevant point, while under the F- and C-terms the delivery point is related to the handing over of the goods to the carrier in the country of dispatch or shipment (see the comments to A4 of these terms). In the terms used for goods intended to be carried by sea, reference is made to delivery alongside the named vessel (FAS) or delivery onboard the vessel (FOB, CFR, CIF).

Premature passing of risk

The buyer's failure to notify the seller of the vessel name, loading place and required delivery time may result in a premature passing of the risk, as it cannot be accepted that the buyer should be able to delay the delivery and passing of the risk longer than contemplated when the contract of sale was made. Thus, his failure to notify according to B7 will cause the risk to pass "from the agreed date or the expiry date of the period stipulated for delivery".

A further problem can arise if the vessel fails to arrive in time, since in these cases the goods cannot be placed alongside as contemplated. Consequently, a premature passing of the risk could occur in these circumstances. The same result could also occur if the vessel is "unable to take the goods, or closes for cargo earlier than the stipulated time". In this latter case, the goods will remain at the buyer's risk.

For the risk to pass prematurely, it is required that the goods be identified as the contract goods (for example, they have to be "appropriated to the contract"). When the goods have been prepared for dispatch they have also normally been appropriated to the contract. But a failure of the buyer to give sufficient notice of the date or period of shipment according to B7 causes the seller to defer his preparations. If so, it may not be possible to identify some goods stored at the seller's premises or in an independent cargo terminal as the contract goods on the "agreed date or the expiry date of any period stipulated for delivery". The risk would then not pass until the appropriation has been made.

B6   Division of costs

The buyer must pay

- ■ all costs relating to the goods from the time they have been delivered in accordance with A4; and

- ■ any additional costs incurred, either because the vessel nominated by him has failed to arrive on time, or is unable to take the goods, or closes for cargo earlier than the time notified in accordance with B7, or because the buyer has failed to give appropriate notice in accordance with B7 provided, however, that the goods have been duly appropriated to the contract, that is to say, clearly set aside or otherwise identified as the contract goods; and

■ where applicable[8], all duties, taxes and other charges as well as the costs of carrying out customs formalities payable upon import of the goods and for their transit through any country.

Comments Under FAS the seller fulfils his delivery obligation according to A4 by placing the goods alongside the vessel. The buyer must pay the freight and other costs occurring subsequently.

Since under FAS the buyer has to contract for carriage and nominate the ship, he also has to pay any additional costs incurred "because the vessel named by him has failed to arrive on time, or will be unable to take the goods, or will close for cargo earlier than the stipulated time" (see the corresponding rule for the premature passing of the risk in the comments to B5).

The failure of the buyer to notify the seller according to B7 will not only cause the risk of loss of or damage to the goods to pass prematurely, but will also make the buyer liable to pay any additional costs caused thereby, for example, extra costs for storage and insurance.

For the buyer to be liable for additional costs according to B6, the goods to which these costs relate must be identifiable as the contract goods (see the comments on "appropriation" under B5).

B7 Notice to the seller

The buyer must give the seller sufficient notice of the vessel name, loading point and required delivery time.

Comments As discussed in the comments to B5 and B6, the failure of the buyer to notify the seller of the name of the vessel, the loading place and the required delivery time may cause the risk of the loss of or damage to the goods to pass before the goods have been delivered according to A4, and also make the buyer liable to pay any additional costs the seller incurs as a result of the buyer's failure.

B8 Proof of delivery, transport document or equivalent electronic message

The buyer must accept the proof of delivery in accordance with A8.

Comments The buyer must accept the seller's proof of delivery if the proof is adequate. If the buyer nevertheless rejects it (for example, by instructions to a bank not to pay the seller under a documentary credit), he commits a breach of contract which will give the seller remedies for the breach available under the contract of sale (for example, a right to cancel the contract or to claim damages for breach). However, the buyer is not obliged to accept a document which does not provide adequate proof of delivery. If there are notations on the document showing that the goods are defective or that they have been provided in less than the agreed quantity, the document is then considered to be "unclean".

B9 Inspection of goods

The buyer must pay the costs of any pre-shipment inspection, except when such inspection is mandated by the authorities of the country of export.

Comments As noted in the comments to A9, the buyer has to pay for any costs of checking the goods, unless the contract determines that these costs should be wholly or partly borne by the seller. In some cases, the contract may provide that the costs should be borne by the seller if the inspection reveals that the goods do not conform with the contract.

---

8 Refer to Introduction to *Incoterms 2000* paragraph 14. (See reproduced pages 184-185 in this text.)

In some countries, where import licences or permission to obtain foreign currency for the payment of the price may be required, the authorities may demand an inspection of the goods before shipment to ensure that the goods are in conformity with the contract. (This is usually called pre-shipment inspection, PSI.) If this is the case, the inspection is normally arranged by instructions from the authorities to an inspection company, which they appoint.

The costs following from this inspection have to be paid by the authorities. Any reimbursement to the authorities for the inspection costs, however, must be made by the buyer, unless otherwise specifically agreed between the buyer and the seller.

B10 Other obligations

The buyer must pay all costs and charges incurred in obtaining the documents or equivalent electronic messages mentioned in A10 and reimburse those incurred by the seller in rendering his assistance in accordance therewith.

Comments As discussed in the comments to A10, the seller has to render the buyer assistance in obtaining the documents or electronic messages which may be required for the transit and import of the goods. However, this assistance is rendered at the buyer's risk and expense. Therefore, B10 stipulates that the buyer must pay all costs and charges incurred in obtaining these documents or electronic messages. He will also have to reimburse the seller for the seller's costs in rendering his assistance in these matters.

"Free on Board" means that the seller delivers when the goods pass the ship's rail at the named port of shipment. This means that the buyer has to bear all costs and risks of loss of or damage to the goods from that point. The FOB term requires the seller to clear the goods for export. This term can be used only for sea or inland waterway transport. If the parties do not intend to deliver the goods across the ship's rail, the FCA term should be used.

FOB

Free On Board
(…named port of shipment)

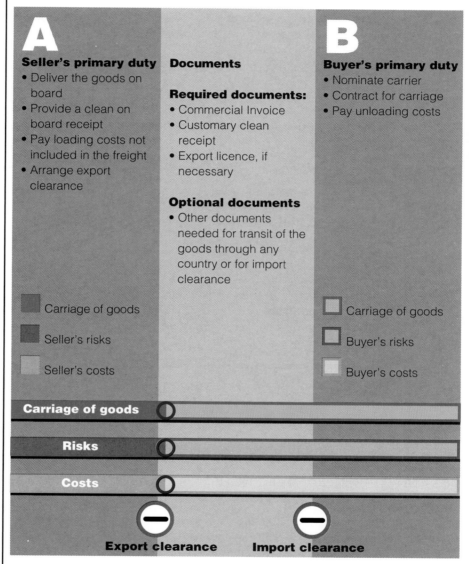

A

Seller's primary duty
- Deliver the goods on board
- Provide a clean on board receipt
- Pay loading costs not included in the freight
- Arrange export clearance

Documents

Required documents:
- Commercial Invoice
- Customary clean receipt
- Export licence, if necessary

Optional documents
- Other documents needed for transit of the goods through any country or for import clearance

B

Buyer's primary duty
- Nominate carrier
- Contract for carriage
- Pay unloading costs

Carriage of goods

Seller's risks

Seller's costs

Carriage of goods

Buyer's risks

Buyer's costs

Carriage of goods

Risks

Costs

Export clearance   **Import clearance**

Critical points

Carriage to be arranged by the buyer

Risk transfer from the seller to the buyer when the goods pass the ship's rail

Cost transfer from the seller to the buyer when the goods pass the ship's rail

FOB

A THE SELLER'S OBLIGATIONS

A1 Provision of goods in conformity with the contract

The seller must provide the goods and the commercial invoice, or its equivalent electronic message, in conformity with the contract of sale and any other evidence of conformity which may be required by the contract.

Comments   The seller must provide the goods in conformity with the contract. It is also usual practice that the seller, in order to be paid, has to invoice the buyer. In addition, the seller must submit any other evidence stipulated in the contract itself that the goods conform with the contract.

This text only serves as a reminder of the seller's main obligation under the contract of sale.

A2 Licences, authorizations and formalities

The seller must obtain at his own risk and expense any export licence or other official authorization and carry out, where applicable[1], all customs formalities necessary for the export of the goods.

Comments   The seller has to clear the goods for export and assume any risk or expense which this involves. Consequently, if there is an export prohibition or if there are particular taxes on the export of the goods – and if there are other government-imposed requirements which may render the export of the goods more expensive than contemplated – all of these risks and costs must be borne by the seller. However, contracts of sale usually contain particular provisions which the seller may invoke to protect himself in the event of these contingencies. Under CISG and corresponding provisions in various national Sale of Goods Acts, unforeseen or reasonably unforeseeable export prohibitions may relieve the seller from his obligations under the contract of sale.

A3 Contracts of carriage and insurance

a) Contract of carriage

No obligation[2].

b) Contract of insurance

No obligation[3].

Comments   The seller has no obligation to contract for carriage and would not be requested to do so if the FOB term is used for the carriage of full ship loads of bulk commodities.

Freight rates are often fixed according to standards determined by liner conferences. In these cases, it does not matter whether the seller or the buyer contracts for carriage; indeed, the seller or his freight forwarder can often do this more easily in the port of shipment. Nevertheless, ICC considered it inappropriate to repeat here the reference in FCA A3 to the seller's additional service in contracting for carriage at the buyer's risk and expense, since FOB should normally not be used for carriage of general cargo unless the cargo is handed over for carriage at the ship's rail.

---

1 Refer to Introduction to *Incoterms 2000* paragraph 14. (See reproduced pages 184-185 in this text.)
2 Refer to Introduction to *Incoterms 2000* paragraph 10. (See reproduced pages 184-185 in this text.)
3 Refer to Introduction to *Incoterms 2000* paragraph 10. (See reproduced pages 184-185 in this text.)

A4   Delivery

The seller must deliver the goods on the date or within the agreed period at the named port of shipment and in the manner customary at the port on board the vessel nominated by the buyer.

Comments   The seller's obligation to place the goods onboard the ship in due time is the essence of the FOB term. Through the centuries the ship's rail has assumed an inordinate importance as an imaginary border between the seller's and the buyer's territory. But using the ship's rail as a point for the division of functions, costs and risks between the parties is not, and never has been, quite appropriate. To divide the functions between the parties while the goods are swinging across the ship's rail seems impracticable. In the words of an often-cited English court decision: "Only the most enthusiastic lawyer could watch with satisfaction the spectacle of liabilities shifting uneasily as the cargo sways at the end of a derrick across a notional perpendicular projecting from the ship's rail." (Pyrene v. Scindia Navigation [1954] 2 Q.B. 402 at p. 419).

The reference in FOB A4 to "the manner customary at the port" highlights the problem of using the passing of the ship's rail as the guiding factor in practice. The parties in these circumstances will have to follow the custom of the port regarding the actual measures to be taken in delivering the goods onboard. Usually the task is performed by stevedoring companies, and the practical problem normally lies in deciding who should bear the costs of their services.

The seller's obligation to place the goods onboard may be extended by a phrase added to FOB, for example "FOB stowed" or "FOB stowed and trimmed". Though these additional words are primarily intended to make sure the seller has to pay all of the loading costs, it is doubtful whether they are also intended to move the "delivery point" to the extent that the seller would be considered to have failed to fulfil his delivery obligation until the loading, stowing and trimming have been completed (see Understanding Incoterms page 32) and comments to FOB A5, A6 and FOB B5, B6).

A5   Transfer of risks

The seller must, subject to the provisions of B5, bear all risks of loss of or damage to the goods until such time as they have passed the ship's rail at the named port of shipment.

Comments   All Incoterms are based on the same principle that the risk of loss of or damage to the goods is transferred from the seller to the buyer when the seller has fulfilled his delivery obligation according to A4. A5 of FOB, CFR and CIF further specifies that the risk is transferred when the goods "have passed the ship's rail at the named port of shipment".

All Incoterms, in conformity with the general principle of CISG, connect the transfer of the risk with the delivery of the goods and not with other circumstances, such as the passing of ownership or the time of the conclusion of the contract. Neither Incoterms nor CISG deals with transfer of title to the goods or other property rights with respect to the goods.

The passing of risk for loss of or damage to the goods concerns the risk of fortuitous events (accidents) and does not include loss or damage caused by the seller or the buyer, for example through inadequate packing or marking of the goods. Therefore, even if damage occurs subsequent to the transfer of the risk, the seller may still be responsible if the damage could be attributed to the fact that the goods were not delivered in conformity with the contract (see A1 and the comments to A9).

A5 of all Incoterms contain the phrase "subject to the provisions of B5". This means that there are exceptions to the main rule in the circumstances described in B5 which may result in a premature passing of the risk because of the buyer's failure properly to fulfil his obligations (see the comments to B5).

FOB

A6 Division of costs

The seller must, subject to the provisions of B6, pay

■ all costs relating to the goods until such time as they have passed the ship's rail at the named port of shipment; and

■ where applicable[4], the costs of customs formalities necessary for export as well as all duties, taxes and other charges payable upon export.

Comments As is the case with the transfer of the risk of loss of or damage to the goods, all Incoterms follow the same rule, that the division of costs occurs at the delivery point. All costs occurring before the seller has fulfilled his obligation to deliver according to A4 are for his account, while further costs are for the account of the buyer (see the comments to B6). This rule is made subject to the provisions of B6, which indicates that the buyer may have to bear additional costs incurred by his failure to give appropriate notice to the seller.

The seller must pay the costs of customs formalities necessary for export as well as all duties, taxes and other official charges payable upon export.

A7 Notice to the buyer

The seller must give the buyer sufficient notice that the goods have been delivered in accordance with A4.

Comments The seller must give the buyer sufficient notice concerning when the goods have been delivered onboard. There is no stipulation in Incoterms spelling out the consequences of the seller's failure to give this notice. But it follows from Incoterms that the seller's failure constitutes a breach of contract. This means that the seller could be held responsible for the breach according to the law applicable to the contract of sale.

A8 Proof of delivery, transport document or equivalent electronic message

The seller must provide the buyer at the seller's expense with the usual proof of delivery in accordance with A4.

Unless the document referred to in the preceding paragraph is the transport document, the seller must render the buyer, at the latter's request, risk and expense, every assistance in obtaining a transport document for the contract of carriage (for example, a negotiable bill of lading, a non-negotiable sea waybill, an inland waterway document, or a multimodal transport document).

Where the seller and the buyer have agreed to communicate electronically, the document referred to in the preceding paragraph may be replaced by an equivalent electronic data interchange (EDI) message.

Comments Since the seller has to hand over the goods for carriage, the carrier normally gives him a receipt which is usually identical to the transport document. If so, that document serves not only as evidence of the contract of carriage – which under F-terms is made by or on behalf of the buyer – but also as evidence of the delivery of the goods to the carrier.

If, however, the seller receives a document other than the transport document – for example, a so-called mate's receipt when the goods have been loaded onboard a ship chartered by the buyer – he should, upon the buyer's request, assist the buyer to obtain the transport document. This assistance is rendered at the buyer's risk and expense.

Whenever the parties have agreed to communicate electronically, documents may be replaced by EDI messages.

---

[4] Refer to Introduction to *Incoterms 2000* paragraph 14. (See reproduced pages 184-185 in this text.)

A9 Checking – packaging – marking

The seller must pay the costs of those checking operations (such as checking quality, measuring, weighing, counting) which are necessary for the purpose of delivering the goods in accordance with A4.

The seller must provide at his own expense packaging (unless it is usual for the particular trade to ship the goods of the contract description unpacked) which is required for the transport of the goods, to the extent that the circumstances relating to the transport (for example modalities, destination) are made known to the seller before the contract of sale is concluded. Packaging is to be marked appropriately.

Comments The goods must also be adequately packed. But the seller may not know the buyer's intentions with respect to the ultimate destination. There is a considerable difference between a short journey to an adjoining country and an intercontinental carriage by sea, which may expose the goods to the risk of breakage or corrosion from humidity and condensation.

A10 Other obligations

The seller must render the buyer at the latter's request, risk and expense, every assistance in obtaining any documents or equivalent electronic messages (other than those mentioned in A8) issued or transmitted in the country of shipment and/or of origin which the buyer may require for the import of the goods and, where necessary, for their transit through any country.

The seller must provide the buyer, upon request, with the necessary information for procuring insurance.

Comments It is for the buyer to do whatever is necessary with respect to transit and import clearance. He may also need the seller's assistance to obtain documents (for example, a certificate of origin, a health certificate, a clean report of finding, an import licence) or equivalent EDI messages issued or transmitted in the country of shipment and/or origin. But any cost incurred by the seller in rendering this assistance must be reimbursed to him by the buyer, according to B10.

Also, the seller may be requested to provide the buyer with information relating to the goods which the buyer may require for insurance purposes, if this information does not follow from the description of the goods in the contract of sale.

FOB

FOB

B THE BUYER'S OBLIGATIONS

B1 Payment of the price

The buyer must pay the price as provided in the contract of sale.

Comments The buyer must pay the price agreed in the contract of sale. B1 constitutes a reminder of this main obligation, which corresponds with the seller's obligation to provide the goods in conformity with the contract of sale, as stipulated in A1.

B2 Licences, authorizations and formalities

The buyer must obtain at his own risk and expense any import licence or other official authorization and carry out, where applicable[5], all customs formalities for the import of the goods and, where necessary, for their transit through any country.

Comments The buyer must take care of the import clearance and bear any costs and risks in connection with it. Therefore, an import prohibition will not relieve the buyer of his obligation to pay for the goods, unless there is a particular "relief clause" in the contract of sale which he invokes to obtain this relief. Such clauses may provide for the extension of time or the right to avoid the contract under the applicable law (see the comments to A2).

B3 Contracts of carriage and insurance

a) Contract of carriage

The buyer must contract at his own expense for the carriage of the goods from the named port of shipment.

b) Contract of insurance

No obligation[6].

Comments The buyer has to contract for carriage so that the goods can be placed onboard. However, the seller – as in FCA A3 – may assist the buyer in contracting for carriage (see the comments to A3). If so, the assistance is rendered at the buyer's risk and expense.

B4 Taking delivery

The buyer must take delivery of the goods when they have been delivered in accordance with A4.

Comments The buyer must take delivery of the goods when they have been placed onboard the vessel named by the buyer at the named port of shipment. His failure to do so will not relieve him of his obligation to pay the price and could further result in a premature passing of the risk of loss of or damage to the goods, or make him liable to pay additional costs according to B5 and B6.

B5 Transfer of risks

The buyer must bear all risks of loss of or damage to the goods

- from the time they have passed the ship's rail at the named port of shipment; and
- from the agreed date or the expiry date of the agreed period for delivery which arise because he fails to give notice in accordance with B7, or because the vessel nominated by him fails to arrive on time, or is unable to take the goods, or closes for cargo earlier than the time notified in accordance with B7, provided, however, that the goods have been

---

[5] Refer to Introduction to *Incoterms 2000* paragraph 14. (See reproduced pages 184-185 in this text.)
[6] Refer to Introduction to *Incoterms 2000* paragraph 10. (See reproduced pages 184-185 in this text.)

duly appropriated to the contract, that is to say, clearly set aside or otherwise identified as the contract goods.

Comments According to the main rule, while the seller under A5 bears the risk of loss of or damage to the goods until the delivery point, the buyer has to bear the risk thereafter. The delivery point is different under the different terms. In EXW and all D-terms, the goods are simply placed "at the disposal of the buyer" at the relevant point, while under the F- and C-terms the delivery point is related to the handing over of the goods to the carrier in the country of dispatch or shipment (see the comments to A4 of these terms). In the terms used for goods intended to be carried by sea, reference is made to delivery alongside the named vessel (FAS) or delivery onboard the vessel (FOB, CFR, CIF).

Premature passing of risk

The buyer's failure to notify the seller of the vessel name, loading place and required delivery time may result in a premature passing of the risk, as it cannot be accepted that the buyer should be able to delay the delivery and passing of the risk longer than contemplated when the contract of sale was made. Thus, his failure to notify according to B7 will cause the risk to pass "from the agreed date or the expiry date of the period stipulated for delivery".

A further problem could arise if the vessel is not named or if it fails to arrive in time, since then the goods cannot be placed onboard as contemplated. Moreover, a premature passing of the risk could occur in these circumstances. B5 also stipulates that the same could result if the vessel is "unable to take the goods, or close for cargo earlier than the stipulated time".

For risk to pass prematurely, it is required that the goods be identified as the contract goods (i.e., they have to be "appropriated to the contract"). When the goods have been prepared for dispatch they have also usually been appropriated to the contract. But a failure of the buyer to give sufficient notice of the date or period of shipment according to B7 causes the seller to defer his preparations. If so, it may not be possible to identify some goods stored at the seller's premises, in an independent cargo terminal, or on the quay as the contract goods on the "agreed date or the expiry date of any period stipulated for delivery". The risk would then not pass until the appropriation has been made.

B6 Division of costs

The buyer must pay

- all costs relating to the goods from the time they have passed the ship's rail at the named port of shipment; and

- any additional costs incurred, either because the vessel nominated by him fails to arrive on time, or is unable to take the goods, or closes for cargo earlier than the time notified in accordance with B7, or because the buyer has failed to give appropriate notice in accordance with B7, provided, however, that the goods have been duly appropriated to the contract, that is to say, clearly set aside or otherwise identified as the contract goods; and

- where applicable[7], all duties, taxes and other charges as well as the costs of carrying out customs formalities payable upon import of the goods and for their transit through any country.

Comments Under FOB the seller fulfils his delivery obligation according to A4 by placing the goods onboard the vessel at the loading place.

Since under FOB the buyer has to contract for carriage and nominate the ship, he also has to pay any additional costs incurred "because the vessel named by him has failed to

FOB

---

7 Refer to Introduction to *Incoterms 2000* paragraph 14. (See reproduced pages 184-185 in this text.)

FOB

arrive on time, or will be unable to take the goods, or will close for cargo earlier than the stipulated time" (see the corresponding rule for the premature passing of the risk in the comments to B5).

The failure of the buyer to notify the seller according to B7 would not only cause the risk of loss of or damage to the goods to pass prematurely but would also make the buyer liable to pay any additional costs caused thereby, for example, extra costs for storage and insurance.

For the buyer to be liable for additional costs according to B6, the goods to which these costs relate must be identifiable as the contract goods (see the comments on "appropriation" under B5).

Under FOB, because the buyer has to clear the goods for import, he has to pay "all duties, taxes and other official charges as well as the costs of carrying out customs formalities" and to reimburse the seller for any assistance the seller renders him in this regard.

B7   Notice to the seller

 The buyer must give the seller sufficient notice of the vessel name, loading point and required delivery time.

Comments   As discussed in the comments to B5 and B6, the failure of the buyer to notify the seller of the name of the vessel, the loading place and the required delivery time may cause the risk of the loss of or damage to the goods to pass before the goods have been delivered according to A4 and also make the buyer liable to pay any additional costs the seller incurs as a result of the buyer's failure.

B8   Proof of delivery, transport document or equivalent electronic message

The buyer must accept the proof of delivery in accordance with A8.

Comments   The buyer must accept the seller's proof of delivery if the proof is adequate. If the buyer nevertheless rejects it (for example, by instructions to a bank not to pay the seller under a documentary credit), he commits a breach of contract which will give the seller remedies for the breach available under the contract of sale (for example, a right to cancel the contract or to claim damages for breach). However, the buyer is not obliged to accept a document which does not provide adequate proof of delivery. If there are notations on the document showing that the goods are defective or that they have been provided in less than the agreed quantity, the document is then considered to be "unclean".

B9   Inspection of goods

 The buyer must pay the costs of any pre-shipment inspection except when such inspection is mandated by the authorities of the country of export.

Comments   As noted in the comments to A9, the buyer has to pay for any costs of checking the goods, unless the contract determines that these costs should be wholly or partly borne by the seller. In some cases, the contract may provide that the costs should be borne by the seller if the inspection reveals that the goods do not conform with the contract. In some countries, where import licences or permission to obtain foreign currency for the payment of the price may be required, the authorities may demand an inspection of the goods before shipment, to ensure that the goods are in conformity with the contract. (This is usually called pre-shipment inspection, PSI.) If this is the case, the inspection is normally arranged by instructions from the authorities to an inspection company, which they appoint. The costs following from this inspection have to be paid by the authorities.

Any reimbursement to the authorities for the inspection costs, however, must be made by the buyer, unless otherwise specifically agreed between the buyer and the seller.

B10 Other obligations

The buyer must pay all costs and charges incurred in obtaining the documents or equivalent electronic messages mentioned in A10 and reimburse those incurred by the seller in rendering his assistance in accordance therewith.

Comments As discussed in the comments to A10, the seller has to render the buyer assistance in obtaining the documents or electronic messages which may be required for the transit and import of the goods. However, this assistance is rendered at the buyer's risk and expense. Therefore, B10 stipulates that the buyer must pay all costs and charges incurred in obtaining these documents or electronic messages. He will also have to reimburse the seller for the seller's costs in rendering his assistance.

FOB

"Cost and Freight" means that the seller delivers when the goods pass the ship's rail in the port of shipment.

The seller must pay the costs and freight necessary to bring the goods to the named port of destination BUT the risk of loss of or damage to the goods, as well as any additional costs due to events occurring after the time of delivery, are transferred from the seller to the buyer.

The CFR term requires the seller to clear the goods for export.

This term can be used only for sea and inland waterway transport. If the parties do not intend to deliver the goods across the ship's rail, the CPT term should be used.

CFR

Cost and FReight
(...named port of destination)

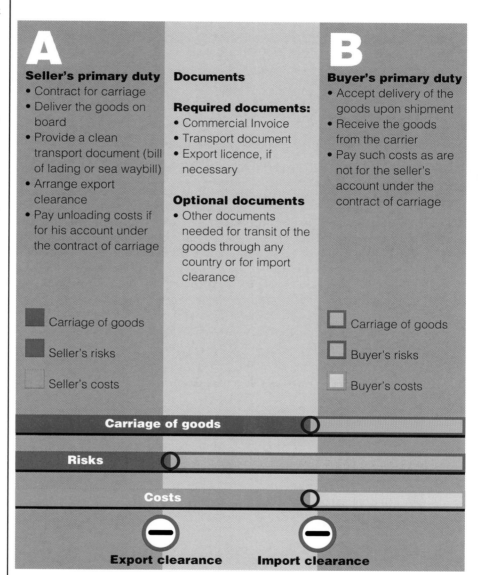

A

Seller's primary duty
- Contract for carriage
- Deliver the goods on board
- Provide a clean transport document (bill of lading or sea waybill)
- Arrange export clearance
- Pay unloading costs if for his account under the contract of carriage

Documents

Required documents:
- Commercial Invoice
- Transport document
- Export licence, if necessary

Optional documents
- Other documents needed for transit of the goods through any country or for import clearance

B

Buyer's primary duty
- Accept delivery of the goods upon shipment
- Receive the goods from the carrier
- Pay such costs as are not for the seller's account under the contract of carriage

Carriage of goods

Seller's risks

Seller's costs

Carriage of goods

Buyer's risks

Buyer's costs

Carriage of goods

Risks

Costs

Export clearance   **Import clearance**

Critical points

- Carriage to be arranged by the seller

- Risk transfer from the seller to the buyer when the goods pass the ship's rail

- Cost transfer at port of destination, buyer paying such costs as are not for the seller's account under the contract of carriage

A   THE SELLER'S OBLIGATIONS

A1   Provision of goods in conformity with the contract

The seller must provide the goods and the commercial invoice, or its equivalent electronic message, in conformity with the contract of sale and any other evidence of conformity which may be required by the contract.

Comments The seller must provide the goods in conformity with the contract. It is also usual practice that the seller, in order to be paid, has to invoice the buyer. In addition, the seller must submit any other evidence stipulated in the contract itself that the goods conform with that contract.

This text only serves as a reminder of the seller's main obligation under the contract of sale.

A2   Licences, authorizations and formalities

The seller must obtain at his own risk and expense any export licence or other official authorization and carry out, where applicable[1], all customs formalities necessary for the export of the goods.

Comments The seller has to clear the goods for export and assume any risk or expense which this involves. Consequently, if there is an export prohibition or if there are particular taxes on the export of the goods – and if there are other government-imposed requirements which may render the export of the goods more expensive than contemplated – all of these risks and costs must be borne by the seller. However, contracts of sale usually contain particular provisions which the seller may invoke to protect himself in the event of these contingencies. Under CISG and corresponding provisions in various national Sale of Goods Acts, unforeseen or reasonably unforeseeable export prohibitions may relieve the seller from his obligations under the contract of sale.

A3   Contracts of carriage and insurance

a) Contract of carriage

The seller must contract on usual terms at his own expense for the carriage of the goods to the named port of destination by the usual route in a seagoing vessel (or inland waterway vessel as the case may be) of the type normally used for the transport of goods of the contract description.

b) Contract of insurance

No obligation[2].

Comments Although the CFR seller fulfils his obligations by shipping the goods (see section A4 below), he has to arrange and pay for the contract of carriage to the named port of destination. Unless the contract contains specific stipulations as to the nature of the contract of carriage, the seller may contract "on usual terms" and for carriage "by the usual route".

The CFR term can be used only for sea and inland waterway transport. (Section A8 requires the seller to provide a negotiable bill of lading, which is not possible to obtain for modes of transport other than carriage of goods by sea.) But the vessel need not necessarily be "seagoing", since the CFR term may also be used for carriage by inland waterways. In this latter case, an "inland waterway vessel" may be used.

The vessel should be of a kind normally used for the transport of the goods of the

---

1 Refer to Introduction to *Incoterms 2000* paragraph 14. (See reproduced pages 184-185 in this text.)
2 Refer to Introduction to *Incoterms 2000* paragraph 10. (See reproduced pages 184-185 in this text.)

contract description. It may be unacceptable, for example, to arrange for the carriage of containerized cargo on deck if the ship is not designed for carriage of containers, since the carriage may then expose the cargo to additional risks and even render the insurance cover ineffective.

Differences between goods carried in liner trade and bulk cargoes carried in chartered ships

There is a considerable difference between goods normally carried in so-called liner trade and bulk cargoes, which are normally carried in chartered ships. In most cases, it should be clear what kind of carriage the seller should arrange, since break bulk cargo now is normally containerized or otherwise carried by regular transport in transportation units (flats, pallets, etc.) from port to port.

In these cases, the carrier frequently undertakes to carry the goods, not only from port to port but from an interior point in the country of shipment to an interior point in the country of destination. It is then inappropriate to use the CFR term, and the parties are advised to use the CPT term instead (see the comments on CPT).

When it is uncertain whether the goods should be carried by regular shipping lines or by chartered ships, it is advisable that the matter be specifically dealt with in the contract of sale. It often happens that carriage by chartered ships is permitted, but that the carriage must nevertheless be contracted for on "liner terms". If so, the freight costs would ordinarily include loading and unloading costs. A charter party, however, may well provide that these costs should be "free" to the carrier. This is the so-called FIO-clause – which stands for "Free In" and "Free Out".

In any case, the expression "liner terms" is vague and ambiguous, and it is recommended that the parties specifically deal with the conditions of the contract of carriage in the contract of sale when carriage is not to be arranged by regular, well-known shipping lines.

A4   Delivery

The seller must deliver the goods on board the vessel at the port of shipment on the date or within the agreed period.

Comments   As noted above, delivery under the CFR term occurs at the moment the goods are placed onboard the vessel at the port of shipment. Thus, the CFR term, like the FOB term, is evidence of a shipment contract. Since the point of destination is mentioned after CFR, for example "CFR London" by a seller in New York, the legal nature of a CFR contract is frequently misunderstood by traders. This is quite understandable, because the critical point where the seller fulfils his obligation is usually omitted. CFR contracts do not usually provide that shipment shall take place at a particular port, for example "CFR London shipment from New York", since this would restrict the seller's options to ship the goods from alternative ports of shipment.

It must be emphasized that the CFR term, as distinguished from the FOB term, contains two critical points. The first represents the point at which delivery takes place upon shipment according to A4, namely when the goods are placed onboard the vessel. The second represents the point at destination, up to which the seller shall arrange for carriage of the goods.

Avoid stipulating date of delivery at destination

One essential point of the CFR term is sometimes ignored in commercial practice. When, for example, the contract stipulates that delivery should take place not later than a specified date at destination (for example "arrival London not later than ..."), this kind of stipulation defeats the object of the CFR term and leaves room for different interpretations of the contract.

CFR

One option would be to interpret this stipulation to mean that the parties have agreed on an arrival contract rather than a shipment contract. If that is the case, the seller is not considered to have fulfilled the contract until the goods have actually arrived at destination. If in such a case the goods are delayed because of casualties after shipment or are even lost, the seller would not be free from his obligations under the contract of sale unless, of course, he has the protection of a particular relief clause or force majeure clause in the contract of sale. Such a contract is, of course, different from a CFR contract under which the seller fulfils the contract in the port of shipment.

The other option would be to interpret the stipulation in a way which would allow the basic nature of the CFR contract to supersede the particular wording the parties use, even in cases when the parties have stipulated that the goods should arrive before a particular date at destination. If that is done, the contract would be interpreted to mean that the goods must be placed onboard the ship at such time as would normally suffice for its arrival at destination at the stipulated date.

Since it is uncertain which of these options will be used to interpret CFR with this or similar language added, the parties are strongly advised to abstain from using such additions.

A5   Transfer of risks

The seller must, subject to the provisions of B5, bear all risks of loss of or damage to the goods until such time as they have passed the ship's rail at the port of shipment.

Comments   All Incoterms are based on the same principle that the risk of loss of or damage to the goods is transferred from the seller to the buyer when the seller has fulfilled his delivery obligation according to A4. A5 of FOB, CFR and CIF further specifies that the risk is transferred when the goods "have passed the ship's rail at the port of shipment".

All Incoterms, in conformity with the general principle of CISG, connect the transfer of the risk with the delivery of the goods and not with other circumstances, such as the passing of ownership or the time of the conclusion of the contract. As noted, neither Incoterms nor CISG deals with transfer of title to the goods or other property rights with respect to the goods.

The passing of risk of loss of or damage to the goods concerns the risk of fortuitous events (accidents) and does not include loss or damage caused by the seller or the buyer, for example, inadequate packing or marking of the goods. Therefore, even if damage occurs subsequent to the transfer of the risk, the seller may still be responsible if the damage could be attributed to the fact that the goods were not delivered in conformity with the contract (see A1 and the comments to A9).

A5 of all Incoterms contain the phrase "subject to the provisions of B5". This means that there are exceptions to the main rule concerning the passing of risk under the circumstances mentioned in B5, which may result in a premature passing of the risk because of the buyer's failure properly to fulfil his obligations (see the comments to B5).

A6   Division of costs

The seller must, subject to the provisions of B6, pay

- all costs relating to the goods until such time as they have been delivered in accordance with A4; and

- the freight and all other costs resulting from A3 a), including the costs of loading the goods on board and any charges for unloading at the agreed port of discharge which were for the seller's account under the contract of carriage; and

- where applicable[3], the costs of customs formalities necessary for export as well as all duties, taxes and other charges payable upon export, and for their transit through any country if they were for the seller's account under the contract of carriage.

Comments   As is the case with the transfer of the risk of loss of or damage to the goods, all Incoterms follow the same rule, that the division of costs occurs at the delivery point. All costs occurring before the seller has fulfilled his obligation to deliver according to A4 are for his account, while further costs are for the account of the buyer (see the comments to B6). This rule is made subject to the provisions of B6, which indicates that the buyer may have to bear additional costs incurred by his failure to give appropriate notice to the seller.

A7   Notice to the buyer

The seller must give the buyer sufficient notice that the goods have been delivered in accordance with A4 as well as any other notice required in order to allow the buyer to take measures which are normally necessary to enable him to take the goods.

Comments   The seller must give the buyer sufficient notice that the goods have been delivered onboard the vessel, as well as other relevant information, so that the buyer can make preparations in time to take delivery according to B4. There is no stipulation in Incoterms spelling out the consequences of the seller's failure to give such notice. But it follows from Incoterms that the seller's failure constitutes a breach of contract. This means that the seller could be held responsible for the breach according to the law applicable to the contract of sale.

A8   Proof of delivery, transport document or equivalent electronic message

The seller must at his own expense provide the buyer without delay with the usual transport document for the agreed port of destination.

This document (for example a negotiable bill of lading, a non-negotiable sea waybill or an inland waterway document) must cover the contract goods, be dated within the period agreed for shipment, enable the buyer to claim the goods from the carrier at the port of destination and, unless otherwise agreed, enable the buyer to sell the goods in transit by the transfer of the document to a subsequent buyer (the negotiable bill of lading) or by notification to the carrier.

When such a transport document is issued in several originals, a full set of originals must be presented to the buyer.

Where the seller and the buyer have agreed to communicate electronically, the document referred to in the preceding paragraphs may be replaced by an equivalent electronic data interchange (EDI) message.

Comments   It is of vital importance for the buyer to know that the seller has fulfilled his obligation to deliver the goods onboard the ship. The transport document usually constitutes proof of such delivery.

---

3 Refer to Introduction to *Incoterms 2000* paragraph 14. (See reproduced pages 184-185 in this text.)

CFR

Non-negotiable transport documents

Generally, it suffices for the parties to refer to the "usual transport document" obtained from the carrier when the goods are handed over to him. But in maritime carriage different documents can be used. While, traditionally, negotiable bills of lading were used for carriage of goods by sea, other documents have appeared in recent years, for example transport documents which are non-negotiable and similar to those used for other modes of transport. These alternative documents have different names – "liner waybills", "ocean waybills", "cargo quay receipts", "data freight receipts" or "sea waybills". The term "sea waybill" is frequently used to include all of the various non-negotiable transport documents used for carriage of goods by sea.

Unfortunately, international conventions and most national laws do not yet provide specific regulations for these non-negotiable transport documents. (The exception is in the United States, where a non-negotiable bill of lading is recognized; this is the "straight bill of lading".) For this reason, the Comité Maritime International (CMI) in June 1990 adopted Uniform Rules for Sea Waybills. The parties should refer to these Rules in the contract of carriage to avoid any legal uncertainties stemming from the use of non-negotiable documents (see Annex).

Sale of goods in transit

In most cases, goods intended for carriage by regular shipping lines will not be the subject of a further sale in transit. But with respect to goods intended to be carried in chartered ships, the situation is frequently quite different. For example, when commodities are sold on the spot market, they are often sold many times before they reach destination. In these cases the negotiable bill of lading has traditionally been very important, since the possession of the paper document enables the subsequent buyer to claim the goods from the carrier at destination. He does this by surrendering the original bill of lading to the carrier in exchange for the goods.

However, when no sale of the goods in transit is intended, there is no need to use a bill of lading if the buyer's right to claim the goods from the carrier at destination is ensured by other means, such as by reference in the contract to the CMI Uniform Rules for Sea Waybills.

A buyer intending to sell the goods in transit to a subsequent buyer has the right under CFR and CIF terms to claim a negotiable bill of lading from his seller. This sale in transit can also be arranged, however, without a bill of lading. It can occur if the parties involved use a system which calls upon the carrier to follow instructions to hold the goods at the disposition of subsequent buyer(s).

EDI and the bill of lading

Section A8 takes into account that the parties may wish to engage in "paperless trading". If the parties have agreed to communicate electronically, the requirement that a paper document be presented is no longer compulsory.

The traditional bill of lading is out of step with the modern development towards paperless trading. For this reason, the CMI in June 1990 designed the "Uniform Rules for Electronic Bills of Lading", which cover situations in which EDI messages between the parties involved are intended to replace the need for the traditional paper bill of lading.

These Uniform Rules are based on EDI messages to the carrier which serve the same purpose as the words "notification to the carrier" in A8. Parties who have not agreed to use the "Uniform Rules for Electronic Bills of Lading", however, have to continue the traditional practice of requiring negotiable bills of lading. Systems – such as BOLERO – are now being developed for EDI messages not only among the shipper, the carrier and the consignee but also among other parties such as banks, insurers, freight forwarders and customs authorities.

Risk of maritime fraud when issuing several original bills of lading

Unfortunately, the malpractice of issuing bills of lading in several originals has persisted despite the fact that it creates a considerable risk of maritime fraud. A buyer paying for the goods directly or through a bank must therefore ensure that he receives all originals of the bill of lading, if several originals have been issued.

Bills of lading issued upon request of a charterer

When bills of lading are issued upon the request of a charterer by the owner of a chartered ship, the bill of lading may refer to the terms of the charter party (for example, "all other terms as per charter party"). For these cases, Incoterms 1990 stipulated that the seller must also provide a copy of the charter party. This stipulation has been deleted in Incoterms 2000.

A9 Checking – packaging – marking

The seller must pay the costs of those checking operations (such as checking quality, measuring, weighing, counting) which are necessary for the purpose of delivering the goods in accordance with A4.

The seller must provide at his own expense packaging (unless it is usual for the particular trade to ship the goods of the contract description unpacked) which is required for the transport of the goods arranged by him. Packaging is to be marked appropriately.

Comments It is necessary for the buyer to ensure that the seller has duly fulfilled his obligation with respect to the condition of the goods. This is particularly important if the buyer is called upon to pay for the goods before he has received and checked them. However, the seller has no duty to arrange and pay for inspection of the goods before shipment, unless this has been specifically agreed in the contract of sale.

The goods must also be adequately packed. Since the seller arranges the carriage, he is in a good position to decide the packing required for the transport of the goods. The goods should also be marked in accordance with applicable standards and regulations.

A10 Other obligations

The seller must render the buyer at the latter's request, risk and expense, every assistance in obtaining any documents or equivalent electronic messages (other than those mentioned in A8) issued or transmitted in the country of shipment and/or of origin which the buyer may require for the import of the goods and, where necessary, for their transit through any country.

The seller must provide the buyer, upon request, with the necessary information for procuring insurance.

Comments The seller has the obligation to clear the goods for export, but he has no obligation after shipment to bear any costs or risks connected either with the transit through another country or with import clearance of the goods at destination. However, he has the duty to render assistance to the buyer in obtaining any documents (for example, a certificate of origin, a health certificate, a clean report of findings, an import licence) or equivalent electronic messages which may be required for these purposes. The buyer, however, must reimburse the seller for any expenses which the seller might have incurred in connection with this assistance. Moreover, if something goes wrong, the buyer will have to assume the risk.

Also, the seller may be requested to provide the buyer with such information relating to the goods as the buyer may require for insurance purposes, if this information does not follow from the description of the goods in the contract of sale.

CFR

B THE BUYER'S OBLIGATIONS

B1 Payment of the price

The buyer must pay the price as provided in the contract of sale.

Comments The buyer must pay the price agreed in the contract of sale. B1 constitutes a reminder of this main obligation, which corresponds with the seller's obligation to provide the goods in conformity with the contract of sale, as stipulated in A1.

B2 Licences, authorizations and formalities

The buyer must obtain at his own risk and expense any import licence or other official authorization and carry out, where applicable[4], all customs formalities for the import of the goods and for their transit through any country.

Comments The buyer must take care of the import clearance and bear any costs and risks in connection with it. Therefore, an import prohibition will not relieve the buyer of his obligation to pay for the goods, unless there is a particular "relief clause" in the contract of sale which he invokes to obtain this relief. Such clauses may provide for the extension of time or the right to avoid the contract under the applicable law (see the comments to A2).

The buyer must also do whatever may be needed to pass the goods through a third country after they have been shipped (dispatched) from the seller's country, unless this obligation is for the seller's account under the contract of carriage.

B3 Contracts of carriage and insurance

a) Contract of carriage

No obligation[5].

b) Contract of insurance

No obligation[6].

Comments Although B3 merely stipulates "No obligation" for the buyer, on-carriage from the port of destination is necessary in most cases, and it is the buyer's responsibility to do whatever is required for this purpose. But the seller is not concerned with the further carriage of the goods, and the buyer has no obligation to the seller in this respect. The words "No obligation" mean that whatever the buyer does is in his own interest and is not covered by the contract of sale.

B4 Taking delivery

The buyer must accept delivery of the goods when they have been delivered in accordance with A4 and receive them from the carrier at the named port of destination.

Comments Here, the two critical points under a CFR sale appear again. Since the seller fulfils his obligation by delivering the goods onboard the vessel at the port of shipment (A4), it is for the buyer to accept such delivery under B4. But the buyer also has a further obligation to receive the goods from the carrier at the named port of destination. This is not something he does only in his own interest (as in B3) but is an obligation to the seller, who has concluded the contract of carriage with the carrier.

Unless the buyer frees the goods from the ship when they duly arrive, the seller may incur additional costs debited to him by the carrier. These costs must be borne by the buyer if he is in breach of his obligation to receive the goods from the carrier.

---

4 Refer to Introduction to *Incoterms 2000* paragraph 14. (See reproduced pages 184-185 in this text.)
5 Refer to Introduction to *Incoterms 2000* paragraph 10. (See reproduced pages 184-185 in this text.)
6 Refer to Introduction to *Incoterms 2000* paragraph 10. (See reproduced pages 184-185 in this text.)

That the buyer "must accept delivery of the goods when they have been delivered in accordance with A4" does not, of course, preclude him from raising claims against the seller if the goods do not conform with the contract.

Charter party loading and discharge

In the charter party trade, problems frequently arise in ports of loading as well as in ports of discharge when the time for loading and discharging the cargo exceeds the "free" time according to the charter party terms (the "lay-time"). In these cases, the charterer has to pay particular compensation ("demurrage") to the owner.

Needless to say, it is vital for sellers and buyers to agree, not only in the charter party but also in the contract of sale, how much time should be available for loading and discharge respectively, and which of the parties should bear the costs of any demurrage charged by the shipowner. Charter parties may also provide that the shipowner should pay compensation if the time of loading and/or discharge is less than a certain stipulated time This is so-called dispatch, or despatch, money. In this case, it is also important to stipulate in the contract of sale which of the parties should be entitled to this compensation.

B5   Transfer of risks

The buyer must bear all risks of loss of or damage to the goods from the time they have passed the ship's rail at the port of shipment.

The buyer must, should he fail to give notice in accordance with B7, bear all risks of loss of or damage to the goods from the agreed date or the expiry date of the period fixed for shipment provided, however, that the goods have been duly appropriated to the contract, that is to say, clearly set aside or otherwise identified as the contract goods.

Comments   According to the main rule, while the seller under A5 bears the risk of loss of or damage to the goods until the delivery point, the buyer has to bear the risk thereafter. The delivery point is different under the different terms. In EXW and all D-terms, the goods are simply placed "at the disposal of the buyer" at the relevant point, while under the F- and C-terms the delivery point is related to the handing over of the goods to the carrier in the country of dispatch or shipment (see the comments to A4 of these terms). In the terms used for goods intended to be carried by sea, reference is made to delivery alongside the named vessel (FAS) or delivery onboard the vessel (FOB, CFR, CIF).

Since the seller is relieved from any further risk of loss of or damage to the goods when they have passed the ship's rail, it follows that the buyer has to assume these risks subsequent to the passing of that critical point. According to the terms of the contract of sale, the buyer may be given the option to determine the time for shipping the goods. This option may also include the right to later name the port to which the goods should be shipped. In these cases, it is necessary that the seller be given timely and sufficient notice (see comments to B7).

Premature transfer of risk

If the buyer fails to give appropriate notice to the seller, he could be exposed to additional costs and risks if the goods have to be stored in the port of loading, pending shipping instructions. B5 stipulates that in these cases the risk may be transferred from the seller to the buyer before the time when the goods have passed the ship's rail. This is an important exception to the main rule.

This premature transfer of the risks could occur at one of two points: (1) when, as a result of the buyer's failure to give sufficient notice, the goods cannot be shipped at an agreed date or (2) on the expiry date, in cases when the buyer has been given a period during which to determine the time for shipment.

In accordance with the general principle of Incoterms, this premature transfer of the risks will never occur until the goods have been duly appropriated to the contract. In other words, the goods have to be clearly set aside or otherwise identified as the contract goods for the premature transfer of the risks to occur.

CFR

B6   Division of costs

The buyer must, subject to the provisions of A3 a), pay

- all costs relating to the goods from the time they have been delivered in accordance with A4; and

- all costs and charges relating to the goods whilst in transit until their arrival at the port of destination, unless such costs and charges were for the seller's account under the contract of carriage; and

- unloading costs including lighterage and wharfage charges, unless such costs and charges were for the seller's account under the contract of carriage; and

- all additional costs incurred if he fails to give notice in accordance with B7, for the goods from the agreed date or the expiry date of the period fixed for shipment, provided, however, that the goods have been duly appropriated to the contract, that is to say, clearly set aside or otherwise identified as the contract goods; and

- where applicable[7], all duties, taxes and other charges as well as the costs of carrying out customs formalities payable upon import of the goods and, where necessary, for their transit through any country unless included within the cost of the contract of carriage.

Comments   While the seller has to pay all costs required to bring the goods to the port of shipment and to deliver the goods onboard the vessel (as well as unloading charges at the port of discharge, provided they have been included in the freight), the buyer has to pay any further costs which may arise after the seller has delivered the goods onboard the vessel. In this sense, the transfer of the risk also determines the division of costs. If something occurs as a result of contingencies after shipment – such as strandings, collisions, strikes, government directions, hindrances because of ice or other weather conditions – any additional costs charged by the carrier as a result of these contingencies, or otherwise occurring, will be for the account of the buyer.

The buyer is free from paying the further costs only if these costs "were for the seller's account under the contract of carriage". This does not mean, however, that the buyer must pay for costs and charges payable under the contract of carriage in the ordinary course of events (for example, when the shipper has been given credit by the carrier, i.e., "collect freight").

Failure to give notice and buyer's additional costs
The failure to give appropriate notice in accordance with B7 not only results in a premature transfer of the risks (see comments to B5) but also imposes on the buyer the responsibility to pay any additional costs as a consequence. In this case, the obligation to pay these additional costs occurs only if the goods have been duly appropriated to the contract (as discussed in the comments to B5).

Buyer's duties in clearing goods for import
As noted in the comments to B2, the buyer has the duty to clear the goods for import; it is then established in B6 that he has to pay the costs arising from the clearance ("duties, taxes and other official charges as well as the costs of carrying out customs formalities"). The buyer also has to pay any duties, taxes and other charges arising in connection with the transit of the goods through another country after they have been delivered by the seller in accordance with A4, unless such costs were for the seller's account under the contract of carriage.

---

7 Refer to Introduction to *Incoterms 2000* paragraph 14. (See reproduced pages 184-185 in this text.)

CFR

B7   Notice to the seller

The buyer must, whenever he is entitled to determine the time for shipping the goods and/or the port of destination, give the seller sufficient notice thereof.

Comments   As discussed in the comments to B5 and B6, the failure of the buyer to notify the seller of the time for shipping the goods or the destination – when the buyer in the contract of sale has been given the option to determine these matters – may cause the risk of the loss of or damage to the goods to pass before the goods have been delivered according to A4. In addition, it can make the buyer liable to pay any additional costs incurred by the seller as a result of the buyer's failure.

B8   Proof of delivery, transport document or equivalent electronic message

The buyer must accept the transport document in accordance with A8 if it is in conformity with the contract.

Comments   The buyer has to accept the transport document if it conforms with the contract and with the requirements of A8 (see the comments to A8). If the buyer rejects the transport document (for example, by instructions to a bank not to pay the seller under a documentary credit), he commits a breach of contract, which would give the seller remedies available for such a breach under the contract of sale.

These remedies could include, for example, a right to cancel the contract or to claim damages for breach. However, the buyer is not obliged to accept a document which does not provide adequate proof of delivery, for example, one which has notations on it showing that the goods are defective or that they have been provided in less than the agreed quantity. In these cases, the document is termed "unclean".

B9   Inspection of goods

The buyer must pay the costs of any pre-shipment inspection except when such inspection is mandated by the authorities of the country of export.

Comments   As noted in the comments to A9, the buyer has to pay for any costs of checking the goods, unless the contract determines that these costs should be wholly or partly borne by the seller. In some cases, the contract may provide that the costs should be borne by the seller if the inspection reveals that the goods do not conform with the contract.

In some countries, where import licences or permission to obtain foreign currency for the payment of the price may be required, the authorities may demand an inspection of the goods before shipment, to ensure that the goods are in conformity with the contract. (This is usually called pre-shipment inspection, PSI.) If this is the case, the inspection is normally arranged by instructions from the authorities to an inspection company, which they appoint. The costs following from this inspection have to be paid by the authorities. Any reimbursement to the authorities for the inspection costs, however, must be made by the buyer, unless otherwise specifically agreed between the buyer and the seller.

B10   Other obligations

The buyer must pay all costs and charges incurred in obtaining the documents or equivalent electronic messages mentioned in A10 and reimburse those incurred by the seller in rendering his assistance in accordance therewith.

Comments   As discussed in the comments to A10, the seller has to render the buyer assistance in obtaining the documents or electronic messages which may be required for the transit and import of the goods. However, this assistance is rendered at the buyer's risk and expense. Therefore, B10 stipulates that the buyer must pay all costs and charges incurred in obtaining these documents or electronic messages. He will also have to reimburse the seller for the seller's costs in rendering his assistance in these matters.

CFR

CIF

Cost, Insurance and Freight
(…named port of destination)

"Cost, Insurance and Freight" means that the seller delivers when the goods pass the ship's rail in the port of shipment.

The seller must pay the costs and freight necessary to bring the goods to the named port of destination BUT the risk of loss of or damage to the goods, as well as any additional costs due to events occurring after the time of delivery, are transferred from the seller to the buyer. However, in CIF the seller also has to procure marine insurance against the buyer's risk of loss of or damage to the goods during the carriage.

Consequently, the seller contracts for insurance and pays the insurance premium. The buyer should note that under the CIF term the seller is required to obtain insurance only on minimum cover.[1]

Should the buyer wish to have the protection of greater cover, he would either need to agree as much expressly with the seller or to make his own extra insurance arrangements.

The CIF term requires the seller to clear the goods for export.

This term can be used only for sea and inland waterway transport. If the parties do not intend to deliver the goods across the ship's rail, the CIP term should be used.

1 Refer to the introduction of *Incoterms 2000*, ICC publication N°560, paragraph 9.3. (See reproduced pages 184-185 in this text.)

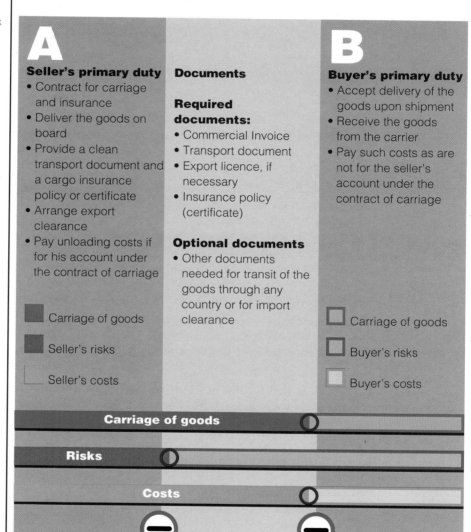

A

Seller's primary duty
- Contract for carriage and insurance
- Deliver the goods on board
- Provide a clean transport document and a cargo insurance policy or certificate
- Arrange export clearance
- Pay unloading costs if for his account under the contract of carriage

Carriage of goods

Seller's risks

Seller's costs

Documents

Required documents:
- Commercial Invoice
- Transport document
- Export licence, if necessary
- Insurance policy (certificate)

Optional documents
- Other documents needed for transit of the goods through any country or for import clearance

B

Buyer's primary duty
- Accept delivery of the goods upon shipment
- Receive the goods from the carrier
- Pay such costs as are not for the seller's account under the contract of carriage

Carriage of goods

Buyer's risks

Buyer's costs

Carriage of goods

Risks

Costs

Export clearance Import clearance

Critical points

- Carriage and insurance to be arranged by the seller
- Risk transfer from the seller to the buyer when the goods pass the ship's rail
- Cost transfer at port of destination, buyer paying such costs as are not for the seller's account under the contract of carriage

A   THE SELLER'S OBLIGATIONS

A1, A2, A4 to A10

See the comments to CFR A1, A2, A4 to A10.

A3   Contracts of carriage and insurance

a) Contract of carriage

The seller must contract on usual terms at his own expense for the carriage of the goods to the named port of destination by the usual route in a seagoing vessel (or inland waterway vessel as the case may be) of the type normally used for the transport of goods of the contract description.

b) Contract of insurance

The seller must obtain at his own expense cargo insurance as agreed in the contract, such that the buyer, or any other person having an insurable interest in the goods, shall be entitled to claim directly from the insurer and provide the buyer with the insurance policy or other evidence of insurance cover.

The insurance shall be contracted with underwriters or an insurance company of good repute and, failing express agreement to the contrary, be in accordance with minimum cover of the Institute Cargo Clauses (Institute of London Underwriters) or any similar set of clauses. The duration of insurance cover shall be in accordance with B5 and B4. When required by the buyer, the seller shall provide at the buyer's expense war, strikes, riots and civil commotion risk insurances if procurable. The minimum insurance shall cover the price provided in the contract plus ten per cent (i.e. 110%) and shall be provided in the currency of the contract.

Comments   The only difference between the CFR and the CIF term is that the latter requires the seller also to obtain and pay for cargo insurance. This is particularly important for the buyer, since under CIF the risk for loss of or damage to the goods will pass from the seller to the buyer when the goods pass the ship's rail at the port of shipment (see A5 under CFR).

In addition, it is vital for the buyer to be given the right to claim against the insurer independently of the seller. For this purpose it may be necessary to provide the buyer with the insurance policy under which the insurer makes his undertaking directly to the buyer.

Seller need only provide "minimum cover"

It is important to note that the seller only has to provide for "minimum cover". Such limited cover is suitable only for bulk cargoes, which normally do not suffer loss or damage in transit unless something happens to the ship as well as to the cargo (strandings, collisions, fire, etc.). The buyer and seller are therefore advised to agree that the seller should provide a more suitable insurance cover. The buyer should then specify the extended cover he prefers.

The insurance cover according to the so-called Institute Cargo Clauses is available in categories A, B and C. The C category provides the minimum cover, and the cover is extended progressively in categories B and A. However, even the most extended cover in A does not provide for what is misleadingly called "all-risk insurance". Furthermore, there are other important exceptions which category A insurance does not cover, for example, cases when the loss of the goods has been caused by insolvency or fraud, or when financial loss has been incurred by delay in delivery.

Duration of insurance cover

The duration of the insurance cover must coincide with the carriage and must protect the buyer from the moment he has to bear the risk of loss of or damage to the goods (i.e., from the moment the goods pass the ship's rail at the port of shipment). It must extend until the goods arrive at the agreed port of destination.

Some risks require additional cover

Some particular risks require additional insurance, and if the buyer requests it, the seller must arrange this additional cover at the buyer's expense – for example, insurance against the risks of war, strikes, riots and civil commotion – if this cover can possibly be arranged.

Amount of the insurance cover

The amount of the insurance should correspond to the price provided in the contract, plus 10 per cent. The additional 10 per cent is intended to cover the average profit that buyers of goods expect from the sale. The insurance should be provided in the same currency as stipulated in the contract for the price of the goods. Consequently, if the price of the goods is to be paid in convertible currency, the seller may not provide insurance in other than convertible currency.

CIF

B THE BUYER'S OBLIGATIONS

B1 to B9

See the comments to CFR B1 to B9.

B10   Other obligations

The buyer must pay all costs and charges incurred in obtaining the documents or equivalent electronic messages mentioned in A10 and reimburse those incurred by the seller in rendering his assistance in accordance therewith.

The buyer must provide the seller, upon request, with the necessary information for procuring insurance.

Comments   It is vital for the buyer to understand that the seller only has to take out minimum insurance cover. This cover in most cases is insufficient when manufactured goods are involved. In the contract of sale, therefore, the buyer should require the seller to take out additional cover, usually according to the Institute Clauses A or a corresponding cover. If, however, the contract does not deal with this matter at all, the seller's obligation is limited as stipulated in A3, and the buyer has to arrange and pay for any additional insurance cover required.

In most cases the seller will know how to arrange the insurance from the contract of sale (from the invoice value of the goods, their destination, etc.). But if this is not the case, the buyer has to provide the seller, upon the latter's request, with any additional necessary information.

(See also the comments to CFR B10.)

"Carriage paid to..." means that the seller delivers the goods to the carrier nominated by him but the seller must in addition pay the cost of carriage necessary to bring the goods to the named destination. This means that the buyer bears all risks and any other costs occurring after the goods have been so delivered.

"Carrier" means any person who, in a contract of carriage, undertakes to perform or to procure the performance of transport, by rail, road, air, sea, inland waterway or by a combination of such modes.

If subsequent carriers are used for the carriage to the agreed destination, the risk passes when the goods have been delivered to the first carrier.

The CPT term requires the seller to clear the goods for export.

This term may be used irrespective of the mode of transport including multimodal transport.

CPT

Carriage Paid To
(...named place of destination)

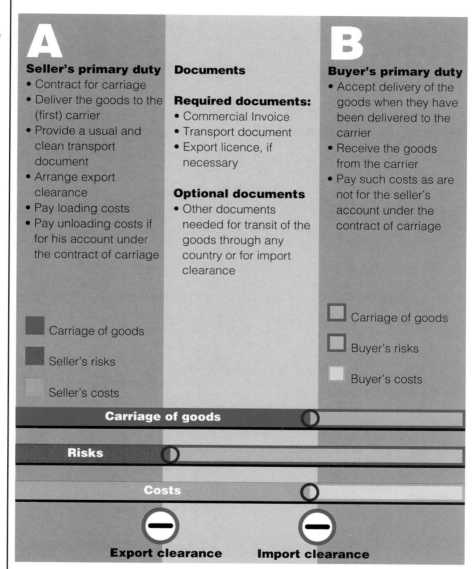

A

Seller's primary duty
- Contract for carriage
- Deliver the goods to the (first) carrier
- Provide a usual and clean transport document
- Arrange export clearance
- Pay loading costs
- Pay unloading costs if for his account under the contract of carriage

Documents

Required documents:
- Commercial Invoice
- Transport document
- Export licence, if necessary

Optional documents
- Other documents needed for transit of the goods through any country or for import clearance

B

Buyer's primary duty
- Accept delivery of the goods when they have been delivered to the carrier
- Receive the goods from the carrier
- Pay such costs as are not for the seller's account under the contract of carriage

■ Carriage of goods

■ Seller's risks

□ Seller's costs

□ Carriage of goods

□ Buyer's risks

□ Buyer's costs

Carriage of goods

Risks

Costs

Export clearance   **Import clearance**

Critical points

 Carriage to be arranged by the seller

 Risk transfer from the seller to the buyer when the goods have been delivered to the carrier

 Cost transfer at place of destination, buyer paying such costs as are not for the seller's account under the contract of carriage

A THE SELLER'S OBLIGATIONS

CPT

A1 Provision of goods in conformity with the contract

The seller must provide the goods and the commercial invoice, or its equivalent electronic message, in conformity with the contract of sale and any other evidence of conformity which may be required by the contract.

Comments   The seller must provide the goods in conformity with the contract. It is also usual practice that the seller, in order to be paid, has to invoice the buyer. In addition, the seller must submit any other evidence stipulated in the contract itself that the goods conform with that contract.

This text only serves as a reminder of the seller's main obligation under the contract of sale.

A2 Licences, authorizations and formalities

The seller must obtain at his own risk and expense any export licence or other official authorization and carry out, where applicable[1], all customs formalities necessary for the export of the goods.

Comments   The seller has to clear the goods for export and assume any risk or expense which this involves. Consequently, if there is an export prohibition or if there are particular taxes on the export of the goods – and if there are other government-imposed requirements which may render the export of the goods more expensive than contemplated – all of these risks and costs must be borne by the seller. However, contracts of sale usually contain particular provisions which the seller may invoke to protect himself in the event of these contingencies. Under CISG and corresponding provisions in various national Sale of Goods Acts, unforeseen or reasonably unforeseeable export prohibitions may relieve the seller from his obligations under the contract of sale.

A3 Contracts of carriage and insurance

a) Contract of carriage

The seller must contract on usual terms at his own expense for the carriage of the goods to the agreed point at the named place of destination by a usual route and in a customary manner. If a point is not agreed or is not determined by practice, the seller may select the point at the named place of destination which best suits his purpose.

b) Contract of insurance

No obligation[2].

Comments   The seller's obligation to contract for carriage is basically the same under all C-terms, in that the seller fulfils his delivery obligation upon handing over the goods for carriage in the country of shipment, but with the additional obligation to arrange and pay for the carriage up to the agreed point in the country of destination. Since CFR and CIF can only be used when the goods are intended for carriage by sea or inland waterway transport, CPT and CIP respectively must be used as alternatives to CFR and CIF when the goods are intended to be carried by other modes of transport (air, road, rail, unnamed or multimodal transport). But they should also be used whenever the goods are not handed over for sea transport over the ship's rail, for example, transport of containerized cargo or in roll on-roll off traffic when the goods are carried in railway wagons, trailers or semi-trailers on ferries.

---

1 Refer to Introduction to *Incoterms 2000* paragraph 14. (See reproduced pages 184-185 in this text.)
2 Refer to Introduction to *Incoterms 2000* paragraph 10. (See reproduced pages 184-185 in this text.)

In all C-terms, the seller must, unless otherwise agreed, contract for carriage "on usual terms" and "by a usual route". In CFR and CIF reference is made to a vessel "of the type normally used for the transport of goods of the contract description". Since CPT and CIP are not confined to sea carriage but may be used for all modes of transport, reference is not made to the vehicle of transport but instead to the "customary manner" of transportation.

A4   Delivery

The seller must deliver the goods to the carrier contracted in accordance with A3 or, if there are subsequent carriers to the first carrier, for transport to the agreed point at the named place on the date or within the agreed period.

Comments   While delivery under CFR and CIF must be made "onboard the vessel at the port of shipment", the goods under CPT and CIP must be delivered "to the carrier'. Therefore, the delivery obligation is no longer related to the means of conveyance – the vessel – but to the carrier as such.

CPT and CIP should be the preferred terms, even when in practice delivery is not intended to be made directly to a vessel. When the parties intend to use several carriers – for example, a pre-carriage by road or rail from the seller's premises at an inland point for further carriage by sea to the agreed destination – the seller has fulfilled his delivery obligation under CPT and CIP when the goods have been handed over for carriage to the first carrier. In this respect, there is an important difference between CPT and CIP on the one hand and CFR and CIF on the other.

In the latter two terms, delivery is not completed until the goods have reached a vessel at the port of shipment. Therefore, the principle that the delivery is completed when the goods have been handed over to the first carrier cannot apply under CFR and CIF unless the pre-carriage is performed by sea, for example, by a so-called feeder ship to an ocean-going vessel for further carriage.

A5   Transfer of risks

The seller must, subject to the provisions of B5, bear all risks of loss of or damage to the goods until such time as they have been delivered in accordance with A4.

Comments   All Incoterms are based on the same principle that the risk of loss of or damage to the goods is transferred from the seller to the buyer when the seller has fulfilled his delivery obligation according to A4. A5 of FOB, CFR and CIF further specifies that the risk is transferred when the goods "have passed the ship's rail at the port of shipment".

All Incoterms, in conformity with the general principle of CISG, connect the transfer of the risk with the delivery of the goods and not with other circumstances, such as the passing of ownership or the time of the conclusion of the contract. Neither Incoterms nor CISG deals with transfer of title to the goods or other property rights with respect to the goods.

The passing of risk of loss of or damage to the goods concerns the risk of fortuitous events (accidents) and does not include loss or damage caused by the seller or the buyer, for example, inadequate packing or marking of the goods. Therefore, even if damage occurs subsequent to the transfer of the risk, the seller may still be responsible if the damage could be attributed to the fact that the goods were not delivered in conformity with the contract (see A1 and the comments to A9).

A5 of all Incoterms contain the phrase "subject to the provisions of B5". This means that there are exceptions to the main rule concerning the passing of risk under the circumstances mentioned in B5, which may result in a premature passing of the risk because of the buyer's failure to fulfil his obligations properly (see the comments to B5).

CPT

A6   Division of costs

The seller must, subject to the provisions of B6, pay

■ all costs relating to the goods until such time as they have been delivered in accordance with A4 as well as the freight and all other costs resulting from A3 a), including the costs of loading the goods and any charges for unloading at the place of destination which were for the seller's account under the contract of carriage; and

■ where applicable[3], the costs of customs formalities necessary for export as well as all duties, taxes or other charges payable upon export, and for their transit through any country if they were for the seller's account under the contract of carriage.

Comments   As is the case with the transfer of the risk for loss of or damage to the goods, all Incoterms follow the same rule, that the division of costs occurs at the delivery point.

All costs occurring before the seller has fulfilled his obligation to deliver according to A4 are for his account, while further costs are for the account of the buyer (see the comments to B6). This rule is made subject to the provisions of B6, which indicates that the buyer may have to bear additional costs incurred by his failure to give appropriate notice to the seller.

A7   Notice to the buyer

The seller must give the buyer sufficient notice that the goods have been delivered in accordance with A4 as well as any other notice required in order to allow the buyer to take measures which are normally necessary to enable him to take the goods.

Comments   The seller must give the buyer sufficient notice that the goods have been dispatched, as well as other relevant information, so that the buyer can make preparations in time to take delivery according to B4. There is no stipulation in Incoterms spelling out the consequences of the seller's failure to give such notice. But it follows from Incoterms that the seller's failure constitutes a breach of contract. This means that the seller could be held responsible for the breach according to the law applicable to the contract of sale.

A8   Proof of delivery, transport document or equivalent electronic message

The seller must provide the buyer at the seller's expense, if customary, with the usual transport document or documents (for example a negotiable bill of lading, a non-negotiable sea waybill, an inland waterway document, an air waybill, a railway consignment note, a road consignment note, or a multimodal transport document) for the transport contracted in accordance with A3.

Where the seller and the buyer have agreed to communicate electronically, the document referred to in the preceding paragraph may be replaced by an equivalent electronic data interchange (EDI) message.

Comments   In all shipment contracts – and particularly contracts under the so-called C-terms, which require the seller to arrange and pay for the contract of carriage – it is vital for the buyer to know that the seller has fulfilled his obligation to perform these tasks and to deliver the goods to the carrier. The transport document constitutes proof of such delivery.

Non-negotiable transport documents

Generally, it suffices for the parties to refer to the "usual transport document" obtained from the carrier when the goods are handed over to him. But in maritime carriage, different documents can be used. While traditionally, negotiable bills of lading were used for carriage of goods by sea, other documents have appeared in recent years, for example, transport documents which are non-negotiable and similar to those used for other modes of transport. These alternative documents have different names – "liner waybills", "ocean waybills", "cargo quay receipts", "data freight receipts" or "sea waybills". The term "sea waybill" is frequently used to include all of the various non-negotiable transport

---

3 Refer to Introduction to *Incoterms 2000* paragraph 14. (See reproduced pages 184-185 in this text.)

documents used for carriage of goods by sea.

Unfortunately, international conventions and national laws do not yet provide specific regulations for these non-negotiable transport documents. (The exception is in the United States, where a non-negotiable bill of lading is recognized; this is the "straight bill of lading".) For this reason, the Comité Maritime International (CMI) in June 1990 adopted Uniform Rules for Sea Waybills. The parties should refer to these Rules in the contract of carriage to avoid any legal uncertainties stemming from the use of non-negotiable documents (see Appendix).

Electronic communication and the bill of lading

Section A8 takes into account that the parties may wish to engage in "paperless trading". If the parties have agreed to communicate electronically, the requirement that a paper document be presented is no longer compulsory.

However, with respect to maritime carriage, particular problems arise in replacing the bill of lading with electronic communication (see the comments to CFR A8).

CPT

A9   Checking – packaging – marking

The seller must pay the costs of those checking operations (such as checking quality, measuring, weighing, counting) which are necessary for the purpose of delivering the goods in accordance with A4.

The seller must provide at his own expense packaging (unless it is usual for the particular trade to send the goods of the contract description unpacked) which is required for the transport of the goods arranged by him. Packaging is to be marked appropriately.

Comments   It is necessary for the buyer to ensure that the seller has duly fulfilled his obligation with respect to the condition of the goods. This is particularly important if the buyer is called upon to pay for the goods before he has received and checked them. However, the seller has no duty to arrange and pay for inspection of the goods before shipment, unless this has been specifically agreed in the contract of sale.

The goods must also be adequately packed. Since the seller arranges the carriage, he is in a good position to decide the packing required for the transport of the goods. The goods should also be marked in accordance with applicable standards and regulations.

A10   Other obligations

The seller must render the buyer at the latter's request, risk and expense, every assistance in obtaining any documents or equivalent electronic messages (other than those mentioned in A8) issued or transmitted in the country of dispatch and/or of origin which the buyer may require for the import of the goods and for their transit through any country.

The seller must provide the buyer, upon request, with the necessary information for procuring insurance.

Comments   The seller has the obligation to clear the goods for export, but he has no obligation after shipment to bear any costs or risks connected either with the transit through another country or with import clearance of the goods at destination. However, he has the duty to render assistance to the buyer in obtaining any documents or equivalent electronic messages which may be required for these purposes. The buyer, however, must reimburse the seller for any expenses which the seller might have incurred in connection with this assistance. Moreover, if something goes wrong, the buyer will have to assume the risk.

The seller may also be requested to provide the buyer with information related to the goods which the buyer requires for insurance purposes, if this information does not follow from the description of the goods in the contract of sale.

CPT

B THE BUYER'S OBLIGATIONS

B1 Payment of the price

The buyer must pay the price as provided in the contract of sale.

Comments
The buyer must pay the price agreed in the contract of sale. B1 constitutes a reminder of this main obligation, which corresponds with the seller's obligation to provide the goods in conformity with the contract of sale, as stipulated in A1.

B2 Licences, authorizations and formalities

The buyer must obtain at his own risk and expense any import licence or other official authorization and carry out, where applicable[4], all customs formalities for the import of the goods and for their transit through any country.

Comments
The buyer must take care of the import clearance and bear any costs and risks in connection with it. Therefore, an import prohibition will not relieve the buyer of his obligation to pay for the goods, unless there is a particular "relief clause" in the contract of sale which he invokes to obtain this relief. Such clauses may provide for the extension of time or the right to avoid the contract under the applicable law (see the comments to A2).

The buyer must also do whatever may be needed to pass the goods through a third country after they have been shipped (dispatched) from the seller's country, unless this obligation is for the seller's account under the contract of carriage.

B3 Contracts of carriage and insurance

a) Contract of carriage

No obligation[5].

b) Contract of insurance

No obligation[6].

Comments
Although B3 merely stipulates "No obligation" for the buyer, on-carriage from the port of destination is necessary in most cases, and it is the buyer's responsibility to do whatever is required for this purpose. But the seller is not concerned with the further carriage of the goods, and the buyer has no obligation to the seller in this respect. The words "No obligation" mean that whatever the buyer does is in his own interest and is not covered by the contract of sale.

B4 Taking delivery

The buyer must accept delivery of the goods when they have been delivered in accordance with A4 and receive them from the carrier at the named place.

Comments
Here, the two critical points under the C-term appear again. Since the seller fulfils his obligation by handing over the goods to the carrier at the place of dispatch (A4), it is for the buyer to accept such delivery under B4. But the buyer also has a further obligation to receive the goods from the carrier at the named port of destination. This is not something he does only in his own interest (as in B3) but is an obligation to the seller, who has concluded the contract of carriage with the carrier.

That the buyer "must accept delivery of the goods as soon as they have been delivered in accordance with A4" does not, of course, preclude him from raising claims against the seller if the goods do not conform with the contract.

4 Refer to Introduction to *Incoterms 2000* paragraph 14. (See reproduced pages 184-185 in this text.)
5 Refer to Introduction to *Incoterms 2000* paragraph 10. (See reproduced pages 184-185 in this text.)
6 Refer to Introduction to *Incoterms 2000* paragraph 10. (See reproduced pages 184-185 in this text.)

CPT

B5   Transfer of risks

The buyer must bear all risks of loss of or damage to the goods from the time they have been delivered in accordance with A4.

The buyer must, should he fail to give notice in accordance with B7, bear all risks of the goods from the agreed date or the expiry date of the period fixed for delivery provided, however, that the goods have been duly appropriated to the contract, that is to say, clearly set aside or otherwise identified as the contract goods.

Comments   According to the main rule, while the seller under A5 bears the risk of loss of or damage to the goods until the delivery point, the buyer has to bear the risk thereafter. The delivery point is different under the different terms. In EXW and all D-terms the goods are simply placed "at the disposal of the buyer" at the relevant point, while under the F- and C-terms the delivery point is related to the handing over of the goods to the carrier in the country of dispatch or shipment (see the comments to A4 of these terms). In the terms used for goods intended to be carried by sea, reference is made to delivery alongside the named vessel (FAS) or delivery on board the vessel (FOB, CFR, CIF).

The buyer's failure to give notice according to B7, which relates to the "time for dispatching the goods and/or the destination" (see the comments to B7) may result in a premature passing of the risk: it is unacceptable to allow the buyer to delay the delivery and passing of the risk longer than contemplated when the contract of sale was made. Therefore, his failure to notify according to B7 will cause the risk to pass "from the agreed date or the expiry date of the period fixed for delivery".

The risk, however, cannot pass until the goods "have been appropriated to the contract". If the goods are unascertained – i.e. goods of a certain kind which the seller will deliver to various buyers – appropriation occurs only when the goods are "clearly set aside as the contract goods".

B6   Division of costs

The buyer must, subject to the provisions of A3 a), pay

- all costs relating to the goods from the time they have been delivered in accordance with A4; and

- all costs and charges relating to the goods whilst in transit until their arrival at the agreed place of destination, unless such costs and charges were for the seller's account under the contract of carriage; and

- unloading costs unless such costs and charges were for the seller's account under the contract of carriage; and

- all additional costs incurred if he fails to give notice in accordance with B7, for the goods from the agreed date or the expiry date of the period fixed for dispatch, provided, however, that the goods have been duly appropriated to the contract, that is to say, clearly set aside or otherwise identified as the contract goods; and

- where applicable[7], all duties, taxes and other charges as well as the costs of carrying out customs formalities payable upon import of the goods and for their transit through any country unless included within the cost of the contract of carriage.

Comments   While the seller has to pay all costs required to bring the goods to the place of dispatch and to deliver the goods to the carrier (as well as unloading charges at the place of destination, provided they have been included in the freight), the buyer has to pay any further costs which may arise after the seller has fulfilled these obligations. In this sense, the transfer of the risk also determines the division of costs; if something occurs as a result of contingencies after shipment – such as strandings, collisions, strikes, government

---

7 Refer to Introduction to *Incoterms 2000* paragraph 14. (See reproduced pages 184-185 in this text.)

CPT

directions, hindrances because of ice or other weather conditions – any additional costs charged by the carrier as a result of these contingencies, or otherwise occurring, will be for the account of the buyer.

Failure to give notice and premature passing of risk

The failure to give appropriate notice in accordance with B7 not only results in a premature transfer of the risks (see comments to B5) but also imposes on the buyer the responsibility to pay any additional costs as a consequence. In this case, the obligation to pay these additional costs occurs only if the goods have been duly appropriated to the contract (as discussed in the comments to B5).

Buyer's duties in clearing goods for import

As noted in the comments to B2, the buyer has the duty to clear the goods for import; it is then established in B6 that he has to pay the costs arising from the clearance ("duties, taxes and other charges as well as the costs of carrying out customs formalities"). The buyer also has to pay any duties, taxes and other charges arising in connection with the transit of the goods through another country after they have been delivered by the seller in accordance with A4 unless these costs were for the seller's account under the contract of carriage.

B7 Notice to the seller

The buyer must, whenever he is entitled to determine the time for dispatching the goods and/or the destination, give the seller sufficient notice thereof.

Comments As discussed in the comments to B5 and B6, the failure of the buyer to notify the seller of the time for shipping the goods or the destination – when the buyer in the contract of sale has been given the option to determine these matters – may cause the risk of the loss of or damage to the goods to pass before the goods have been delivered according to A4. In addition, it can make the buyer liable to pay any additional costs incurred by the seller as a result of the buyer's failure.

B8 Proof of delivery, transport document or equivalent electronic message

The buyer must accept the transport document in accordance with A8 if it is in conformity with the contract.

Comments The buyer has to accept the transport document if it conforms with the contract and with the requirements of A8 (see the comments to A8). If the buyer rejects the transport document (for example, by instructions to a bank not to pay the seller under a documentary credit), he commits a breach of contract, which would give the seller remedies available for such a breach under the contract of sale.

These remedies could include, for example, a right to cancel the contract or to claim damages for breach. However, the buyer is not obliged to accept a document which does not provide adequate proof of delivery, for example, one which has notations on it showing that the goods are defective or that they have been provided in less than the agreed quantity. In these cases, the document is termed "unclean".

B9 Inspection of goods

The buyer must pay the costs of any pre-shipment inspection except when such inspection is mandated by the authorities of the country of export.

Comments As discussed in the comments to A9, the buyer has to pay for any costs of checking the goods unless the contract states that these costs should be borne wholly or partly by the seller. In some cases, the contract may provide that the costs should be borne by the seller if the inspection reveals that the goods do not conform with the contract.

In some countries, where import licences or permission to obtain foreign currency for the payment of the price may be required, the authorities may demand an inspection of the goods before shipment, to ensure that the goods are in conformity with the contract. (This is usually called pre-shipment inspection, PSI.) If this is the case, the inspection is normally arranged by instructions from the authorities to an inspection company, which they appoint. The costs following from this inspection have to be paid by the authorities. Any reimbursement to the authorities for the inspection costs, however, must be made by the buyer, unless otherwise specifically agreed between the buyer and the seller.

B10   Other obligations

The buyer must pay all costs and charges incurred in obtaining the documents or equivalent electronic messages mentioned in A10 and reimburse those incurred by the seller in rendering his assistance in accordance therewith.

Comments   As discussed in the comments to A10, the seller has to render the buyer assistance in obtaining the documents or electronic messages which may be required for the transit and import of the goods. However, this assistance is rendered at the buyer's risk and expense. Therefore, B10 stipulates that the buyer must pay all costs and charges incurred in obtaining these documents or electronic messages. He will also have to reimburse the seller for the seller's costs in rendering his assistance in these matters.

CPT

"Carriage and Insurance paid to..." means that the seller delivers the goods to the carrier nominated by him but the seller must in addition pay the cost of carriage necessary to bring the goods to the named destination. This means that the buyer bears all risks and any additional costs occurring after the goods have been so delivered. However, in CIP the seller also has to procure insurance against the buyer's risk of loss of or damage to the goods during the carriage.

Consequently, the seller contracts for insurance and pays the insurance premium.

The buyer should note that under the CIP term the seller is required to obtain insurance only on minimum cover.[1]

Should the buyer wish to have the protection of greater cover, he would either need to agree as much expressly with the seller or to make his own extra insurance arrangements.

"Carrier" means any person who, in a contract of carriage, undertakes to perform or to procure the performance of transport, by rail, road, air, sea, inland waterway or by a combination of such modes.

If subsequent carriers are used for the carriage to the agreed destination, the risk passes when the goods have been delivered to the first carrier.

The CIP term requires the seller to clear the goods for export.

This term may be used irrespective of the mode of transport including multimodal transport.

1 Refer to the introduction of *Incoterms 2000*, ICC publication Nº560, paragraph 9.3. (See reproduced pages 184-185 in this text.)

CIP

Carriage and Insurance Paid to
(…named place of destination)

Group ⓒ
main carriage
paid by the seller

A

Seller's primary duty
- Contract for carriage and insurance
- Deliver the goods to the (first) carrier
- Provide a usual and clean transport document and a cargo insurance policy or certificate
- Arrange export clearance
- Pay loading costs
- Pay unloading costs if for his account under the contract of carriage

■ Carriage of goods

■ Seller's risks

□ Seller's costs

Documents

Required documents:
- Commercial Invoice
- Transport document
- Export licence, if necessary
- Insurance policy (certificate)

Optional documents
- Other documents needed for transit of the goods through any country or for import clearance

B

Buyer's primary duty
- Accept delivery of the goods when they have been delivered to the carrier
- Receive the goods from the carrier
- Pay such costs as are not for the seller's account under the contract of carriage

□ Carriage of goods

□ Buyer's risks

□ Buyer's costs

Carriage of goods

Risks

Costs

Export clearance   **Import clearance**

Critical points

◐ Carriage and insurance to be arranged by the seller

◐ Risk transfer from the seller to the buyer when the goods have been delivered to the carrier

◑ Cost transfer at place of destination, the buyer paying such costs as are not for the seller's account under the contract of carriage

CIP

A THE SELLER'S OBLIGATIONS

A1, A2, A4 to A10

See the comments to CPT A1, A2, A4 to A10.

A3 Contracts of carriage and insurance

a) Contract of carriage

The seller must contract on usual terms at his own expense for the carriage of the goods to the agreed point at the named place of destination by a usual route and in a customary manner. If a point is not agreed or is not determined by practice, the seller may select the point at the named place of destination which best suits his purpose.

b) Contract of insurance

The seller must obtain at his own expense cargo insurance as agreed in the contract, such that the buyer, or any other person having an insurable interest in the goods, shall be entitled to claim directly from the insurer and provide the buyer with the insurance policy or other evidence of insurance cover.

The insurance shall be contracted with underwriters or an insurance company of good repute and, failing express agreement to the contrary, be in accordance with minimum cover of the Institute Cargo Clauses (Institute of London Underwriters) or any similar set of clauses. The duration of insurance cover shall be in accordance with B5 and B4. When required by the buyer, the seller shall provide at the buyer's expense war, strikes, riots and civil commotion risk insurances if procurable. The minimum insurance shall cover the price provided in the contract plus ten per cent (i.e. 110 %) and shall be provided in the currency of the contract.

Comments
The only difference between the CPT and the CIP term is that the latter requires the seller to also obtain and pay for cargo insurance. This is particularly important for the buyer, since under CIP the risk of loss of or damage to the goods will pass from the seller to the buyer when the goods have been delivered to the carrier at the place of dispatch (see CPT A5).

In addition, it is vital for the buyer to be given the right to claim against the insurer independently of the seller. For this purpose it may be necessary to provide the buyer with the insurance policy under which the insurer makes his undertaking directly to the buyer.

Seller need only provide "minimum cover"
It is important to note that the seller only has to provide for so-called "minimum cover". Such limited cover is suitable only for bulk cargoes, which normally do not suffer loss or damage in transit unless something happens to the means of conveyance as well as to the cargo (strandings, collisions, fire, etc.). The buyer and seller are therefore advised to agree that the seller should provide a more suitable insurance cover. The buyer should then specify the extended cover he prefers.

The insurance cover according to the so-called Institute Cargo Clauses is available in categories A, B and C. The C category provides the minimum cover, and the cover is extended progressively in categories B and A. However, even the most extended cover in A does not provide for what is misleadingly called "all-risk insurance". Furthermore, there are other important exceptions which category A insurance does not cover, for example, cases when the loss of the goods has been caused by insolvency or fraud, or when financial loss has been incurred by delay in delivery.

Duration of insurance cover
The duration of the insurance cover must coincide with the carriage and must protect the buyer from the moment he has to bear the risk of loss of or damage to the goods

(i.e. from the moment the goods have been delivered to the carrier at the place of dispatch). It must extend until the goods arrive at the agreed place of destination.

Some risks require additional cover

Some particular risks require additional insurance, and if the buyer requests it, the seller must arrange this additional cover at the buyer's expense – for example, insurance against the risks of war, strikes, riots and civil commotion – if this cover can possibly be arranged.

Amount of the insurance cover

The amount of the insurance should correspond to the price provided in the contract, plus 10 per cent. The additional 10 per cent is intended to cover the average profit which buyers of goods expect from the sale. The insurance should be provided in the same currency as stipulated in the contract for the price of the goods. Consequently, if the price of the goods is to be paid in convertible currency, the seller may not provide insurance in other than convertible currency.

CIP

B BUYER'S OBLIGATIONS

B1 to B9

See the comments to CPT B1 to B9.

B10 Other obligations

The buyer must pay all costs and charges incurred in obtaining the documents or equivalent electronic messages mentioned in A10 and reimburse those incurred by the seller in rendering his assistance in accordance therewith.

The buyer must provide the seller, upon request, with the necessary information for procuring any additional insurance.

Comments   It is vital for the buyer to understand that the seller only has to take out minimum insurance cover. This cover in most cases is insufficient when manufactured goods are involved. In the contract of sale, therefore, the buyer should require the seller to take out additional cover, usually according to the Institute Clauses A or a corresponding cover. If, however, the contract does not deal with this matter at all, the seller's obligation is limited as stipulated in A3, and the buyer has to arrange and pay for any additional insurance cover required.

In most cases the seller will know how to arrange the insurance from the contract of sale (from the invoice value of the goods, their destination, etc.). But if this is not the case, the buyer has to provide the seller, upon the latter's request, with any additional necessary information. (See also the comments to CPT B10.)

"Delivered at Frontier" means that the seller delivers when the goods are placed at the disposal of the buyer on the arriving means of transport not unloaded, cleared for export, but not cleared for import at the named point and place at the frontier, but before the customs border of the adjoining country. The term "frontier" may be used for any frontier including that of the country of export. Therefore, it is of vital importance that the frontier in question be defined precisely by always naming the point and place in the term. However, if the parties wish the seller to be responsible for the unloading of the goods from the arriving means of transport and to bear the risks and costs of unloading, this should be made clear by adding explicit wording to this effect in the contract of sale.[1]

This term may be used irrespective of the mode of transport when goods are to be delivered at a land frontier. When delivery is to take place in the port of destination, on board a vessel or on the quay (wharf), the DES or DEQ terms should be used.

1 Refer to the introduction of *Incoterms 2000,* ICC publication N°560, paragraph 11. (See reproduced pages 184-185 in this text.)

DAF

Delivered At Frontier
(…named place)

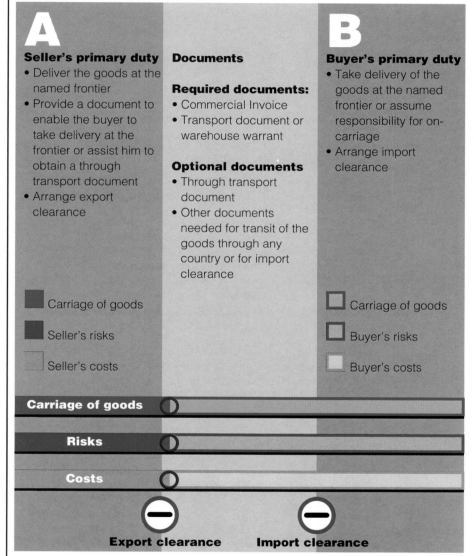

A

Seller's primary duty
- Deliver the goods at the named frontier
- Provide a document to enable the buyer to take delivery at the frontier or assist him to obtain a through transport document
- Arrange export clearance

Documents

Required documents:
- Commercial Invoice
- Transport document or warehouse warrant

Optional documents
- Through transport document
- Other documents needed for transit of the goods through any country or for import clearance

B

Buyer's primary duty
- Take delivery of the goods at the named frontier or assume responsibility for on-carriage
- Arrange import clearance

Carriage of goods

Seller's risks

Seller's costs

Carriage of goods

Buyer's risks

Buyer's costs

Carriage of goods

Risks

Costs

Export clearance   Import clearance

Critical points

- Carriage to be arranged by the seller
- Risk transfer from the seller to the buyer when the goods have been delivered at the frontier
- Cost transfer from the seller to the buyer when the goods have been delivered at the frontier

DAF

A THE SELLER'S OBLIGATIONS

A1 Provision of goods in conformity with the contract

The seller must provide the goods and the commercial invoice, or its equivalent electronic message, in conformity with the contract of sale and any other evidence of conformity which may be required by the contract.

Comments   The seller must provide the goods in conformity with the contract. It is also usual practice that the seller, in order to be paid, has to invoice the buyer. In addition, the seller must submit any other evidence stipulated in the contract itself that the goods conform with that contract.

This text only serves as a reminder of the seller's main obligation under the contract of sale.

A2 Licences, authorizations and formalities

The seller must obtain at his own risk and expense any export licence or other official authorization or other document necessary for placing the goods at the buyer's disposal.

The seller must carry out, where applicable[2], all customs formalities necessary for the export of the goods to the named place of delivery at the frontier and for their transit through any country.

Comments   The seller has to clear the goods for export and assume any risk or expense which this involves. Consequently, if there is an export prohibition or if there are particular taxes on the export of the goods – and if there are other government-imposed requirements which may render the export of the goods more expensive than contemplated – all of these risks and costs must be borne by the seller. However, contracts of sale usually contain particular provisions which the seller may invoke to protect himself in the event of these contingencies. Under CISG and corresponding provisions in various national Sale of Goods Acts, unforeseen or reasonably unforeseeable export prohibitions may relieve the seller from his obligations under the contract of sale.

A2 stipulates that the seller has to do whatever may be necessary with respect to prior transit formalities. This is the case even when the goods are to be carried through several countries before they reach the point named after DAF in the contract of sale. DAF is frequently used in these circumstances, usually with the goods being carried by rail. Non-compliance with the above requirements would prevent the seller from reaching the agreed place of delivery.

A3 Contracts of carriage and insurance

a) Contract of carriage

i) The seller must contract at his own expense for the carriage of the goods to the named point, if any, at the place of delivery at the frontier. If a point at the named place of delivery at the frontier is not agreed or is not determined by practice, the seller may select the point at the named place of delivery which best suits his purpose.

ii) However, if requested by the buyer, the seller may agree to contract on usual terms at the buyer's risk and expense for the on-going carriage of the goods beyond the named place at the frontier to the final destination in the country of import named by the buyer. The seller may decline to make the contract and, if he does, shall promptly notify the buyer accordingly.

b) Contract of insurance

No obligation[3].

---

2 Refer to Introduction to *Incoterms 2000* paragraph 14. (See reproduced pages 184-185 in this text.)
3 Refer to Introduction to *Incoterms 2000* paragraph 10. (See reproduced pages 184-185 in this text.)

Comments   Under all D-terms, the seller must ensure that the goods actually arrive at destination. It follows from this that the seller must arrange and pay for any carriage of the goods. Under the D-terms, the seller's choice of transport is only of importance to the buyer insofar as it affects the buyer's obligation to receive the goods from the carrier. If the seller chooses an unusual mode of transport which makes it more difficult or expensive for the buyer to receive the goods from the carrier, any additional costs or risks caused by the seller's choice of transport will be for the seller's account.

Normally, the point mentioned after the D-term will indicate where the goods should be delivered at destination. But if there are several alternatives available, and the contract of sale or commercial practice does not indicate which alternative the seller must choose, he "may select the point at the named place of delivery which best suits his purpose". In Incoterms 2000 an addition has been made for the not-unusual case where the buyer requests the seller to contract for on-carriage at the buyer's risk and expense beyond the named place at the frontier.

A4   Delivery

The seller must place the goods at the disposal of the buyer on the arriving means of transport not unloaded at the named place of delivery at the frontier on the date or within the agreed period.

Comments   Under all D-terms the seller must "place the goods at the disposal of the buyer" at destination. The precise point for the delivery of the goods depends upon the D-term chosen. According to DAF A4, the goods should be placed at the disposal of the buyer "at the named place of delivery at the frontier". Incoterms 2000 specify that the goods are placed at the disposal of the buyer "on the arriving means of transport not unloaded" (see also DDU and DDP A4).

If in the contract of sale only the frontier of the country concerned is named and not the place at that frontier where the delivery should take place (the contract may say, for example, "DAF Italian border"), the seller can then select the place at the border which best suits his purpose.

DAF may be used irrespective of the intended mode of transport, though it is more frequently used for rail carriage. The rail carriage usually continues past the border without any discharge of the goods from the railway wagon and re-loading on to another one. Consequently, there will be no real "placing of the goods at the disposal of the buyer". Instead, the seller, on the buyer's request, will provide the buyer with a through railway consignment note to the place of final destination in the country of import (see the comments to A3 a) ii) and A8).

A5   Transfer of risks

The seller must, subject to the provisions of B5, bear all risks of loss of or damage to the goods until such time as they have been delivered in accordance with A4.

Comments   All Incoterms are based on the same principle that the risk of loss of or damage to the goods is transferred from the seller to the buyer when the seller has fulfilled his delivery obligation according to A4. A5 of FOB, CFR and CIF further specifies that the risk is transferred when the goods "have passed the ship's rail at the port of shipment".

All Incoterms, in conformity with the general principle of CISG, connect the transfer of the risk with the delivery of the goods and not with other circumstances, such as the passing of ownership or the time of the conclusion of the contract. Neither Incoterms nor CISG deals with transfer of title to the goods or other property rights with respect to the goods.

The passing of risk of loss of or damage to the goods concerns the risk of fortuitous events (accidents) and does not include loss or damage caused by the seller or the buyer, for example, inadequate packing or marking of the goods. Therefore, even if damage occurs subsequent to the transfer of the risk, the seller may still be responsible if the damage could be attributed to the fact that the goods were not delivered in conformity with the contract (see A1 and the comments to A9).

A5 of all Incoterms contains the phrase "subject to the provisions of B5". This means that there are exceptions to the main rule concerning the passing of risk under the circumstances mentioned in B5, which may result in a premature passing of the risk because of the buyer's failure to fulfil his obligations properly (see the comments to B5).

A6   Division of costs

The seller must, subject to the provisions of B6, pay

- in addition to the costs resulting from A3 a), all costs relating to the goods until such time as they have been delivered in accordance with A4; and

- where applicable[4], the costs of customs formalities necessary for export as well as all duties, taxes or other charges payable upon export of the goods and for their transit through any country prior to delivery in accordance with A4.

Comments   As is the case with the transfer of the risk of loss of or damage to the goods, all Incoterms follow the same rule, that the division of costs occurs at the delivery point. All costs occurring before the seller has fulfilled his obligation to deliver according to A4 are for his account, while further costs are for the account of the buyer (see the comments to B6). This rule is made subject to the provisions of B6, which indicates that the buyer may have to bear additional costs incurred by his failure to give appropriate notice to the seller.

Since under D-terms the seller does not fulfil his obligation until the goods have actually arrived at destination and been placed at the disposal of the buyer, the seller has to do everything required to achieve this. A3 in all D-terms still stipulates that the seller must contract for carriage; and A6 of all D-terms stipulates that he must pay the costs resulting from A3 for the carriage of the goods and, where applicable, the costs relating to customs formalities, duties, taxes and other charges prior to delivery in accordance with A4. Needless to say, any transit costs incurred subsequent to delivery will have to be paid by the buyer.

A7   Notice to the buyer

The seller must give the buyer sufficient notice of the dispatch of the goods to the named place at the frontier as well as any other notice required in order to allow the buyer to take measures which are normally necessary to enable him to take delivery of the goods.

Comments   The seller must give the buyer sufficient notice as to when the goods are available at the agreed or chosen delivery point, so that the buyer can make preparations in time to take delivery according to B4. There is no stipulation in Incoterms spelling out the consequences of the seller's failure to give such notice. But it follows from Incoterms that the seller's failure constitutes a breach of contract. This means that the seller could be held responsible for the breach according to the law applicable to the contract of sale.

A8 Proof of delivery, transport document or equivalent electronic message

i) The seller must provide the buyer at the seller's expense with the usual document or other evidence of the delivery of the goods at the named place at the frontier in accordance with A3 a) i).

ii) The seller must, should the parties agree on on-going carriage beyond the frontier in accordance with A3 a) ii), provide the buyer at the latter's request, risk and expense, with the through document of transport normally obtained in the country of dispatch covering on usual terms the transport of the goods from the point of dispatch in that country to the place of final destination in the country of import named by the buyer.

Where the seller and the buyer have agreed to communicate electronically, the document referred to in the preceding paragraph may be replaced by an equivalent electronic data interchange (EDI) message.

DAF

Comments   When the goods have actually been delivered physically at the frontier, the seller, at his own expense, has to provide the buyer "with the usual document or other evidence of the delivery". However, as noted in the comments to DAF A4, goods carried by rail will frequently remain on the railway wagon and continue to the final destination. The seller must then provide the buyer with the usual "through document of transport" if the seller has agreed to contract for on-carriage in accordance with A3 a) ii). These documents can be replaced by EDI messages when the parties have agreed to communicate electronically.

A9 Checking – packaging – marking

The seller must pay the costs of those checking operations (such as checking quality, measuring, weighing, counting) which are necessary for the purpose of delivering the goods in accordance with A4.

The seller must provide at his own expense packaging (unless it is agreed or usual for the particular trade to deliver the goods of the contract description unpacked) which is required for the delivery of the goods at the frontier and for the subsequent transport to the extent that the circumstances (for example modalities, destination) are made known to the seller before the contract of sale is concluded. Packaging is to be marked appropriately.

Comments   It is important that the buyer ensure that the seller has duly fulfilled his obligation with respect to the condition of the goods, particularly if the buyer is called upon to pay for the goods before he has received and checked them. However, the seller has no duty to arrange and pay for the inspection of the goods before shipment, unless this is specifically agreed in the contract of sale.

A10 Other obligations

The seller must render the buyer at the latter's request, risk and expense, every assistance in obtaining any documents or equivalent electronic messages (other than those mentioned in A8) issued or transmitted in the country of dispatch and/or origin which the buyer may require for the import of the goods and, where necessary, for their transit through any country.

The seller must provide the buyer, upon request, with the necessary information for procuring insurance.

Comments   The seller has the obligation to carry out all customs formalities for the export of the goods and for their prior transit. But he has no obligation after the goods have reached the frontier to bear any costs and risks for their transit through another country or for import clearance. However, he has the duty to render the buyer assistance in obtaining the documents (for example, a certificate of origin, a health certificate, a clean report of findings, an import licence) or equivalent electronic messages which may be required for import clearance of the goods.

The buyer, in turn, must reimburse the seller for any expenses which the seller might have incurred in connection with this assistance. Moreover, if something goes wrong, the buyer will have to assume the risk.

The seller may also be requested to provide the buyer with any information relating to the goods which the buyer might require for insurance purposes, if this information is not provided in the description of the goods in the contract of sale.

B   THE BUYER'S OBLIGATIONS

B1   Payment of the price

The buyer must pay the price as provided in the contract of sale.

Comments   The buyer must pay the price agreed in the contract of sale. B1 constitutes a reminder of this main obligation, which corresponds with the seller's obligation to provide the goods in conformity with the contract of sale, as stipulated in A1.

B2   Licences, authorizations and formalities

The buyer must obtain at his own risk and expense any import licence or other official authorization or other documents and carry out, where applicable[5], all customs formalities necessary for the import of the goods, and for their subsequent transport.

Comments   The buyer must take care of the import clearance and bear any costs and risks in connection with it. Therefore, an import prohibition will not relieve the buyer of his obligation to pay for the goods, unless there is a particular "relief clause" in the contract of sale which he invokes to obtain this relief. Such clauses may provide for the extension of time or the right to avoid the contract under the applicable law (see the comments to A2).

B3   Contracts of carriage and insurance

a) Contract of carriage

No obligation[6].

b) Contract of insurance

No obligation[7].

Comments   Although B3 merely stipulates "No obligation" for the buyer, on-carriage from the place of delivery is necessary in most cases, and it is the buyer's responsibility to do whatever is required for this purpose unless he has agreed with the seller that the latter should do it (see A3 a) ii)). Otherwise, the seller is not concerned with the further carriage of the goods and the buyer has no obligation to the seller in this respect. The words "No obligation" mean that whatever the buyer does is in his own interest and is not covered by the contract of sale.

---

5 Refer to Introduction to *Incoterms 2000* paragraph 14. (See reproduced pages 184-185 in this text.)
6 Refer to Introduction to *Incoterms 2000* paragraph 10. (See reproduced pages 184-185 in this text.)
7 Refer to Introduction to *Incoterms 2000* paragraph 10. (See reproduced pages 184-185 in this text.)

B4   Taking delivery

The buyer must take delivery of the goods when they have been delivered in accordance with A4.

Comments   As in all D-terms, B4 has wording stating that the buyer shall take delivery as soon as the goods have been placed at his disposal in accordance with A4. The seller, according to A4 in the D-terms, shall place the goods at the buyer's disposal "on the date or within the agreed period".

If the goods are placed at the buyer's disposal earlier than agreed, the buyer is not obliged to take delivery before the agreed time, though it may normally be in his own interest to do so. If the goods are placed at the buyer's disposal too late, the buyer may hold the seller responsible for breach of contract according to the applicable law. He may also recover damages from the seller or, in the event of a fundamental breach, cancel the contract.

B5   Transfer of risks

The buyer must bear all risks of loss of or damage to the goods from the time they have been delivered in accordance with A4.

The buyer must, should he fail to give notice in accordance with B7, bear all risks of loss of or damage to the goods from the agreed date or the expiry date of the agreed period for delivery provided, however, that the goods have been duly appropriated to the contract, that is to say, clearly set aside or otherwise identified as the contract goods.

Comments   According to the main rule, while the seller under A5 bears the risk of loss of or damage to the goods until the delivery point, the buyer has to bear the risk thereafter. The delivery point is different under the different terms. In EXW and all D-terms the goods are simply placed "at the disposal of the buyer" at the relevant point, while under the F- and C-terms the delivery point is related to the handing over of the goods to the carrier in the country of dispatch or shipment (see the comments to A4 of these terms). In the terms used for goods intended to be carried by sea, reference is made to delivery alongside the named vessel (FAS) or delivery onboard the vessel (FOB, CFR, CIF).

Consequences of buyer's failure to give notice
While the seller under EXW and all D-terms can transfer the risk by his own act of placing the goods at the buyer's disposal, he may be prevented from doing so by the buyer's failure to give notice according to B7. This can occur when it is the buyer's responsibility to determine (1) the time within a stipulated period when the goods are to be made available or (2) the place of delivery (see the comments to B7). The failure to perform these tasks results in a premature passing of the risk: it is not acceptable that the buyer should be able to delay the delivery and passing of the risk longer than contemplated when the contract of sale was made. Therefore, his failure to notify according to B7 will cause the risk to pass "from the agreed date or the expiry date of the agreed period for delivery".

Appropriation and the passing of risk
The risk, however, cannot pass until the goods "have been duly appropriated to the contract". If the goods are unascertained – i.e., goods of a certain kind which the seller will deliver to various buyers – appropriation occurs only when the goods are "clearly set aside or otherwise identified as the contract goods".

This appropriation will normally be made when the seller has handed over the goods for carriage and the consignment has been marked as intended for the buyer – unless the cargo is carried in bulk and intended to be appropriated between different buyers only upon the arrival of the goods at destination.

DAF

B6   Division of costs

The buyer must pay

- all costs relating to the goods from the time they have been delivered in accordance with A4 including the expenses of unloading necessary to take delivery of the goods from the arriving means of transport at the named place of delivery at the frontier; and

- all additional costs incurred if he fails to take delivery of the goods when they have been delivered in accordance with A4, or to give notice in accordance with B7, provided, however, that the goods have been appropriated to the contract, that is to say, clearly set aside or otherwise identified as the contract goods; and

- where applicable[8], the cost of customs formalities as well as all duties, taxes and other charges payable upon import of the goods and for their subsequent transport.

Comments   If, as stipulated in A4, the goods are placed at the disposal of the buyer at the named place of delivery at the frontier, the buyer, under DAF B6 and under all other D-terms, would have to pay all costs from the time the goods have been made available to him in this manner. The seller has to pay all costs of discharge required in order to place the goods at the disposal of the buyer. But if the goods are intended to be re-loaded upon an on-carrying vehicle, the parties are advised to stipulate specifically who should perform the unloading and re-loading operations, for example, by adding the words "loaded upon on-carrying vehicle" after the Incoterm.

When DAF is used for railway traffic, the goods will usually remain on the same railway wagon, and the point mentioned in the contract will then primarily serve as a point for dividing the railway freight between the parties (i.e., as a tariff point). The seller has to bear all costs and risks until that point has been reached.

Under all D-terms, the buyer has to take delivery of the goods at the agreed point and time. The same principle governs even if there is no delivery in the physical sense, for example, if the goods remain on the same vehicle when it passes the agreed delivery point. If the buyer fails to take delivery or to take the required measures for on-carriage, he will have to bear any additional costs incurred thereby.

Appropriation required if goods arrive in bulk

At the delivery stage, the seller will normally have identified the goods as the contract goods (through "appropriation"). But if he has not done so – for example, if the goods arrive at destination in bulk for later appropriation by delivery orders or otherwise – the buyer does not have to bear any additional costs relating to the goods until they have been duly appropriated.

Subject to the goods having been appropriated, the buyer then has to pay any additional costs incurred as a result of his failure to notify the seller of the time or place of taking delivery according to B7, for example, additional storage and insurance costs.

Buyer's duties in clearing goods for import

As noted in the comments to B2, the buyer has the duty to clear the goods for import; B6 declares that he also has to pay the costs arising in that connection ("the costs of customs formalities as well as all duties, taxes and other charges"). The buyer also has to pay any duties, taxes and other charges arising with regard to the transit of the goods through another country, after they have been delivered by the seller in accordance with A4.

B7   Notice to the seller

The buyer must, whenever he is entitled to determine the time within an agreed period and/or the point of taking delivery at the named place, give the seller sufficient notice thereof.

---

8 Refer to Introduction to *Incoterms 2000* paragraph 14. (See reproduced pages 184-185 in this text.)

Comments   As discussed in the comments to B5 and B6, the failure of the buyer to notify the seller of the time and place of taking delivery – when the buyer in the contract of sale has been given the option to determine these matters – may cause the risk of the loss of or damage to the goods to pass before the goods have been delivered according to A4. In addition, it can make the buyer liable to pay any additional costs incurred by the seller as a result of the buyer's failure.

B8   Proof of delivery, transport document or equivalent electronic message

The buyer must accept the transport document and/or other evidence of delivery in accordance with A8.

Comments   The buyer has to accept the document if it conforms with the contract and with the requirements of A8 (see the comments to A8). If the buyer rejects the document (for example, by instructions to a bank not to pay the seller under a documentary credit), he commits a breach of contract, which would give the seller remedies available for such a breach under the contract of sale.

These remedies could include, for example, a right to cancel the contract or to claim damages for breach. However, the buyer is not obliged to accept a document which does not provide adequate proof of delivery, for example, one which has notations on it showing that the goods are defective or that they have been provided in less than the agreed quantity. In these cases, the document is termed "unclean".

B9   Inspection of goods

The buyer must pay the costs of any pre-shipment inspection except when such inspection is mandated by the authorities of the country of export.

Comments   As noted in the comments to A9, the buyer has to pay for any costs of checking the goods, unless the contract determines that these costs should be wholly or partly borne by the seller. In some cases, the contract may provide that the costs should be borne by the seller if the inspection reveals that the goods do not conform with the contract.

In some countries, where import licences or permission to obtain foreign currency for the payment of the price may be required, the authorities may demand an inspection of the goods before shipment, to ensure that the goods are in conformity with the contract. (This is usually called pre-shipment inspection, PSI.) If this is the case, the inspection is normally arranged by instructions from the authorities to an inspection company, which they appoint. The costs following from this inspection have to be paid by the authorities. Any reimbursement to the authorities for the inspection costs, however, must be made by the buyer, unless otherwise specifically agreed between the buyer and the seller.

B10   Other obligations

The buyer must pay all costs and charges incurred in obtaining the documents or equivalent electronic messages mentioned in A10 and reimburse those incurred by the seller in rendering his assistance in accordance therewith.

If necessary, according to A3 a) ii), the buyer must provide the seller at his request and the buyer's risk and expense with the exchange control authorization, permits, other documents or certified copies thereof, or with the address of the final destination of the goods in the country of import for the purpose of obtaining the through document of transport or any other document contemplated in A8 ii).

Comments   As discussed in the comments to A10, the seller has to render the buyer assistance in obtaining the documents or electronic messages which may be required for the transit and import of the goods. However, this assistance is rendered at the buyer's risk and expense. Therefore, B10 stipulates that the buyer must pay all costs and charges incurred in obtaining these documents or electronic messages. He will also have to reimburse the seller for the seller's costs in rendering his assistance in these matters.

According to A3aii and A8, the seller may have to provide the buyer with a through document of transport. This may also involve other measures, such as obtaining "exchange control authorization, permits, other documents or certified copies thereof". The buyer must, at his risk and expense, provide the seller with these documents, when the seller requests that he do so.

DAF

"Delivered Ex Ship" means that the seller delivers when the goods are placed at the disposal of the buyer on board the ship not cleared for import at the named port of destination. The seller has to bear all the costs and risks involved in bringing the goods to the named port of destination before discharging. If the parties wish the seller to bear the costs and risks of discharging the goods, then the DEQ term should be used.

This term can be used only when the goods are to be delivered by sea or inland waterway or multimodal transport on a vessel in the port of destination.

DES

Delivered Ex Ship
(...named port of destination)

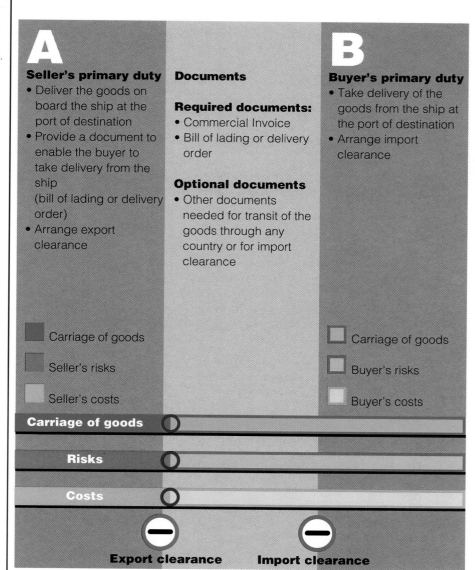

A

Seller's primary duty
- Deliver the goods on board the ship at the port of destination
- Provide a document to enable the buyer to take delivery from the ship (bill of lading or delivery order)
- Arrange export clearance

Documents

Required documents:
- Commercial Invoice
- Bill of lading or delivery order

Optional documents
- Other documents needed for transit of the goods through any country or for import clearance

B

Buyer's primary duty
- Take delivery of the goods from the ship at the port of destination
- Arrange import clearance

Carriage of goods

Seller's risks

Seller's costs

Carriage of goods

Buyer's risks

Buyer's costs

Carriage of goods

Risks

Costs

Export clearance   Import clearance

Critical points

Carriage to be arranged by the seller

Risk transfer from the seller to the buyer when the goods are placed at the disposal of the buyer on board the ship

Cost transfer from the seller to the buyer when the goods are placed at the disposal of the buyer on board the ship

DES

A   THE SELLER'S OBLIGATIONS

A1   Provision of goods in conformity with the contract

The seller must provide the goods and the commercial invoice, or its equivalent electronic message, in conformity with the contract of sale and any other evidence of conformity which may be required by the contract.

Comments
The seller must provide the goods in conformity with the contract. It is also usual practice that the seller, in order to be paid, has to invoice the buyer. In addition, the seller must submit any other evidence stipulated in the contract itself that the goods conform with that contract.

This text only serves as a reminder of the seller's main obligation under the contract of sale.

A2   Licences, authorizations and formalities

The seller must obtain at his own risk and expense any export licence or other official authorization or other documents and carry out, where applicable[1], all customs formalities necessary for the export of the goods and for their transit through any country.

Comments
The seller has to clear the goods for export and assume any risk or expense which this involves. Consequently, if there is an export prohibition or if there are particular taxes on the export of the goods – and if there are other government-imposed requirements which may render the export of the goods more expensive than contemplated – all of these risks and costs must be borne by the seller. However, contracts of sale usually contain particular provisions which the seller may invoke to protect himself in the event of these contingencies. Under CISG and corresponding provisions in various national Sale of Goods Acts, unforeseen or reasonably unforeseeable export prohibitions would relieve the seller from his obligations under the contract of sale.

A3   Contracts of carriage and insurance

a) Contract of carriage

The seller must contract at his own expense for the carriage of the goods to the named point, if any, at the named port of destination. If a point is not agreed or is not determined by practice, the seller may select the point at the named port of destination which best suits his purpose.

b) Contract of insurance

No obligation[2].

Comments
Under all D-terms, the seller must ensure that the goods actually arrive at destination. It follows from this that the seller must arrange and pay for any carriage of the goods.

Under the D-terms, the seller's choice of transport is only of importance to the buyer insofar as it affects the buyer's obligation to receive the goods from the carrier. If the seller chooses an unusual transport which makes it more difficult or expensive for the buyer to receive the goods from the carrier, any additional costs or risks caused by the seller's choice of transport will be for the seller's account.

Normally, the point mentioned after the D-term will indicate where the goods should be delivered at destination. But if there are several alternatives available, and the contract of sale or commercial practice does not indicate which alternative the seller must choose, he "may select the point at the named port of destination which best suits his purpose".

---

1 Refer to Introduction to *Incoterms 2000* paragraph 14. (See reproduced pages 184-185 in this text.)
2 Refer to Introduction to *Incoterms 2000* paragraph 10. (See reproduced pages 184-185 in this text.)

A4   Delivery

The seller must place the goods at the disposal of the buyer on board the vessel at the unloading point referred to in A3 a), in the named port of destination on the date or within the agreed period, in such a way as to enable them to be removed from the vessel by unloading equipment appropriate to the nature of the goods.

Comments   Under all D-terms, the seller must "place the goods at the disposal of the buyer" at destination. The precise point for the delivery of the goods depends upon the D-term chosen. According to DES A4, the goods should be made available to the buyer "on board the vessel at the unloading point". This has to be done "in such a way as to enable them to be removed from the vessel by unloading equipment appropriate to the nature of the goods".

A5   Transfer of risks

The seller must, subject to the provisions of B5, bear all risks of loss of or damage to the goods until such time as they have been delivered in accordance with A4.

Comments   All Incoterms are based on the same principle that the risk of loss of or damage to the goods is transferred from the seller to the buyer when the seller has fulfilled his delivery obligation according to A4. A5 of FOB, CFR and CIF further specifies that the risk is transferred when the goods "have passed the ship's rail at the port of shipment".

All Incoterms, in conformity with the general principle of CISG, connect the transfer of the risk with the delivery of the goods and not with other circumstances, such as the passing of ownership or the time of the conclusion of the contract. Neither Incoterms nor CISG deals with transfer of title to the goods or other property rights with respect to the goods.

The passing of risk of loss of or damage to the goods concerns the risk of fortuitous events (accidents) and does not include loss or damage caused by the seller or the buyer, for example, inadequate packing or marking of the goods. Therefore, even if damage occurs subsequent to the transfer of the risk, the seller may still be responsible if the damage could be attributed to the fact that the goods were not delivered in conformity with the contract (see A1 and the comments to A9).

A5 of all Incoterms contain the phrase "subject to the provisions of B5". This means that there are exceptions to the main rule concerning the passing of risk under the circumstances mentioned in B5, which may result in a premature passing of the risk because of the buyer's failure properly to fulfil his obligations (see the comments to B5).

A6   Division of costs

The seller must, subject to the provisions of B6, pay

■   in addition to costs resulting from A3 a), all costs relating to the goods until such time as they have been delivered in accordance with A4; and

■   where applicable[3], the costs of customs formalities necessary for export as well as all duties, taxes or other charges payable upon export of the goods and for their transit through any country prior to delivery in accordance with A4.

Comments   As is the case with the transfer of the risk for loss of or damage to the goods, all Incoterms follow the same rule, that the division of costs occurs at the delivery point. All costs occurring before the seller has fulfilled his obligation to deliver according to A4 are for his account, while further costs are for the account of the buyer (see the comments to B6). This rule is made subject to the provisions of B6, which indicates that the buyer may have to bear additional costs incurred by his failure to give appropriate notice to the seller.

---

3 Refer to Introduction to *Incoterms 2000* paragraph 14. (See reproduced pages 184-185 in this text.)

DES

Since under D-terms, the seller does not fulfil his obligation until the goods have actually arrived at destination and been placed at the disposal of the buyer, the seller has to do everything required to achieve this. Nevertheless, A3 in all D-terms still stipulates that the seller must contract for carriage; and A6 of all D-terms stipulates that he must pay the costs resulting from A3 for the carriage of the goods "and, where applicable, the costs of customs formalities… as well as all duties, taxes and other charges… prior to delivery in accordance with A4". Needless to say, any transit costs incurred subsequent to delivery will have to be paid by the buyer.

A7 Notice to the buyer

The seller must give the buyer sufficient notice of the estimated time of arrival of the nominated vessel in accordance with A4 as well as any other notice required in order to allow the buyer to take measures which are normally necessary to enable him to take delivery of the goods.

Comments The seller must give the buyer sufficient notice as to the estimated time of arrival (ETA) of the vessel and other essential notices, so that the buyer can make preparations in time to take delivery according to B4. There is no stipulation in Incoterms spelling out the consequences of the seller's failure to give such notice. But it follows from Incoterms that the seller's failure constitutes a breach of contract. This means that the seller could be held responsible for the breach according to the law applicable to the contract of sale.

A8 Proof of delivery, transport document or equivalent electronic message

The seller must provide the buyer at the seller's expense with the delivery order and/or the usual transport document (for example a negotiable bill of lading, a non-negotiable sea waybill, an inland waterway document, or a multimodal transport document) to enable the buyer to claim the goods from the carrier at the port of destination.

Where the seller and the buyer have agreed to communicate electronically, the document referred to in the preceding paragraph may be replaced by an equivalent electronic data interchange (EDI) message.

Comments In most cases the buyer will require a document in order to be able to obtain the goods from the carrier. Traditionally, the relevant document is a negotiable bill of lading, and this is still the predominant document when DES is used for carriage of bulk commodities. However, bills of lading are often replaced by delivery orders splitting up the total bill of lading quantity into smaller lots for several buyers.

Documents can be replaced by EDI messages when the parties have agreed to communicate electronically.

A9 Checking – packaging – marking

The seller must pay the costs of those checking operations (such as checking quality, measuring, weighing, counting) which are necessary for the purpose of delivering the goods in accordance with A4.

The seller must provide at his own expense packaging (unless it is usual for the particular trade to deliver the goods of the contract description unpacked) which is required for the delivery of the goods. Packaging is to be marked appropriately.

Comments It is important that the buyer ensure that the seller has duly fulfilled his obligation with respect to the condition of the goods, particularly if the buyer is called upon to pay for the goods before he has received and checked them. However, the seller has no duty to arrange and pay for the inspection of the goods unless this is specifically agreed in the contract of sale.

A10   Other obligations

The seller must render the buyer at the latter's request, risk and expense, every assistance in obtaining any documents or equivalent electronic messages (other than those mentioned in A8) issued or transmitted in the country of dispatch and/or of origin which the buyer may require for the import of the goods.

The seller must provide the buyer, upon request, with the necessary information for procuring insurance.

Comments
The seller has the obligation to clear the goods for export. But he has no obligation to bear any costs or risks for import clearance of the goods at destination. However, he has the duty to render the buyer assistance in obtaining the documents (for example, a certificate of origin, a health certificate, a clean report of findings, an import licence) or equivalent electronic messages which may be required for this purpose. The buyer, in turn, must reimburse the seller for any expenses which the seller might have incurred in connection with this assistance. Moreover, if something goes wrong, the buyer will have to assume the risk.

The seller may also be requested to provide the buyer with any information relating to the goods which the buyer might require for insurance purposes, if this information is not provided in the description of the goods in the contract of sale.

B   THE BUYER'S OBLIGATIONS

B1   Payment of the price

The buyer must pay the price as provided in the contract of sale.

Comments
The buyer must pay the price agreed in the contract of sale. B1 constitutes a reminder of this main obligation, which corresponds with the seller's obligation to provide the goods in conformity with the contract of sale, as stipulated in A1.

B2   Licences, authorizations and formalities

The buyer must obtain at his own risk and expense any import licence or other official authorization and carry out, where applicable[4], all customs formalities necessary for the import of the goods.

Comments
The buyer must take care of the import clearance and bear any costs and risks in connection with it. Therefore, an import prohibition will not relieve the buyer of his obligation to pay for the goods, unless there is a particular "relief clause" in the contract of sale which he invokes to obtain this relief. Such clauses may provide for the extension of time or the right to avoid the contract under the applicable law (see the comments to A2).

B3   Contracts of carriage and insurance

a) Contract of carriage

No obligation[5].

b) Contract of insurance

No obligation[6].

---

4 Refer to Introduction to *Incoterms 2000* paragraph 14. (See reproduced pages 184-185 in this text.)
5 Refer to Introduction to *Incoterms 2000* paragraph 10. (See reproduced pages 184-185 in this text.)
6 Refer to Introduction to *Incoterms 2000* paragraph 10. (See reproduced pages 184-185 in this text.)

Comments   Although B3 merely stipulates "No obligation" for the buyer, on-carriage from the port of destination is necessary in most cases, and it is the buyer's responsibility to do whatever is required for this purpose. But the seller is not concerned with the further carriage of the goods, and the buyer has no obligation to the seller in this respect. The words "No obligation" mean that whatever the buyer does is in his own interest and is not covered by the contract of sale.

B4   Taking delivery

The buyer must take delivery of the goods when they have been delivered in accordance with A4.

Comments   As in all D-terms, B4 has wording stating that the buyer shall take delivery as soon as the goods have been placed at his disposal in accordance with A4. (The same wording is also used in EXW B4, but under EXW the placing of the goods at the buyer's disposal usually occurs at the seller's own premises.) The seller, according to A4 in the D-terms, shall place the goods at the buyer's disposal "on the date or within the agreed period".

If the goods are placed at the buyer's disposal earlier than agreed, the buyer is not obliged to take delivery before the agreed time, though it may normally be in his own interest to do so. If the goods are placed at the buyer's disposal too late, the buyer may hold the seller responsible for breach of contract according to the applicable law. He may also recover damages from the seller or, in the event of a fundamental breach, cancel the contract.

B5   Transfer of risks

The buyer must bear all risks of loss of or damage to the goods from the time they have been delivered in accordance with A4.

The buyer must, should he fail to give notice in accordance with B7, bear all risks of loss of or damage to the goods from the agreed date or the expiry date of the agreed period for delivery provided, however, that the goods have been duly appropriated to the contract, that is to say, clearly set aside or otherwise identified as the contract goods.

Comments   According to the main rule, while the seller under A5 bears the risk of loss of or damage to the goods until the delivery point, the buyer has to bear the risk thereafter. The delivery point is different under the different terms. In EXW and all D-terms the goods are simply placed "at the disposal of the buyer" at the relevant point, while under the F- and C-terms the delivery point is related to the handing over of the goods to the carrier in the country of dispatch or shipment (see the comments to A4 of these terms). In the terms used for goods intended to be carried by sea, reference is made to delivery alongside the named vessel (FAS) or delivery onboard the vessel (FOB, CFR, CIF).

B6 Division of costs

The buyer must pay

- all costs relating to the goods from the time they have been delivered in accordance with A4, including the expenses of discharge operations necessary to take delivery of the goods from the vessel; and

- all additional costs incurred if he fails to take delivery of the goods when they have been placed at his disposal in accordance with A4, or to give notice in accordance with B7, provided, however, that the goods have been appropriated to the contract, that is to say, clearly set aside or otherwise identified as the contract goods.

- where applicable[7], the costs of customs formalities as well as all duties, taxes and other charges payable upon import of the goods.

Comments Since the goods according to A4 are made available to the buyer "on board the vessel at the usual unloading point in the named port of destination", the buyer has to pay all costs of discharge.

If the buyer fails to take delivery of the goods as agreed – for example, within the stipulated time during which the vessel is available for discharge free of charge (the so-called laytime) – the buyer must pay any additional costs incurred thereby. In particular, he must pay demurrage to the shipowner when the laytime is exceeded. The buyer also has to pay any additional costs which may arise because of his failure to notify the seller of the time or place of delivery according to B7. The obligation of the buyer to pay these additional costs is always subject to the identification of the goods as the contract goods ("appropriation").

B7 Notice to the seller

The buyer must, whenever he is entitled to determine the time within an agreed period and/or the point of taking delivery in the named port of destination, give the seller sufficient notice thereof.

Comments As discussed in the comments to B5 and B6, the failure of the buyer to notify the seller of the time and place of taking delivery – when the buyer in the contract of sale has been given the option to determine these matters – may cause the risk of the loss of or damage to the goods to pass before the goods have been delivered according to A4. In addition, it can make the buyer liable to pay any additional costs incurred by the seller as a result of the buyer's failure.

B8 Proof of delivery, transport document or equivalent electronic message

The buyer must accept the delivery order or the transport document in accordance with A8.

Comments The buyer has to accept the document if it conforms with the contract and with the requirements of A8 (see the comments to A8). If the buyer rejects the document (for example, by instructions to a bank not to pay the seller under a documentary credit), he commits a breach of contract, which would give the seller remedies available for such a breach under the contract of sale.

These remedies could include, for example, a right to cancel the contract or to claim damages for breach. However, the buyer is not obliged to accept a document which does not provide adequate proof of delivery, for example, one which has notations on it showing that the goods are defective or that they have been provided in less than the agreed quantity. In these cases, the document is termed "unclean".

---

7 Refer to Introduction to *Incoterms 2000* paragraph 14. (See reproduced pages 184-185 in this text.)

DES

B9   Inspection of goods

The buyer must pay the costs of any pre-shipment inspection except when such inspection is mandated by the authorities of the country of export.

Comments   As noted in the comments to A9, the buyer has to pay for any costs of checking the goods, unless the contract determines that these costs should be wholly or partly borne by the seller. In some cases, the contract may provide that the costs should be borne by the seller if the inspection reveals that the goods do not conform with the contract.

In some countries, where import licences or permission to obtain foreign currency for the payment of the price may be required, the authorities may demand an inspection of the goods before shipment, to ensure that the goods are in conformity with the contract. (This is usually called pre-shipment inspection, PSI). If this is the case, the inspection is normally arranged by instructions from the authorities to an inspection company, which they appoint. The costs following from this inspection have to be paid by the authorities. Any reimbursement to the authorities for the inspection costs, however, must be made by the buyer, unless otherwise specifically agreed between the buyer and the seller.

B10   Other obligations

The buyer must pay all costs and charges incurred in obtaining the documents or equivalent electronic messages mentioned in A10 and reimburse those incurred by the seller in rendering his assistance in accordance therewith.

Comments   As discussed in the comments to A10, the seller has to render the buyer assistance in obtaining the documents or electronic messages which may be required for the transit and import of the goods. However, this assistance is rendered at the buyer's risk and expense. Therefore, B10 stipulates that the buyer must pay all costs and charges incurred in obtaining these documents or electronic messages. He will also have to reimburse the seller for the seller's costs in rendering his assistance in these matters.

"Delivered Ex Quay" means that the seller delivers when the goods are placed at the disposal of the buyer not cleared for import on the quay (wharf) at the named port of destination. The seller has to bear costs and risks involved in bringing the goods to the named port of destination and discharging the goods on the quay (wharf). The DEQ term requires the buyer to clear the goods for import and to pay for all formalities, duties, taxes and other charges upon import.

THIS IS A REVERSAL FROM PREVIOUS INCOTERMS VERSIONS, WHICH REQUIRED THE SELLER TO ARRANGE FOR IMPORT CLEARANCE.

If the parties wish to include in the seller's obligations all or part of the costs payable upon import of the goods, this should be made clear by adding explicit wording to this effect in the contract of sale.[1]

This term can be used only when the goods are to be delivered by sea or inland waterway or multimodal transport on discharging from a vessel onto the quay (wharf) in the port of destination. However, if the parties wish to include in the seller's obligations the risks and costs of the handling of the goods from the quay to another place (warehouse, terminal, transport station, etc.) in or outside the port, the DDU or DDP terms should be used.

1 Refer to the introduction of *Incoterms 2000*, ICC publication N°560, paragraph 11. (See reproduced pages 184-185 in this text.)

DEQ

Delivered Ex Quay
(...named port of destination)

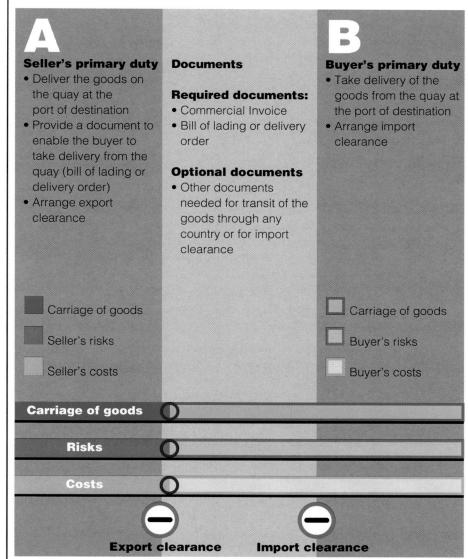

A

Seller's primary duty
- Deliver the goods on the quay at the port of destination
- Provide a document to enable the buyer to take delivery from the quay (bill of lading or delivery order)
- Arrange export clearance

Documents

Required documents:
- Commercial Invoice
- Bill of lading or delivery order

Optional documents
- Other documents needed for transit of the goods through any country or for import clearance

B

Buyer's primary duty
- Take delivery of the goods from the quay at the port of destination
- Arrange import clearance

☐ Carriage of goods

☐ Seller's risks

☐ Seller's costs

☐ Carriage of goods

☐ Buyer's risks

☐ Buyer's costs

Carriage of goods ○

Risks ○

Costs ○

Export clearance **Import clearance**

Critical points

 Carriage to be arranged by the seller

 Risk transfer from the seller to the buyer when the goods are placed at the disposal of the buyer on the quay

 Cost transfer from the seller to the buyer when the goods are placed at the disposal of the buyer on the quay

A   THE SELLER'S OBLIGATIONS

A1   Provision of goods in conformity with the contract

The seller must provide the goods and the commercial invoice, or its equivalent electronic message, in conformity with the contract of sale and any other evidence of conformity which may be required by the contract.

Comments   The seller must provide the goods in conformity with the contract. It is also usual practice that the seller, in order to be paid, has to invoice the buyer. In addition, the seller must submit any other evidence stipulated in the contract itself that the goods conform with that contract.

This text only serves as a reminder of the seller's main obligation under the contract of sale.

A2   Licences, authorizations and formalities

The seller must obtain at his own risk and expense any export licence or other official authorization or other documents and carry out, where applicable[2], all customs formalities for the export of the goods, and for their transit through any country.

Comments   Since the term DEQ is evidence of an arrival contract, the seller has to do whatever may be necessary for the goods to reach the agreed place for delivery. This means the seller is responsible for export clearance of the goods as well as any transit formalities involved in the transport of the goods through another country before arrival at the agreed destination.

Clearance for import is the buyer's obligation
Incoterms 1990 placed the obligation to clear the goods for import on the seller. This has now been changed in Incoterms 2000, so that it is for the buyer to do so.

Unforeseen or reasonably unforeseeable prohibitions
The seller's obligations under DEQ may become more expensive than contemplated as a result of reasonably unforeseeable circumstances. However, contracts of sale usually contain provisions which the seller may invoke to protect himself in the event of these contingencies. Under CISG and corresponding provisions in various national Sale of Goods Acts, unforeseen or reasonably unforeseeable prohibitions may relieve the seller from his obligations under the contract of sale.

Buyer can avoid requirement to clear goods for import
If the buyer wishes to avoid the obligation of clearing the goods for import, he should add the phrase "cleared for import" after DEQ.

A3   Contracts of carriage and insurance

a) Contract of carriage

The seller must contract at his own expense for the carriage of the goods to the named quay (wharf) at the named port of destination. If a specific quay (wharf) is not agreed or is not determined by practice, the seller may select the quay (wharf) at the named port of destination which best suits his purpose.

b) Contract of insurance

No obligation[3].

Comment   Under all D-terms, the seller must ensure that the goods actually arrive at destination. It follows from this that the seller must arrange and pay for any carriage of the goods.

---

2 Refer to Introduction to *Incoterms 2000* paragraph 14. (See reproduced pages 184-185 in this text.)
3 Refer to Introduction to *Incoterms 2000* paragraph 10. (See reproduced pages 184-185 in this text.)

Under the D-terms, the seller's choice of transport is only of importance to the buyer insofar as it affects the buyer's obligation to receive the goods from the carrier. If the seller chooses an unusual mode of transport which makes it more difficult or expensive for the buyer to receive the goods from the carrier, any additional costs or risks caused by the seller's choice of transport will be for the seller's account.

Normally, the point mentioned after the D-term will indicate where the goods should be delivered at destination. But if there are several alternatives available, and the contract of sale or commercial practice does not indicate which alternative the seller must choose, he "may select the point at the named port of destination which best suits his purpose".

A4 Delivery

 The seller must place the goods at the disposal of the buyer on the quay (wharf) referred to in A3 a), on the date or within the agreed period.

Comments   Under all D-terms, the seller must "place the goods at the disposal of the buyer" at destination. The precise point for the delivery of the goods depends upon the D-term chosen. According to DEQ A4, the goods should be placed at the disposal of the buyer "on the quay (wharf)" at the agreed port of destination.

A5 Transfer of risks

The seller must, subject to the provisions of B5, bear all risks of loss of or damage to the goods until such time as they have been delivered in accordance with A4.

Comments   All Incoterms are based on the same principle that the risk of loss of or damage to the goods is transferred from the seller to the buyer when the seller has fulfilled his delivery obligation according to A4. A5 of FOB, CFR and CIF further specifies that the risk is transferred when the goods "have passed the ship's rail at the port of shipment".

All Incoterms, in conformity with the general principle of CISG, connect the transfer of the risk with the delivery of the goods and not with other circumstances, such as the passing of ownership or the time of the conclusion of the contract. Neither Incoterms nor CISG deals with transfer of title to the goods or other property rights with respect to the goods.

The passing of risk of loss of or damage to the goods concerns the risk of fortuitous events (accidents) and does not include loss or damage caused by the seller or the buyer, for example, inadequate packing or marking of the goods. Therefore, even if damage occurs subsequent to the transfer of the risk, the seller may still be responsible if the damage could be attributed to the fact that the goods were not delivered in conformity with the contract (see A1 and the comments to A9).

A5 of all Incoterms contain the phrase "subject to the provisions of B5". This means that there are exceptions to the main rule concerning the passing of risk under the circumstances mentioned in B5, which may result in a premature passing of the risk because of the buyer's failure properly to fulfil his obligations (see the comments to B5).

A6   Division of costs

The seller must, subject to the provisions of B6, pay

- in addition to costs resulting from A3 a), all costs relating to the goods until such time as they are delivered on the quay (wharf) in accordance with A4; and

- where applicable[4], the costs of customs formalities necessary for export as well as all duties, taxes and other charges payable upon export of the goods and for their transit through any country prior to delivery.

Comments   As is the case with the transfer of the risk of loss of or damage to the goods, all Incoterms follow the same rule, that the division of costs occurs at the delivery point. All costs occurring before the seller has fulfilled his obligation to deliver according to A4 are for his account, while further costs are for the account of the buyer (see the comments to B6). This rule is made subject to the provisions of B6, which indicates that the buyer may have to bear additional costs incurred by his failure to give appropriate notice to the seller.

Since under D-terms, the seller does not fulfil his obligation until the goods have actually arrived at destination and been placed at the disposal of the buyer, the seller has to do everything required to achieve this. Nevertheless, A3 in all D-terms still stipulates that the seller must contract for carriage; and A6 of all D-terms stipulates that he must pay the costs resulting from A3 for the carriage of the goods and pay the costs of customs formalities as well as all duties, taxes and other charges payable upon export (and in the case of DDP also import) of the goods, prior to delivery. Needless to say, any transit costs incurred subsequent to delivery will have to be paid by the buyer.

A7   Notice to the buyer

The seller must give the buyer sufficient notice of the estimated time of arrival of the nominated vessel in accordance with A4, as well as any other notice required in order to allow the buyer to take measures which are normally necessary to enable him to take delivery of the goods.

Comments   The seller must give the buyer sufficient notice as to the estimated time of arrival (ETA) of the vessel and other essential notices, so that the buyer can make preparations in time to take delivery according to B4. There is no stipulation in Incoterms spelling out the consequences of the seller's failure to give such notice. But it follows from Incoterms that the seller's failure constitutes a breach of contract. This means that the seller could be held responsible for the breach according to the law applicable to the contract of sale.

A8   Proof of delivery, transport document or equivalent electronic message

The seller must provide the buyer at the seller's expense with the delivery order and/or the usual transport document (for example a negotiable bill of lading, a non-negotiable sea waybill, an inland waterway document or a multimodal transport document) to enable him to take the goods and remove them from the quay (wharf).

Where the seller and the buyer have agreed to communicate electronically, the document referred to in the preceding paragraph may be replaced by an equivalent electronic data interchange (EDI) message.

Comments   In most cases the buyer will require a document in order to be able to obtain the goods from the carrier. Traditionally, the relevant document is a negotiable bill of lading, and this is still the predominant document when DEQ is used for carriage of bulk commodities. However, bills of lading are often replaced by delivery orders splitting up the total bill of lading quantity into smaller lots for several buyers.

Documents can be replaced by EDI messages when the parties have agreed to communicate electronically.

[4] Refer to Introduction to *Incoterms 2000* paragraph 14. (See reproduced pages 184-185 in this text.)

A9   Checking – packaging – marking

The seller must pay the costs of those checking operations (such as checking quality, measuring, weighing, counting) which are necessary for the purpose of delivering the goods in accordance with A4.

The seller must provide at his own expense packaging (unless it is usual for the particular trade to deliver the goods of the contract description unpacked) which is required for the delivery of the goods. Packaging is to be marked appropriately.

Comments   It is important that the buyer ensure that the seller has duly fulfilled his obligation with respect to the condition of the goods, particularly if the buyer is called upon to pay for the goods before he has received and checked them. However, the seller has no duty to arrange and pay for the inspection of the goods unless this is specifically agreed in the contract of sale.

A10   Other obligations

The seller must render the buyer at the latter's request, risk and expense, every assistance in obtaining any documents or equivalent electronic messages (other than those mentioned in A8) issued or transmitted in the country of dispatch and/or origin which the buyer may require for the import of the goods.

The seller must provide the buyer, upon request, with the necessary information for procuring insurance.

Comments   DEQ requires the buyer to clear the goods for import. The buyer has to reimburse the seller for any costs the buyer may incur in rendering any assistance (see B10).

B   THE BUYER'S OBLIGATIONS

B1   Payment of the price

The buyer must pay the price as provided in the contract of sale.

Comments   The buyer must pay the price agreed in the contract of sale. B1 constitutes a reminder of this main obligation, which corresponds with the seller's obligation to provide the goods in conformity with the contract of sale, as stipulated in A1.

B2   Licences, authorizations and formalities

The buyer must obtain at his own risk and expense any import licence or official authorization or other documents and carry out, where applicable[5], all customs formalities necessary for the import of the goods.

Comments   Although the seller has to make the goods available to the buyer in the country of destination and clear the goods for export and transit, it is for the buyer to do whatever is necessary with respect to the clearance of the goods for import (see the comments to A2).

---

5 Refer to Introduction to *Incoterms 2000* paragraph 14. (See reproduced pages 184-185 in this text.)

B3 Contracts of carriage and insurance

a) Contract of carriage

No obligation[6].

b) Contract of insurance

No obligation[7].

Comments Although B3 merely stipulates "No obligation" for the buyer, on-carriage from the port of destination is necessary in most cases, and it is the buyer's responsibility to do whatever is required for this purpose. But the seller is not concerned with the further carriage of the goods, and the buyer has no obligation to the seller in this respect. The words "No obligation" mean that whatever the buyer does is in his own interest and is not covered by the contract of sale.

B4 Taking delivery

The buyer must take delivery of the goods when they have been delivered in accordance with A4.

Comments As in all D-terms, B4 has wording stating that the buyer shall take delivery as soon as the goods have been placed at his disposal in accordance with A4. (The same wording is also used in EXW B4, but under EXW the placing of the goods at the buyer's disposal usually occurs at the seller's own premises.) The seller, according to A4 in the D-terms, shall place the goods at the buyer's disposal "on the date or within the agreed period".

If the goods are placed at the buyer's disposal earlier than agreed, the buyer is not obliged to take delivery before the agreed time, though it may normally be in his own interest to do so. If the goods are placed at the buyer's disposal too late, the buyer may hold the seller responsible for breach of contract according to the applicable law. He may also recover damages from the seller or, in the event of a fundamental breach, cancel the contract.

B5 Transfer of risks

The buyer must bear all risks of loss of or damage to the goods from the time they have been delivered in accordance with A4.

The buyer must, should he fail to give notice in accordance with B7, bear all risks of loss of or damage to the goods from the agreed date or the expiry date of the agreed period for delivery provided, however, that the goods have been duly appropriated to the contract, that is to say, clearly set aside or otherwise identified as the contract goods.

Comments According to the main rule, while the seller under A5 bears the risk of loss of or damage to the goods until the delivery point, the buyer has to bear the risk thereafter. The delivery point is different under the different terms. In EXW and all D-terms the goods are simply placed "at the disposal of the buyer" at the relevant point, while under the F- and C-terms the delivery point is related to the handing over of the goods to the carrier in the country of dispatch or shipment (see the comments to A4 of these terms). In the terms used for goods intended to be carried by sea, reference is made to delivery alongside the named vessel (FAS) or delivery onboard the vessel (FOB, CFR, CIF).

Consequences of buyer's failure to give notice

While the seller under EXW and all D-terms can transfer the risk by his own act of placing the goods at the buyer's disposal, he may be prevented from doing so by the buyer's failure to give notice according to B7. This can occur when it is the buyer's responsibility to determine (1) the time within a stipulated period when the goods are to be made

---

6 Refer to Introduction to *Incoterms 2000* paragraph 14. (See reproduced pages 184-185 in this text.)
7 Refer to Introduction to *Incoterms 2000* paragraph 10. (See reproduced pages 184-185 in this text.)

available or (2) the place of delivery (see the comments to B7). The failure to perform these tasks results in a premature passing of the risk: it is not acceptable that the buyer should be able to delay the delivery and passing of the risk longer than contemplated when the contract of sale was made. Therefore, his failure to notify according to B7 will cause the risk to pass "from the agreed date or the expiry date of any period stipulated for delivery".

Appropriation and the passing of risk

The risk, however, cannot pass until the goods "have been appropriated to the contract". If the goods are unascertained – i.e., goods of a certain kind which the seller will deliver to various buyers – appropriation only occurs when the goods are "clearly set aside or otherwise identified as the contract goods".

This appropriation will normally be made when the seller has handed over the goods for carriage and the consignment has been marked as intended for the buyer – unless the cargo is carried in bulk and intended to be appropriated between different buyers only upon the arrival of the goods at destination.

B6   Division of costs

The buyer must pay

- all costs relating to the goods from the time they have been delivered in accordance with A4, including any costs of handling the goods in the port for subsequent transport or storage in warehouse or terminal; and

- all additional costs incurred if he fails to take delivery of the goods when they have been placed at his disposal in accordance with A4, or to give notice in accordance with B7, provided, however, that the goods have been appropriated to the contract, that is to say, clearly set aside or otherwise identified as the contract goods; and

- where applicable[6], the cost of customs formalities as well as all duties, taxes and other charges payable upon import of the goods and for their subsequent transport.

Comments   Since according to A4 the goods are made available to the buyer "on the quay (wharf)", the buyer is relieved of the obligation to pay for the costs of discharge. However, once the goods have been placed at his disposal in accordance with A4, the buyer must pay any costs for the storage and further carriage of the goods to their final destination.

If the buyer fails to take delivery or to take such measures as are needed for on-carriage, he will have to bear any additional costs incurred thereby. At this stage, the seller will normally have identified the goods as the contract goods (through the process of appropriation). But if he has not done so – for example, if the goods arrive at destination in bulk for later appropriation by delivery orders or otherwise – the buyer does not have to bear any additional costs relating to the goods until they have been duly appropriated.

Subject to the goods having been appropriated as noted above, the buyer also has to pay any additional costs incurred as a result of his failure to notify the seller according to B7 of the time or place of taking delivery, for example additional storage and insurance costs.

B7   Notice to the seller

The buyer must, whenever he is entitled to determine the time within an agreed period and/or the point of taking delivery in the named port of destination, give the seller sufficient notice thereof.

---

6 Refer to Introduction to *Incoterms 2000* paragraph 14. (See reproduced pages 184-185 in this text.)

Comments   As discussed in the comments to B5 and B6, the failure of the buyer to notify the seller of the time and place of taking delivery – when the buyer in the contract of sale has been given the option to determine these matters – may cause the risk of the loss of or damage to the goods to pass before the goods have been delivered according to A4. In addition, it can make the buyer liable to pay any additional costs incurred by the seller as a result of the buyer's failure.

B8   Proof of delivery, transport document or equivalent electronic message

The buyer must accept the delivery order or transport document in accordance with A8.

Comments   The buyer has to accept the document if it conforms with the contract and with the requirements of A8 (see the comments to A8). If the buyer rejects the document (for example, by instructions to a bank not to pay the seller under a documentary credit), he commits a breach of contract, which would give the seller remedies available for such a breach under the contract of sale.

These remedies could include, for example, a right to cancel the contract or to claim damages for breach. However, the buyer is not obliged to accept a document which does not provide adequate proof of delivery, for example, one which has notations on it showing that the goods are defective or that they have been provided in less than the agreed quantity. In these cases, the document is termed "unclean".

B9   Inspection of goods

The buyer must pay the costs of any pre-shipment inspection except when such inspection is mandated by the authorities of the country of export.

Comments   As noted in the comments to A9, the buyer has to pay for any costs of checking the goods, unless the contract determines that these costs should be wholly or partly borne by the seller. In some cases, the contract may provide that the costs should be borne by the seller if the inspection reveals that the goods do not conform with the contract.

In some countries, where import licences or permission to obtain foreign currency for the payment of the price may be required, the authorities may demand an inspection of the goods before shipment, to ensure that the goods are in conformity with the contract. (This is usually called pre-shipment inspection, PSI.) If this is the case, the inspection is normally arranged by instructions from the authorities to an inspection company, which they appoint. The costs following from this inspection have to be paid by the authorities. Any reimbursement to the authorities for the inspection costs, however, must be made by the buyer, unless otherwise specifically agreed between the buyer and the seller.

B10   Other obligations

The buyer must pay all costs and charges incurred in obtaining the documents or equivalent electronic messages mentioned in A10 and reimburse those incurred by the seller in rendering his assistance in accordance therewith.

Comments   Since the buyer has the obligation to clear the goods for import, he may require the seller's assistance to obtain the necessary documents or EDI messages. The seller must render this assistance when requested by the buyer to do so, but the seller does this at the buyer's risk and expense.

"Delivered duty unpaid" means that the seller delivers the goods to the buyer, not cleared for import, and not unloaded from any arriving means of transport at the named place of destination. The seller has to bear the costs and risks involved in bringing the goods thereto, other than, where applicable,[1] any "duty" (which term includes the responsibility for and the risks of the carrying out of customs formalities, and the payment of formalities, customs duties, taxes and other charges) for import in the country of destination. Such "duty" has to be borne by the buyer as well as any costs and risks caused by his failure to clear the goods for import in time.

However, if the parties wish the seller to carry out customs formalities and bear the costs and risks resulting therefrom as well as some of the costs payable upon import of the goods, this should be made clear by adding explicit wording to this effect in the contract of sale.[2]

This term may be used irrespective of the mode of transport but when delivery is to take place in the port of destination on board the vessel or on the quay (wharf), the DES or DEQ terms should be used.

1 Refer to the introduction of *Incoterms 2000*, ICC publication Nº560, paragraph 14. (See reproduced pages 184-185 in this text.)
2 Refer to the introduction of *Incoterms 2000*, ICC publication Nº560, paragraph 11. (See reproduced pages 184-185 in this text.)

DDU

Delivered Duty Unpaid
(...named place of destination)

Group Ⓓ
arrival

DDU

A

Seller's primary duty
- Deliver the goods at the named place of destination
- Provide a document to enable the buyer to take delivery
- Arrange export clearance

Documents

Required documents:
- Commercial Invoice
- Document needed for taking delivery

Optional documents
- Other documents needed for transit of the goods through any country or for import clearance

B

Buyer's primary duty
- Take delivery of the goods from the named place of destination
- Arrange import clearance

◼ Carriage of goods

◼ Seller's risks

◼ Seller's costs

◻ Carriage of goods

◻ Buyer's risks

◻ Buyer's costs

Carriage of goods ⊙

Risks ⊙

Costs ⊙

⊖ **Export clearance**　　⊖ **Import clearance**

Critical points

◐ Carriage to be arranged by the seller

◐ Risk transfer from the seller to the buyer when the goods are placed at the disposal of the buyer

◐ Cost transfer from the seller to the buyer when the goods are placed at the disposal of the buyer

DDU

A THE SELLER'S OBLIGATIONS

A1 Provision of the goods in conformity with the contract

The seller must provide the goods and the commercial invoice, or its equivalent electronic message, in conformity with the contract of sale and any other evidence of conformity which may be required by the contract.

Comments The seller must provide the goods in conformity with the contract. It is also usual practice that the seller, in order to be paid, has to invoice the buyer. In addition, the seller must submit any other evidence stipulated in the contract itself that the goods conform with that contract.

This text only serves as a reminder of the seller's main obligation under the contract of sale.

A2 Licences, authorizations and formalities

The seller must obtain at his own risk and expense any export licence and other official authorization or other documents and carry out, where applicable[3], all customs formalities necessary for the export of the goods and for their transit through any country.

Comments The seller has to clear the goods for export and assume any risk or expense which this involves. Consequently, if there is an export prohibition or if there are particular taxes on the export of the goods – and if there are other government-imposed requirements which may render the export of the goods more expensive than contemplated – all of these risks and costs must be borne by the seller. However, contracts of sale usually contain particular provisions which the seller may invoke to protect himself in the event of these contingencies. Under CISG and corresponding provisions in various national Sale of Goods Acts, unforeseen or reasonably unforeseeable export prohibitions may relieve the seller from his obligations under the contract of sale.

A3 Contracts of carriage and insurance

a) Contract of carriage
The seller must contract at his own expense for the carriage of the goods to the named place of destination. If a specific point is not agreed or is not determined by practice, the seller may select the point at the named place of destination which best suits his purpose.

b) Contract of insurance
No obligation[4].

Comments Under all D-terms, the seller must ensure that the goods actually arrive at destination. It follows from this that the seller must arrange and pay for any carriage of the goods.

Under the D-terms, the seller's choice of transport is only of importance to the buyer insofar as it affects the buyer's obligation to receive the goods from the carrier. If the seller chooses an unusual transport which makes it more difficult or expensive for the buyer to receive the goods from the carrier, any additional costs or risks caused by the seller's choice of transport will be for the seller's account.

Normally, the point mentioned after the D-term will indicate where the goods should be delivered at destination. But if there are several alternatives available, and the contract of sale or commercial practice does not indicate which alternative the seller must choose, he "may select the point at the named place of destination which best suits his purpose".

---

3 Refer to Introduction to *Incoterms 2000* paragraph 14. (See reproduced pages 184-185 in this text.)
4 Refer to Introduction to *Incoterms 2000* paragraph 10. (See reproduced pages 184-185 in this text.)

A4   Delivery

The seller must place the goods at the disposal of the buyer, or at that of another person named by the buyer, on any arriving means of transport not unloaded, at the named place of destination on the date or within the period agreed for delivery.

Comments   Under DDU the seller must "place the goods at the disposal of the buyer" at the named place of destination. The precise point for the delivery of the goods depends upon the D-term chosen.

Incoterms 2000 specify that if the goods are to be delivered at the buyer's premises or to a place under his control, then delivery is completed when the goods are at his disposal on the arriving vehicle not unloaded. In other cases, delivery is normally completed when the goods have been loaded on to the buyer's collecting vehicle.

A5   Transfer of risks

The seller must, subject to the provisions of B5, bear all risks of loss of or damage to the goods until such time as they have been delivered in accordance with A4.

Comments   All Incoterms are based on the same principle that the risk of loss of or damage to the goods is transferred from the seller to the buyer when the seller has fulfilled his delivery obligation according to A4. A5 of FOB, CFR and CIF further specifies that the risk is transferred when the goods "have passed the ship's rail at the port of shipment".

All Incoterms, in conformity with the general principle of CISG, connect the transfer of the risk with the delivery of the goods and not with other circumstances, such as the passing of ownership or the time of the conclusion of the contract. Neither Incoterms nor CISG deals with transfer of title to the goods or other property rights with respect to the goods.

The passing of risk of loss of or damage to the goods concerns the risk of fortuitous events (accidents) and does not include loss or damage caused by the seller or the buyer, for example, inadequate packing or marking of the goods. Therefore, even if damage occurs subsequent to the transfer of the risk, the seller may still be responsible if the damage could be attributed to the fact that the goods were not delivered in conformity with the contract (see A1 and the comments to A9).

A5 of all Incoterms contains the phrase "subject to the provisions of B5". This means that there are exceptions to the main rule concerning the passing of risk under the circumstances mentioned in B5, which may result in a premature passing of the risk because of the buyer's failure properly to fulfil his obligations (see the comments to B5).

A6   Division of costs

The seller must, subject to the provisions of B6, pay

- in addition to costs resulting from A3 a), all costs relating to the goods until such time as they have been delivered in accordance with A4; and

- where applicable[5], the costs of customs formalities necessary for export as well as all duties, taxes and other charges payable upon export and for their transit through any country prior to delivery in accordance with A4.

Comments   As is the case with the transfer of the risk of loss of or damage to the goods, all Incoterms follow the same rule, that the division of costs occurs at the delivery point. All costs occurring before the seller has fulfilled his obligation to deliver according to A4 are for his account, while further costs are for the account of the buyer (see the comments to B6). This rule is made subject to the provisions of B6, which indicates that the buyer may have to bear additional costs incurred by his failure to give appropriate notice to the seller.

---

5 Refer to Introduction to *Incoterms 2000* paragraph 14. (See reproduced pages 184-185 in this text.)

DDU

Since, under D-terms, the seller does not fulfil his obligation until the goods have actually arrived at destination and been placed at the disposal of the buyer, the seller has to do everything required to achieve this. Nevertheless, A3 in all D-terms still stipulates that the seller must contract for carriage; and A6 of all D-terms stipulates that he must pay the costs resulting from A3 for the carriage of the goods, and, where applicable, the costs of customs formalities necessary for export as well as all duties, taxes and other charges prior to delivery in accordance with A4. Under DDP the seller is also responsible for import charges, as well as duties, taxes and other charges prior to delivery in accordance with A4. Needless to say, any transit costs incurred subsequent to delivery will have to be paid by the buyer.

A7   Notice to the buyer

The seller must give the buyer sufficient notice of the dispatch of the goods as well as any other notice required in order to allow the buyer to take measures which are normally necessary to enable him to take delivery of the goods.

Comments   The seller must give the buyer sufficient notice as to when the goods have been dispatched and when they will be available at the agreed or chosen delivery point, so that the buyer can make preparations in time to take delivery according to B4. There is no stipulation in Incoterms spelling out the consequences of the seller's failure to give such notice. But it follows from Incoterms that the seller's failure constitutes a breach of contract. This means that the seller could be held responsible for the breach according to the law applicable to the contract of sale.

A8   Proof of delivery, transport document or equivalent electronic message

The seller must provide the buyer at the seller's expense the delivery order and/or the usual transport document (for example a negotiable bill of lading, a non-negotiable sea waybill, an inland waterway document, an air waybill, a railway consignment note, a road consignment note, or a multimodal transport document) which the buyer may require to take delivery of the goods in accordance with A4/B4.

Where the seller and the buyer have agreed to communicate electronically, the document referred to in the preceding paragraph may be replaced by an equivalent electronic data interchange (EDI) message.

Comments   In most cases the buyer will require a document in order to be able to obtain the goods from the carrier. Traditionally, the relevant document for carriage by sea is a negotiable bill of lading, and this is still the predominant document when DDU is used for carriage of bulk commodities. However, bills of lading are often replaced by delivery orders splitting up the total bill of lading quantity into smaller lots for several buyers. Documents can be replaced by EDI messages when the parties have agreed to communicate electronically.

A9   Checking – packaging – marking

The seller must pay the costs of those checking operations (such as checking quality, measuring, weighing, counting) which are necessary for the purpose of delivering the goods in accordance with A4.

The seller must provide at his own expense packaging (unless it is usual for the particular trade to deliver the goods of the contract description unpacked) which is required for the delivery of the goods. Packaging is to be marked appropriately.

Comments   It is important that the buyer ensure that the seller has duly fulfilled his obligation with respect to the condition of the goods, particularly if the buyer is called upon to pay for the goods before he has received and checked them. However, the seller has no duty to arrange and pay for the inspection of the goods before dispatch unless this is specifically agreed in the contract of sale.

A10   Other obligations

The seller must render the buyer at the latter's request, risk and expense, every assistance in obtaining any documents or equivalent electronic messages (other than those mentioned in A8) issued or transmitted in the country of dispatch and/or of origin which the buyer may require for the import of the goods.

The seller must provide the buyer, upon request, with the necessary information for procuring insurance.

Comments   As noted in A2, the seller has the obligation to clear the goods for export. But he has no obligation after dispatch to bear any costs and risks with respect to import clearance of the goods at destination. However, he has the duty to render the buyer assistance in obtaining any documents (for example, a certificate of origin, a health certificate, a clean report of findings, an import licence) or equivalent electronic messages which the buyer may require for these purposes. The buyer, on the other hand, must reimburse the seller for any expenses which the seller might have incurred in connection with this assistance. Moreover, if something goes wrong, the buyer, not the seller, will have to assume the risk.

B   THE BUYER'S OBLIGATIONS

B1   Payment of the price

The buyer must pay the price as provided in the contract of sale.

Comments   The buyer must pay the price agreed in the contract of sale. B1 constitutes a reminder of this main obligation, which corresponds with the seller's obligation to provide the goods in conformity with the contract of sale, as stipulated in A1.

B2   Licences, authorizations and formalities

The buyer must obtain at his own risk and expense any import licence or other official authorization or other documents and carry out, where applicable[6], all customs formalities necessary for the import of the goods.

Comments   The buyer must take care of the import clearance and bear any costs and risks in connection with it. Therefore, an import prohibition will not relieve the buyer of his obligation to pay for the goods, unless there is a particular "relief clause" in the contract of sale which he invokes to obtain this relief. Such clauses may provide for the extension of time or the right to avoid the contract under the applicable law (see the comments to A2).

B3   Contracts of carriage and insurance

a) Contract of carriage

No obligation[7].

b) Contract of insurance

No obligation[8].

---

[6] Refer to Introduction to *Incoterms 2000* paragraph 14. (See reproduced pages 184-185 in this text.)
[7] Refer to Introduction to *Incoterms 2000* paragraph 10. (See reproduced pages 184-185 in this text.)
[8] Refer to Introduction to *Incoterms 2000* paragraph 10. (See reproduced pages 184-185 in this text.)

Comments Although B3 merely stipulates "No obligation" for the buyer, on-carriage from the place of destination may be necessary in some cases, and it is the buyer's responsibility to do whatever is required for this purpose. But the seller is not concerned with the further carriage of the goods, and the buyer has no obligation to the seller in this respect. The words "No obligation" mean that whatever the buyer does is in his own interest and is not covered by the contract of sale.

B4 Taking delivery

The buyer must take delivery of the goods when they have been delivered in accordance with A4.

Comments As in all D-terms, B4 has wording stating that the buyer shall take delivery as soon as the goods have been placed at his disposal in accordance with A4. (The same wording is also used in EXW B4, but under EXW the placing of the goods at the buyer's disposal usually occurs at the seller's own premises.) The seller, according to A4 in the D-terms, shall place the goods at the buyer's disposal "on the date or within the agreed period".

If the goods are placed at the buyer's disposal earlier than agreed, the buyer is not obliged to take delivery before the agreed time, though it may normally be in his own interest to do so. If the goods are placed at the buyer's disposal too late, the buyer may hold the seller responsible for breach of contract according to the applicable law. He may also recover damages from the seller or, in the event of a fundamental breach, cancel the contract.

B5 Transfer of risks

The buyer must bear all risks of loss of or damage to the goods from the time they have been delivered in accordance with A4.

The buyer must, should he fail to fulfil his obligations in accordance with B2, bear all additional risks of loss of or damage to the goods incurred thereby.

The buyer must, should he fail to give notice in accordance with B7, bear all risks of loss of or damage to the goods from the agreed date or the expiry date of the agreed period for delivery provided, however, that the goods have been duly appropriated to the contract, that is to say, clearly set aside or otherwise identified as the contract goods.

Comments According to the main rule, while the seller under A5 bears the risk of loss of or damage to the goods until the delivery point, the buyer has to bear the risk thereafter. The delivery point is different under the different terms. In EXW and all D-terms the goods are simply placed "at the disposal of the buyer" at the relevant point, while under the F- and C-terms the delivery point is related to the handing over of the goods to the carrier in the country of dispatch or shipment (see the comments to A4 of these terms). In the terms used for goods intended to be carried by sea, reference is made to delivery alongside the named vessel (FAS) or delivery onboard the vessel (FOB, CFR, CIF).

Consequences of buyer's failure to give notice

While the seller under EXW and all D-terms can transfer the risk by his own act of placing the goods at the buyer's disposal, he may be prevented from doing so by the buyer's failure to give notice according to B7. This can occur when it is the buyer's responsibility to determine (1) the time within a stipulated period when the goods are to be made available or (2) the place of delivery (see the comments to B7). The failure to perform these tasks results in a premature passing of the risk: it is not acceptable that the buyer should be able to delay the delivery and the passing of the risk longer than contemplated when the contract of sale was made. Therefore, his failure to notify according to B7 will cause the risk to pass "from the agreed date or the expiry date of the agreed period for delivery".

Appropriation and the passing of risk

The risk, however, cannot pass until the goods "have been appropriated to the contract". If the goods are unascertained – i.e., goods of a certain kind which the seller will deliver to various buyers – appropriation only occurs when the goods are "clearly set aside or otherwise identified as the contract goods".

This appropriation will normally be made when the seller has handed over the goods for carriage and the consignment has been marked as intended for the buyer – unless the cargo is carried in bulk and intended to be appropriated between different buyers only upon the arrival of the goods at destination.

Buyer's obligation to clear goods for import

Under DDU the buyer has the obligation to clear the goods for import (B2). If he fails to do so, the seller may be prevented from reaching the agreed delivery point. Any "additional risks of loss of or damage to the goods incurred thereby" must then be borne by the buyer. Therefore, the risk may pass even before the goods have reached the agreed delivery point, for example, when the goods are detained at a customs station because of the buyer's failure to fulfil his obligation to clear the goods for import.

B6   **Division of costs**

The buyer must pay

- all costs relating to the goods from the time they have been delivered in accordance with A4; and

- all additional costs incurred if he fails to fulfil his obligations in accordance with B2, or to give notice in accordance with B7, provided, however, that the goods have been duly appropriated to the contract, that is to say, clearly set aside or otherwise identified as the contract goods; and

- where applicable[9], the costs of customs formalities as well as all duties, taxes and other charges payable upon import of the goods.

Comments   While in DAF, DES and DEQ, the place of delivery is inherent in the term itself – the named frontier, the ship and the quay respectively – under DDU the parties have to specify the place themselves. Moreover, the buyer must pay any further costs subsequent to the delivery of the goods to that place.

The buyer must pay any additional costs which may arise because of his failure to take delivery as agreed or to notify the seller of the time and place of delivery according to B7. In DDU the failure of the buyer to clear the goods for import according to B2 may prevent the seller from reaching the agreed delivery point, or it may give rise to additional costs. If so, the buyer has to bear the consequences of these events and pay any additional costs incurred thereby. The buyer's obligation to pay additional costs in these circumstances is subject to the identification of the goods as the contract goods ("appropriation").

As noted in the comments to B2, the buyer has the duty to clear the goods for import; B6 declares that he also has to pay the costs arising in that connection ("the costs of customs formalities as well as all duties, taxes and other charges"). The buyer also has to pay any duties, taxes and other charges arising with regard to the transit of the goods through another country, after they have been delivered by the seller in accordance with A4.

B7   **Notice to the seller**

The buyer must, whenever he is entitled to determine the time within an agreed period and/or the point of taking delivery at the named place, give the seller sufficient notice thereof.

---

9 Refer to Introduction to *Incoterms 2000* paragraph 14. (See reproduced pages 184-185 in this text.)

DDU

Comments   As discussed in the comments to B5 and B6, the failure of the buyer to notify the seller of the time and place of taking delivery – when the buyer in the contract of sale has been given the option to determine these matters – may cause the risk of the loss of or damage to the goods to pass before the goods have been delivered according to A4. In addition, it can make the buyer liable to pay any additional costs incurred by the seller as a result of the buyer's failure.

B8   Proof of delivery, transport document or equivalent electronic message

 The buyer must accept the appropriate delivery order or transport document in accordance with A8.

Comments   The buyer has to accept the document if it conforms with the contract and with the requirements of A8 (see the comments to A8). If the buyer rejects the document (for example, by instructions to a bank not to pay the seller under a documentary credit), he commits a breach of contract, which would give the seller remedies available for such a breach under the contract of sale.

These remedies could include, for example, a right to cancel the contract or to claim damages for breach. However, the buyer is not obliged to accept a document which does not provide adequate proof of delivery, for example, one which has notations on it showing that the goods are defective or that they have been provided in less than the agreed quantity. In these cases, the document is termed "unclean".

B9   Inspection of goods

 The buyer must pay the costs of any pre-shipment inspection except when such inspection is mandated by the authorities of the country of export.

Comments   As noted in the comments to A9, the buyer has to pay for any costs of checking the goods, unless the contract determines that these costs should be wholly or partly borne by the seller. In some cases, the contract may provide that the costs should be borne by the seller if the inspection reveals that the goods do not conform with the contract.

In some countries, where import licences or permission to obtain foreign currency for the payment of the price may be required, the authorities may demand an inspection of the goods before shipment, to ensure that the goods are in conformity with the contract. (This is usually called pre-shipment inspection, PSI.) If this is the case, the inspection is normally arranged by instructions from the authorities to an inspection company, which they appoint. The costs following from this inspection have to be paid by the authorities. Any reimbursement to the authorities for the inspection costs, however, must be made by the buyer, unless otherwise specifically agreed between the buyer and the seller.

B10   Other obligations

The buyer must pay all costs and charges incurred in obtaining the documents or equivalent electronic messages mentioned in A10 and reimburse those incurred by the seller in rendering his assistance in accordance therewith.

Comments   As discussed in the comments to A10, the seller has to render the buyer assistance in obtaining the documents or electronic messages which may be required for the import of the goods. However, this assistance is rendered at the buyer's risk and expense. Therefore, B10 stipulates that the buyer must pay all costs and charges incurred in obtaining these documents or electronic messages. He will also have to reimburse the seller for the seller's costs in rendering his assistance in these matters.

DDP

Delivered Duty Paid
(...named place of destination)

"Delivered duty paid" means that the seller delivers the goods to the buyer, cleared for import, and not unloaded from any arriving means of transport at the named place of destination. The seller has to bear all the costs and risks involved in bringing the goods thereto including, where applicable[1], any "duty" (which term includes the responsibility for and the risk of the carrying out of customs formalities and the payment of formalities, customs duties, taxes and other charges) for import in the country of destination.

Whilst the EXW term represents the minimum obligation for the seller, DDP represents the maximum obligation.

This term should not be used if the seller is unable directly or indirectly to obtain the import licence.

However, if the parties wish to exclude from the seller's obligations some of the costs payable upon import of the goods (such as value-added tax: VAT), this should be made clear by adding explicit wording to this effect in the contract of sale.[2]

If the parties wish the buyer to bear all risks and costs of the import, the DDU term should be used.

This term may be used irrespective of the mode of transport but when delivery is to take place in the port of destination on board the vessel or on the quay (wharf), the DES or DEQ terms should be used.

1 Refer to the introduction of *Incoterms 2000*, ICC publication Nº560, paragraph 14. (See reproduced pages 184-185 in this text.)

2 Refer to the introduction of *Incoterms 2000*, ICC publication Nº560, paragraph 11. (See reproduced pages 184-185 in this text.)

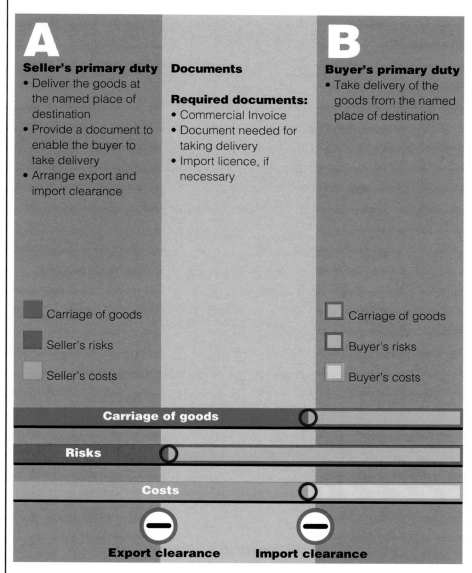

A

Seller's primary duty
- Deliver the goods at the named place of destination
- Provide a document to enable the buyer to take delivery
- Arrange export and import clearance

Documents

Required documents:
- Commercial Invoice
- Document needed for taking delivery
- Import licence, if necessary

B

Buyer's primary duty
- Take delivery of the goods from the named place of destination

Carriage of goods

Seller's risks

Seller's costs

Carriage of goods

Buyer's risks

Buyer's costs

Carriage of goods

Risks

Costs

Export clearance   Import clearance

Critical points

- Carriage to be arranged by the seller
- Risk transfer from the seller to the buyer when the goods are placed at the disposal of the buyer
- Cost transfer from the seller to the buyer when the goods are placed at the disposal of the buyer

DDP

A THE SELLER'S OBLIGATIONS

A1 Provision of the goods in conformity with the contract

The seller must provide the goods and the commercial invoice, or its equivalent electronic message, in conformity with the contract of sale and any other evidence of conformity which may be required by the contract.

Comments   The seller must provide the goods in conformity with the contract. It is also usual practice that the seller, in order to be paid, has to invoice the buyer. In addition, the seller must submit any other evidence stipulated in the contract itself that the goods conform with that contract.

This text only serves as a reminder of the seller's main obligation under the contract of sale.

A2 Licences, authorizations and formalities

The seller must obtain at his own risk and expense any export and import licence and other official authorization or other documents and carry out, where applicable[3], all customs formalities necessary for the export of the goods, for their transit through any country and for their import.

Comments   Since the term DDP is evidence of an arrival contract, the seller has to do whatever may be necessary for the goods to reach the agreed place for delivery. This means the seller is responsible for export and import clearance of the goods, as well as any transit of the goods through third countries.

Before agreeing to sell the goods under DDP, the seller should be sure that the regulations of the buyer's country do not prevent him as a non-resident from applying for any necessary import licence. Normally no such difficulties will be encountered, since the application for licences can be made by freight forwarders (customs brokers) on the seller's behalf.

Advisable to exclude payment of some charges

It may be advisable for the parties to exclude the payment of any charges relating to the "internal" fiscal system in the country of import (such as VAT levied upon import) from the seller's obligation to pay. If this is not done, any right to deduct these expenses or to benefit from particular tax advantages available only to residents could be lost. The charges intended to be excluded should then be identified in conjunction with the DDP term in the contract of sale, for example, by using a phrase such as "DDP VAT unpaid".

Unforeseen or reasonably unforeseeable prohibitions

The seller's obligations under DDP may become more expensive than contemplated as a result of reasonably unforeseeable circumstances.

However, contracts of sale usually contain provisions which the seller may invoke to protect himself in the event of these contingencies. Under CISG and corresponding provisions in various national Sale of Goods Acts, unforeseen or reasonably unforeseeable export prohibitions may relieve the seller from his obligations under the contract of sale.

If the seller wishes to avoid the obligation of clearing the goods for import, he should use DDU or add the phrase "not cleared for import" after DDP.

---

3 Refer to Introduction to *Incoterms 2000* paragraph 14. (See reproduced pages 184-185 in this text.)

A3 Contracts of carriage and insurance

a) Contract of carriage

The seller must contract at his own expense for the carriage of the goods to the named place of destination. If a specific point is not agreed or is not determined by practice, the seller may select the point at the named place of destination which best suits his purpose.

b) Contract of insurance

No obligation[4].

Comments   Under DDP the seller must ensure that the goods actually arrive at destination. It follows from this that the seller must arrange and pay for any carriage of the goods.

Under the D-terms, the seller's choice of transport is only of importance to the buyer insofar as it affects the buyer's obligation to receive the goods from the carrier. If the seller chooses an unusual transport which makes it more difficult or expensive for the buyer to receive the goods from the carrier, any additional costs or risks caused by the seller's choice of transport will be for the seller's account.

Normally, the point mentioned after the D-term will indicate where the goods should be delivered at destination. But if there are several alternatives available, and the contract of sale or commercial practice does not indicate which alternative the seller must choose, he "may select the point at the named place of destination which best suits his purpose".

A4 Delivery

The seller must place the goods at the disposal of the buyer, or at that of another person named by the buyer, on any arriving means of transport not unloaded at the named place of destination on the date or within the period agreed for delivery.

Comments   Under DDP the seller must "place the goods at the disposal of the buyer" at destination. The precise point for the delivery of the goods depends upon the D-term chosen.

Incoterms 2000 specify that if the goods are to be delivered at the buyer's premises or to a place under his control, then delivery is completed when the goods are at his disposal on the arriving vehicle not unloaded. In other cases, delivery is normally completed when the goods have been loaded on the buyer's collecting vehicle.

A5 Transfer of risks

The seller must, subject to the provisions of B5, bear all risks of loss of or damage to the goods until such time as they have been delivered in accordance with A4.

Comments   All Incoterms are based on the same principle that the risk of loss of or damage to the goods is transferred from the seller to the buyer when the seller has fulfilled his delivery obligation according to A4. A5 of FOB, CFR and CIF further specifies that the risk is transferred when the goods "have passed the ship's rail at the port of shipment".

All Incoterms, in conformity with the general principle of CISG, connect the transfer of the risk with the delivery of the goods and not with other circumstances, such as the passing of ownership or the time of the conclusion of the contract. Neither Incoterms nor CISG deals with transfer of title to the goods or other property rights with respect to the goods.

The passing of risk of loss of or damage to the goods concerns the risk of fortuitous events (accidents) and does not include loss or damage caused by the seller or the buyer, for example, inadequate packing or marking of the goods. Therefore, even if damage occurs subsequent to the transfer of the risk, the seller may still be responsible if the

---

4 Refer to Introduction to *Incoterms 2000* paragraph 10. (See reproduced pages 184-185 in this text.)

damage could be attributed to the fact that the goods were not delivered in conformity with the contract (see A1 and the comments to A9).

A5 of all Incoterms contains the phrase "subject to the provisions of B5". This means that there are exceptions to the main rule concerning the passing of risk under the circumstances mentioned in B5, which may result in a premature passing of the risk because of the buyer's failure properly to fulfil his obligations (see the comments to B5).

A6 Division of costs

The seller must, subject to the provisions of B6, pay

- in addition to costs resulting from A3 a), all costs relating to the goods until such time as they have been delivered in accordance with A4; and

- where applicable[5], the costs of customs formalities necessary for export and import as well as all duties, taxes and other charges payable upon export and import of the goods, and for their transit through any country prior to delivery in accordance with A4.

Comments As is the case with the transfer of the risk of loss of or damage to the goods, all Incoterms follow the same rule, that the division of costs occurs at the delivery point. All costs occurring before the seller has fulfilled his obligation to deliver according to A4 are for his account, while further costs are for the account of the buyer (see the comments to B6). This rule is made subject to the provisions of B6, which indicates that the buyer may have to bear additional costs incurred by his failure to give appropriate notice to the seller.

Since under D-terms, the seller does not fulfil his obligation until the goods have actually arrived at destination and been placed at the disposal of the buyer, the seller has to do everything required to achieve this. Nevertheless, A3 in all D-terms still stipulates that the seller must contract for carriage; and A6 of all D-terms stipulates that he must pay the costs resulting from A3 for the carriage of the goods, and, where applicable, the costs of customs formalities necessary for export and import as well as all duties, taxes and other charges prior to delivery in accordance with A4. Needless to say, any transit costs incurred subsequent to delivery will have to be paid by the buyer.

A7 Notice to the buyer

The seller must give the buyer sufficient notice of the dispatch of the goods as well as any other notice required in order to allow the buyer to take measures which are normally necessary to enable him to take delivery of the goods.

Comments The seller must give the buyer sufficient notice as to when the goods have been dispatched and when they will be available at the agreed or chosen delivery point, so that the buyer can make preparations in time to take delivery according to B4. There is no stipulation in Incoterms spelling out the consequences of the seller's failure to give such notice. But it follows from Incoterms that the seller's failure constitutes a breach of contract. This means that the seller could be held responsible for the breach according to the law applicable to the contract of sale.

---

5 Refer to Introduction to *Incoterms 2000* paragraph 14. (See reproduced pages 184-185 in this text.)

A8 Proof of delivery, transport document or equivalent electronic message

The seller must provide the buyer at the seller's expense with the delivery order and/or the usual transport document (for example a negotiable bill of lading, a non-negotiable sea waybill, an inland waterway document, an air waybill, a railway consignment note, a road consignment note, or a multimodal transport document) which the buyer may require to take delivery of the goods in accordance with A4/B4.

Where the seller and the buyer have agreed to communicate electronically, the document referred to in the preceding paragraph may be replaced by an equivalent electronic data interchange (EDI) message.

Comments In most cases the buyer will require a document in order to be able to obtain the goods from the carrier.

Traditionally, the relevant document for carriage by sea is a negotiable bill of lading, and this is still the predominant document when DDP is used for carriage of bulk commodities. However, bills of lading are often replaced by delivery orders splitting up the total bill of lading quantity into smaller lots for several buyers.

Documents can be replaced by EDI messages when the parties have agreed to communicate electronically.

A9 Checking – packaging – marking

The seller must pay the costs of those checking operations (such as checking quality, measuring, weighing, counting) which are necessary for the purpose of delivering the goods in accordance with A4.

The seller must provide at his own expense packaging (unless it is usual for the particular trade to deliver the goods of the contract description unpacked) which is required for the delivery of the goods. Packaging is to be marked appropriately.

Comments It is important that the buyer ensure that the seller has duly fulfilled his obligation with respect to the condition of the goods, particularly if the buyer is called upon to pay for the goods before he has received and checked them. However, the seller has no duty to arrange and pay for the inspection of the goods before dispatch unless this is specifically agreed in the contract of sale.

A10 Other obligations

The seller must pay all costs and charges incurred in obtaining the documents or equivalent electronic messages mentioned in B10 and reimburse those incurred by the buyer in rendering his assistance herewith.

The seller must provide the buyer, upon request, with the necessary information for procuring insurance.

Comments DDP requires the seller to clear the goods for import, but if the seller so requests the buyer must assist in obtaining any documents (for example, a certificate of origin, a health certificate, a clean report of findings, an import licence) or equivalent electronic messages which the seller may require for these purposes. The seller, however, has to reimburse the buyer for any costs the buyer may incur in rendering this assistance.

DDP

DDP

B THE BUYER'S OBLIGATIONS

B1 Payment of the price

▨ The buyer must pay the price as provided in the contract of sale.

Comments   The buyer must pay the price agreed in the contract of sale. B1 constitutes a reminder of this main obligation, which corresponds with the seller's obligation to provide the goods in conformity with the contract of sale, as stipulated in A1.

B2 Licences, authorizations and formalities

▌ The buyer must render the seller at the latter's request, risk and expense, every assistance in obtaining, where applicable[6], any import licence or other official authorization necessary for the import of the goods.

Comments   Since the seller has to make the goods available to the buyer in the country of destination, it is for the seller to do whatever is necessary with respect to the clearance of the goods for export, transit and import.

B3 Contracts of carriage and insurance

▌ a) Contract of carriage

No obligation[7].

b) Contract of insurance

No obligation[8].

Comments   Although B3 merely stipulates "No obligation" for the buyer, on-carriage from the place of destination may be necessary in some cases, and it is the buyer's responsibility to do whatever is required for this purpose. But the seller is not concerned with the further carriage of the goods, and the buyer has no obligation to the seller in this respect. The words "No obligation" mean that whatever the buyer does is in his own interest and is not covered by the contract of sale.

B4 Taking delivery

▌ The buyer must take delivery of the goods when they have been delivered in accordance with A4.

Comments   As in all D-terms, B4 has wording stating that the buyer shall take delivery as soon as the goods have been placed at his disposal in accordance with A4. (The same wording is also used in EXW B4, but EXW B3 specifies that the placing of the goods at the buyer's disposal occurs at the seller's own premises.) The seller, according to A4 in the D-terms, shall place the goods at the buyer's disposal "on the date or within the agreed period".

If the goods are placed at the buyer's disposal earlier than agreed, the buyer is not obliged to take delivery before the agreed time, though it may normally be in his own interest to do so. If the goods are placed at the buyer's disposal too late, the buyer may hold the seller responsible for breach of contract according to the applicable law. He may also recover damages from the seller or, in the event of a fundamental breach, cancel the contract.

---

6 Refer to Introduction to *Incoterms 2000* paragraph 14. (See reproduced pages 184-185 in this text.)
7 Refer to Introduction to *Incoterms 2000* paragraph 10. (See reproduced pages 184-185 in this text.)
8 Refer to Introduction to *Incoterms 2000* paragraph 10. (See reproduced pages 184-185 in this text.)

B5 Transfer of risks

The buyer must bear all risks of loss of or damage to the goods from the time they have been delivered in accordance with A4.

The buyer must, should he fail to fulfil his obligations in accordance with B2, bear all additional risks of loss of or damage to the goods incurred thereby.

The buyer must, should he fail to give notice in accordance with B7, bear all risks of loss of or damage to the goods from the agreed date or the expiry date of the agreed period for delivery provided, however, that the goods have been duly appropriated to the contract, that is to say, clearly set aside or otherwise identified as the contract goods.

Comments According to the main rule, while the seller under A5 bears the risk of loss of or damage to the goods until the delivery point, the buyer has to bear the risk thereafter. The delivery point is different under the different terms. In EXW and all D-terms the goods are simply placed "at the disposal of the buyer" at the relevant point, while under the F- and C-terms the delivery point is related to the handing over of the goods to the carrier in the country of dispatch or shipment (see the comments to A4 of these terms). In the terms used for goods intended to be carried by sea, reference is made to delivery alongside the named vessel (FAS) or delivery onboard the vessel (FOB, CFR, CIF).

Consequences of buyer's failure to give notice

While the seller under EXW and all D-terms can transfer the risk by his own act of placing the goods at the buyer's disposal, he may be prevented from doing so by the buyer's failure to give notice according to B7. This can occur when it is the buyer's responsibility to determine (1) the time within a stipulated period when the goods are to be made available or (2) the place of delivery (see the comments to B7). The failure to perform these tasks results in a premature passing of the risk: it is not acceptable that the buyer should be able to delay the delivery and the passing of the risk longer than contemplated when the contract of sale was made. Therefore, his failure to notify according to B7 will cause the risk to pass "from the agreed date or the expiry date of the agreed period for delivery".

Appropriation and the passing of risk

The risk, however, cannot pass until the goods "have been duly appropriated to the contract". If the goods are unascertained – i.e. goods of a certain kind which the seller will deliver to various buyers – appropriation only occurs when the goods are "clearly set aside as the contract goods".

This appropriation will normally be made when the seller has handed over the goods for carriage and the consignment has been marked as intended for the buyer – unless the cargo is carried in bulk and intended to be appropriated between different buyers only upon the arrival of the goods at destination.

B6 Division of costs

The buyer must pay

- all costs relating to the goods from the time they have been delivered in accordance with A4; and

- all additional costs incurred if he fails to fulfil his obligations in accordance with B2, or to give notice in accordance with B7, provided, however, that the goods have been duly appropriated to the contract, that is to say, clearly set aside or otherwise identified as the contract goods.

DDP

Comments   While in DAF, DES and DEQ, the place of delivery is inherent in the term itself – the named frontier, ship and quay respectively – under DDP the parties have to specify the place themselves. Moreover, the buyer must pay any further costs subsequent to the delivery of the goods to that place.

The buyer must pay any additional costs which may arise if he fails to take delivery as agreed or if he fails to notify the seller of the time and place of delivery according to B7. The buyer's obligation to pay additional costs in these cases is subject to the identification of the goods as the contract goods (appropriation).

Since under DDP the seller has to clear the goods for import, the buyer does not have to pay any costs in that regard.

B7   Notice to the seller

 The buyer must, whenever he is entitled to determine the time within an agreed period and/or the point of taking delivery at the named place, give the seller sufficient notice thereof.

Comments   As discussed in the comments to B5 and B6, the failure of the buyer to notify the seller of the time and place of taking delivery – when the buyer in the contract of sale has been given the option to determine these matters – may cause the risk of the loss of or damage to the goods to pass before the goods have been delivered according to A4. In addition, it can make the buyer liable to pay any additional costs incurred by the seller as a result of the buyer's failure.

B8   Proof of delivery, transport document or equivalent electronic message

 The buyer must accept the appropriate delivery order or transport document in accordance with A8.

Comments   The buyer has to accept the document if it conforms with the contract and with the requirements of A8 (see the comments to A8). If the buyer rejects the document (for example, by instructions to a bank not to pay the seller under a documentary credit), he commits a breach of contract, which would give the seller remedies available for such a breach under the contract of sale.

These remedies could include, for example, a right to cancel the contract or to claim damages for breach. However, the buyer is not obliged to accept a document which does not provide adequate proof of delivery, for example one which has notations on it showing that the goods are defective or that they have been provided in less than the agreed quantity. In these cases, the document is termed "unclean".

B9   Inspection of goods

 The buyer must pay the costs of any pre-shipment inspection except when such inspection is mandated by the authorities of the country of export.

Comments   As noted in the comments to A9, the buyer has to pay for any costs of checking the goods, unless the contract determines that these costs should be wholly or partly borne by the seller. In some cases, the contract may provide that the costs should be borne by the seller if the inspection reveals that the goods do not conform with the contract.

In some countries, where import licences or permission to obtain foreign currency for the payment of the price may be required, the authorities may demand an inspection of the goods before shipment, to ensure that the goods are in conformity with the contract. (This is usually called pre-shipment inspection, PSI.) If this is the case, the inspection is normally arranged by instructions from the authorities to an inspection company, which they appoint. The costs following from this inspection have to be paid by the authorities.

Any reimbursement to the authorities for the inspection costs, however, must be made by the buyer, unless otherwise specifically agreed between the buyer and the seller.

B10   Other obligations

The buyer must render the seller, at the latter's request, risk and expense, every assistance in obtaining any documents or equivalent electronic messages issued or transmitted in the country of import which the seller may require for the purpose of making the goods available to the buyer in accordance therewith.

Comments   Since the seller has the obligation to clear the goods for import, he may require the buyer's assistance to obtain the necessary documents or EDI messages. The buyer must render this assistance when requested by the seller to do so, but this is done at the seller's risk and expense.

DDP

INCOTERMS 2000 AT A GLANCE

Transport obligations, costs and risks

Seller	Carrier	Buyer
Export clearance		Import clearance

Critical points

Group E — Departure

Under EXW, the seller minimizes his risk by only making the goods available at his own premises

EXW — EX Works (...named place)

- Carriage of goods
- Risks
- Costs

- Carriage to be arranged by the buyer
- Risk transfer from the seller to the buyer when the goods are at the disposal of the buyer
- Cost transfer from the seller to the buyer when the goods are at the disposal of buyer

Group F

Main carriage not paid by seller

Under F Terms, and under FCA unless otherwise agreed, the seller arranges and pays for the pre-carriage in the country of export

FCA — Free CArrier (...named place)

- Carriage of goods
- Risks
- Costs

- Carriage to be arranged by the buyer or by the seller on the buyer's behalf
- Risk transfer from the seller to the buyer when the goods have been delivered to the carrier at the named place
- Cost transfer from the seller to the buyer when the goods have been delivered to the carrier at the named place

FAS — Free Alongside Ship (...named port of shipment)

- Carriage of goods
- Risks
- Costs

- Carriage to be arranged by the buyer
- Risk transfer from the seller to the buyer when the goods have been placed alongside the ship
- Cost transfer from the seller to the buyer when the goods have been placed alongside the ship

FOB — Free On Board (...named port of shipment)

- Carriage of goods
- Risks
- Costs

- Carriage to be arranged by the buyer
- Risk transfer from the seller to the buyer when the goods pass the ship's rail
- Cost transfer from the seller to the buyer when the goods pass the ship's rail

Group C

Main carriage paid by seller

Under C Terms the seller arranges and pays for the main carriage but without assuming the risk of the main carriage

CFR — Cost and FReight (...named port of destination)

- Carriage of goods
- Risks
- Costs

- Carriage to be arranged by the seller
- Risk transfer from the seller to the buyer when the goods pass the ship's rail
- Cost transfer at port of destination, buyer paying such costs as are not for the seller's account under the contract of carriage

INCOTERMS 2000 AT A GLANCE

© **International Chamber of Commerce**

This chart is available as a poster
(ICC publication N°614) from ICC Publishing

ANNEXES

Incoterms 2000 (ICC publication No. 560)

Introduction (extracts – see footnotes)

9.   THE TERMS

9.3   (...) There are only two terms which deal with insurance, namely CIF and CIP. Under these terms the seller is obliged to procure insurance for the benefit of the buyer. In other cases it is for the parties themselves to decide whether and to what extent they want to cover themselves by insurance. Since the seller takes out insurance for the benefit of the buyer, he would not know the buyer's precise requirements. Under the Institute Cargo Clauses drafted by the Institute of London Underwriters, insurance is available in "minimum cover" under Clause C, "medium cover" under Clause B and "most extended cover" under Clause A. Since in the sale of commodities under the CIF term the buyer may wish to sell the goods in transit to a subsequent buyer who in turn may wish to resell the goods again, it is impossible to know the insurance cover suitable to such subsequent buyers and, therefore, the minimum cover under CIF has traditionally been chosen with the possibility for the buyer to require the seller to take out additional insurance. Minimum cover is however unsuitable for sale of manufactured goods where the risk of theft, pilferage or improper handling or custody of the goods would require more than the cover available under Clause C. Since CIP, as distinguished from CIF, would normally not be used for the sale of commodities, it would have been feasible to adopt the most extended cover under CIP rather than the minimum cover under CIF. But to vary the seller's insurance obligation under CIF and CIP would lead to confusion and both terms therefore limit the seller's insurance obligation to the minimum cover. It is particularly important for the CIP-buyer to observe this: should additional cover be required, he should agree with the seller that the latter could take out additional insurance or, alternatively, arrange for extended insurance cover himself. There are also particular instances where the buyer may wish to obtain even more protection than is available under Institute Clause A, for example insurance against war, riots, civil commotion, strikes or other labour disturbances. If he wishes the seller to arrange such insurance he must instruct him accordingly in which case the seller would have to provide such insurance if procurable.

10.   THE EXPRESSION "NO OBLIGATION"

As appears from the expressions "the seller must" and "the buyer must" Incoterms are only concerned with the obligations which the parties owe to each other. The words "no obligation" have therefore been inserted whenever one party does not owe an obligation to the other party. Thus, if for instance according to A3 of the respective term the seller has to arrange and pay for the contract of carriage we find the words "no obligation" under the heading "contract of carriage" in B3 a) setting forth the buyer's position. Again, where neither party owes the other an obligation, the words "no obligation" will appear with respect to both parties, for example, with respect to insurance.

In either case, it is important to point out that even though one party may be under "no obligation" towards the other to perform a certain task, this does not mean that it is not in his interest to perform that task. Thus, for example, just because a CFR buyer owes his seller no duty to make a contract of insurance under B4, it is clearly in his interest to make such a contract, the seller being under no such obligation to procure insurance cover under A4.

11.   VARIANTS OF INCOTERMS

In practice, it frequently happens that the parties themselves by adding words to an Incoterm seek further precision than the term could offer. It should be underlined that Incoterms give no guidance whatsoever for such additions. Thus, if the parties cannot rely on a well-established custom of the trade for the interpretation of such additions they may encounter serious problems when no consistent understanding of the additions could be proven.

If for instance the common expressions "FOB stowed" or "EXW loaded" are used, it is impossible to establish a worldwide understanding to the effect that the seller's obligations are extended not only with respect to the cost of actually loading the goods in the ship or on the vehicle respectively but also include the risk of fortuitous loss of or damage to the goods in the process of stowage and loading. For these reasons, the parties are strongly advised to clarify whether they only mean that the function or the cost of the stowage and loading operations should fall upon the seller or whether he should also bear the risk until the stowage and loading has actually been completed. These are questions to which Incoterms do not provide an answer: consequently, if the contract too fails expressly to describe the parties' intentions, the parties may be put to much unnecessary trouble and cost.

Although Incoterms 2000 do not provide for many of these commonly used variants, the preambles to certain trade terms do alert the parties to the need for special contractual terms if the parties wish to go beyond the stipulations of Incoterms.

EXW the added obligation for the seller to load the goods on the buyer's collecting vehicle;
CIF/CIP   the buyer's need for additional insurance;
DEQ the added obligation for the seller to pay for costs after discharge.

In some cases sellers and buyers refer to commercial practice in liner and charter party trade. In these circumstances, it is necessary to clearly distinguish between the obligations of the parties under the contract of carriage and their obligations to each other under the contract of sale. Unfortunately, there are no authoritative definitions of expressions such as "liner terms" and "terminal handling charges" (THC). Distribution of costs under such terms may differ in different places and change from time to time. The parties are recommended to clarify in the contract of sale how such costs should be distributed between themselves.

Expressions frequently used in charterparties, such as "FOB stowed", "FOB stowed and trimmed", are sometimes used in contracts of sale in order to clarify to what extent the seller under FOB has to perform stowage and trimming of the goods onboard the ship. Where such words are added, it is necessary to clarify in the contract of sale whether the added obligations only relate to costs or to both costs and risks.

As has been said, every effort has been made to ensure that Incoterms reflect the most common commercial practice. However in some cases – particularly where Incoterms 2000 differ from Incoterms 1990 – the parties may wish the trade terms to operate differently. They are reminded of such options in the preamble of the terms signalled by the word "However".

14.   CUSTOMS CLEARANCE

The term "customs clearance" has given rise to misunderstandings. Thus, whenever reference is made to an obligation of the seller or the buyer to undertake obligations in connection with passing the goods through customs of the country of export or import it is now made clear that this obligation does not only include the payment of duty and other charges but also the performance and payment of whatever administrative matters are connected with the passing of the goods through customs and the information to the authorities in this connection. Further, it has – although quite wrongfully - been considered in some quarters inappropriate to use terms dealing with the obligation to clear the goods through customs when, as in intra-European Union trade or other free trade areas, there is no longer any obligation to pay duty and no restrictions relating to import or export. In order to clarify the situation, the words "where applicable" have been added in the A2 and B2, A6 and B6 clauses of the relevant Incoterms in order for them to be used without any ambiguity where no customs procedures are required.

It is normally desirable that customs clearance is arranged by the party domiciled in the country where such clearance should take place or at least by somebody acting there on his behalf. Thus, the exporter should normally clear the goods for export, while the importer should clear the goods for import.

Incoterms 1990 departed from this under the trade terms EXW and FAS (export clearance duty on the buyer) and DEQ (import clearance duty on the seller) but in Incoterms 2000 FAS and DEQ place the duty of clearing the goods for export on the seller and to clear them for import on the buyer respectively, while EXW – representing the seller's minimum obligation – has been left unamended (export clearance duty on the buyer). Under DDP the seller specifically agrees to do what follows from the very name of the term – Delivered Duty Paid – namely to clear the goods for import and pay any duty as a consequence thereof.

CMI Uniform Rules for SEA WAYBILLS

Comité Maritime International – Paris, June 29, 1990

1.   Scope of Application

(i) These Rules shall be called the "CMI Uniform Rules for Sea Waybills".

(ii) They shall apply when adopted by a contract of carriage which is not covered by a bill of lading or similar document of title, whether the contract be in writing or not.

2.   Definitions

In these Rules:

"Contract of carriage" shall mean any contract of carriage subject to these Rules which is to be performed wholly or partly by sea.

"Goods" shall mean any goods carried or received for carriage under a contract of carriage.

"Carrier" and "Shipper" shall mean the parties named in or identifiable as such from the contract of carriage.

"Consignee" shall mean the party named in or identifiable as such from the contract of carriage, or any person substituted as consignee in accordance with rule 6(i).

"Right of Control" shall mean the rights and obligations referred to in rule 6.

3.   Agency

(i) The shipper on entering into the contract of carriage does so not only on his own behalf but also as agent for and on behalf of the consignee, and warrants to the carrier that he has authority so to do.

(ii) This rule shall apply if, and only if, it be necessary by the law applicable to the contract of carriage so as to enable the consignee to sue and be sued thereon. The consignee shall be under no greater liability than he would have been had the contract of carriage been covered by a bill of lading or similar document of title.

4.   Rights and Responsibilities

(i) The contract of carriage shall be subject to any International Convention or National Law which is, or if the contract of carriage had been covered by a bill of lading or similar document of title would have been, compulsorily applicable thereto. Such convention or law shall apply notwithstanding anything inconsistent therewith in the contract of carriage.

(ii) Subject always to subrule (i), the contract of carriage is governed by:

    (a) these Rules;

    (b) unless otherwise agreed by the parties, the carrier's standard terms and conditions for the trade, if any, including any terms and conditions relating to the non-sea part of the carriage;

    (c) any other terms and conditions agreed by the parties.

(iii) In the event of any inconsistency between the terms and conditions mentioned under subrule (ii)(b) or (c) and these Rules, these Rules shall prevail.

5.   Description of the Goods

(i) The shipper warrants the accuracy of the particulars furnished by him relating to the goods, and shall indemnify the carrier against any loss, damage or expense resulting from any inaccuracy.

(ii) In the absence of reservation by the carrier, any statement in a sea waybill or similar document as to the quantity or condition of the goods shall

    (a) as between the carrier and the shipper be prima facie evidence of receipt of the goods as so stated;

    (b) as between the carrier and the consignee be conclusive evidence of receipt of the goods as so stated, and proof to the contrary shall not be permitted, provided always that the consignee has acted in good faith.

6.   Right of Control

(i) Unless the shipper has exercised his option under subrule (ii) below, he shall be the only party entitled to give the carrier instructions in relation to the contract of carriage. Unless prohibited by the applicable law, he shall be entitled to change the name of the consignee at any time up to the consignee claiming delivery of the goods after their arrival at destination, provided he gives the carrier reasonable notice in writing, or by some other means acceptable to the carrier, and thereby undertaking to indemnify the carrier against any additional expense caused thereby.

(ii) The shipper shall have the option, to be exercised not later than the receipt of the goods by the carrier, to transfer the right of control to the consignee. The exercise of this option must be noted on the sea waybill or similar document, if any. Where the option has been exercised the consignee shall have such rights as are referred to in subrule (i) above and the shipper shall cease to have such rights.

7. Delivery

(i) The carrier shall deliver the goods to the consignee upon production of proper identification.

(ii) The carrier shall be under no liability for wrong delivery if he can prove that he has exercised reasonable care to ascertain that the party claiming to be the consignee is in fact that party.

8. Validity

In the event of anything contained in these Rules or any such provisions as are incorporated into the contract of carriage by virtue of Rule 4, being inconsistent with the provisions of any International Convention or National Law compulsorily applicable to the contract of carriage, such Rules and provisions shall to that extent but no further be null and void.

CMI Rules for ELECTRONIC BILLS of LADING

Comité Maritime International – Paris, June 29, 1990

1. Scope of Application

These rules shall apply whenever the parties so agree.

2. Definitions

a. "Contract of Carriage" means any agreement to carry goods wholly or partly by sea.

b. "EDI" means Electronic Data Interchange, i.e. the interchange of trade data effected by teletransmission.

c. "UN/EDIFACT" means the United Nations Rules for Electronic Data Interchange for Administration, Commerce and Transport.

d. "Transmission" means one or more messages electronically sent together as one unit of dispatch which includes heading and terminating data.

e. "Confirmation" means a Transmission which advises that the content of a Transmission appears to be complete and correct, without prejudice to any subsequent consideration or action that the content may warrant.

f. "Private Key" means any technically appropriate form, such as a combination of numbers and/or letters, which the parties may agree for securing the authenticity and integrity of a Transmission.

g. "Holder" means the party who is entitled to the rights described in Article 7(a) by virtue of its possession of a valid Private Key.

h. "Electronic Monitoring System" means the device by which a computer system can be examined for the transactions that it recorded, such as a Trade Data Log or an Audit Trail.

i. "Electronic Storage" means any temporary, intermediate or permanent storage of electronic data including the primary and the back-up storage of such data.

3. Rules of Procedure

a. When not in conflict with these Rules, the Uniform Rules of Conduct for Interchange of Trade Data by Teletransmission, 1987 (UNCID) shall govern the conduct between the parties.

b. The EDI under these Rules should conform with the relevant UN/EDIFACT standards. However, the parties may use any other method of trade data interchange acceptable to all of the users.

c. Unless otherwise agreed, the document format for the Contract of Carriage shall conform to the UN Layout Key of compatible national standard for bills of lading.

d. Unless otherwise agreed, a recipient of a Transmission is not authorized to act on a Transmission unless he has sent a Confirmation.

e. In the event of a dispute arising between the parties as to the data actually transmitted, an Electronic Monitoring System may be used to verify the data received. Data concerning other transactions not related to the data in dispute are to be considered as trade secrets and thus not available for examination. If such data are unavoidably revealed as part of the examination of the Electronic Monitoring System, they must be treated as confidential and not released to any outside party or used for any other purpose.

f. Any transfer of rights to the goods shall be considered to be private information, and shall not be released to any outside party not connected to the transport or clearance of the goods.

4. Form and Content of the Receipt Message

a. The carrier, upon receiving the goods from the shipper, shall give notice of the receipt of the goods to the shipper by a message at the electronic address specified by the shipper.

b. This receipt message shall include:

   i. the name of the shipper;

   ii. the description of the goods, with any representations and reservations, in the same tenor as would be required if a paper bill of lading were issued;

   iii. the date and place of the receipt of the goods;

   iv. a reference to the carrier's terms and conditions of carriage; and

   v. the Private Key to be used in subsequent Transmissions.

   The shipper must confirm this receipt message to the carrier, upon which Confirmation the shipper shall be the Holder.

c. Upon demand of the Holder, the receipt message shall be updated with the date and place of shipment as soon as the goods have been loaded on board.

d. The information contained in (ii), (iii) and (iv) of paragraph (b) above, including the date and place of shipment if updated in accordance with paragraph (c) of this Rule, shall have the same force and effect as if the receipt message were contained in a paper bill of lading.

5. Terms and Conditions of the Contract of Carriage

a. It is agreed and understood that whenever the carrier makes a reference to its terms and conditions of carriage, these terms and conditions shall form part of the Contract of Carriage.

b. Such terms and conditions must be readily available to the parties to the Contract of Carriage.

c. In the event of any conflict or inconsistency between such terms and conditions and these Rules, these Rules shall prevail.

6. Applicable Law

The Contract of Carriage shall be subject to any international convention or national law which would have been compulsorily applicable if a paper bill of lading had been issued.

7. Right of Control and Transfer

a. The Holder is the only party who may, as against the carrier:

   (1) claim delivery of the goods;

   (2) nominate the consignee or substitute a nominated consignee for any other party, including itself;

   (3) transfer the Right of Control and Transfer to another party;

   (4) instruct the carrier on any other subject concerning the goods, in accordance with the terms and conditions of the Contract of Carriage, as if he were the holder of a paper bill of lading.

b. A transfer of the Right of Control and Transfer shall be effected: (i) by notification of the current Holder to the carrier of its intention to transfer its Right of Control and Transfer to a proposed new Holder, and (ii) Confirmation by the carrier of such notification message, whereupon (iii) the carrier shall transmit the information as referred to in article 4 [except for the Private Key] to the proposed new Holder, whereafter (iv) the proposed new Holder shall advise the carrier of its acceptance of the Right of Control and Transfer, whereupon (v) the carrier shall cancel the current Private Key and issue a new Private Key to the new Holder.

c. If the proposed new Holder advises the carrier that it does not accept the Right of Control and Transfer or fails to advise the carrier of such acceptance within a reasonable time, the proposed transfer of the

Right of Control and Transfer shall not take place. The carrier shall notify the current Holder accordingly and the current Private Key shall retain its validity.

d. The transfer of the Right of Control and Transfer in the manner described above shall have the same effect as the transfer of such rights under a paper bill of lading.

8. The Private Key

a. The Private Key is unique to each successive Holder. It is not transferable by the Holder. The carrier and the Holder shall each maintain the security of the Private Key.

b. The carrier shall only be obliged to send a Confirmation of an electronic message to the last Holder to whom it issued a Private Key, when such Holder secures the Transmission containing such electronic message by the use of the Private Key.

c. The Private Key must be separate and distinct from any means used to identify the Contract of Carriage, and any security password or identification used to access the computer network.

9. Delivery

a. The carrier shall notify the Holder of the place and date of intended delivery of the goods. Upon such notification the Holder has a duty to nominate a consignee and to give adequate delivery instructions to the carrier with verification by the Private Key. In the absence of such nomination, the Holder will be deemed to be the consignee.

b. The carrier shall deliver the goods to the consignee upon production of proper identification in accordance with the delivery instructions specified in paragraph (a) above; such delivery shall automatically cancel the Private Key.

c. The carrier shall be under no liability for misdelivery if it can prove that it exercised reasonable care to ascertain that the party who claimed to be the consignee was in fact that party.

10. Option to Receive a Paper Document

a. The Holder has the option at any time prior to delivery of the goods to demand from the carrier a paper bill of lading. Such document shall be made available at a location to be determined by the Holder, provided that no carrier shall be obliged to make such document available at a place where it has no facilities and in such instance the carrier shall only be obliged to make the document available at the facility nearest to the location determined by the Holder. The carrier shall not be responsible for delays in delivering the goods resulting from the Holder exercising the above option.

b. The carrier has the option at any time prior to delivery of the goods to issue to the Holder a paper bill of lading unless the exercise of such option could result in undue delay or disrupts the delivery of the goods.

c. A bill of lading issued under Rules 10(a) or (b) shall include: (i) the information set out in the receipt message referred to in Rule 4 (except for the Private Key); and (ii) a statement to the effect that the bill of lading has been issued upon termination of the procedures for EDI under the CMI Rules for Electronic Bills of Lading. The aforementioned bill of lading shall be issued at the option of the Holder either to the order of the Holder < whose name for this purpose shall then be inserted in the bill of lading > or to bearer.

d. The issuance of a paper bill of lading under Rule 10(a) or (b) shall cancel the Private Key and terminate the procedures for EDI under these Rules. Termination of these procedures by the Holder or the carrier will not relieve any of the parties to the Contract of Carriage of their rights, obligations or liabilities while performing under the present Rules nor of their rights, obligations or liabilities under the Contract of Carriage.

e. The Holder may demand at any time the issuance of a print-out of the receipt message referred to in Rule 4 (except for the Private Key) marked as ``non-negotiable copy.'' The issuance of such a print-out shall not cancel the Private Key nor terminate the procedures for EDI.

11. Electronic Data is Equivalent to Writing

The carrier and the shipper and all subsequent parties utilizing these procedures agree that any national or local law, custom or practice requiring the Contract of Carriage to be evidenced in writing and signed, is satisfied by the transmitted and confirmed electronic data residing on computer data storage media displayable in human language on a video screen or as printed out by a computer. In agreeing to adopt these Rules, the parties shall be taken to have agreed not to raise the defense that this contract is not in writing.

COMBITERMS 2000

Cost distribution between seller and buyer according to Incoterms 2000 in summary sea transport only

Trade terms[1]

Code	Term	Description	003	004	008	009	016	017
003	**FAS**	Free Alongside Ship (named port of shipment)						
004	**FOB**	Free On Board (named port of shipment)						
008	**CFR**	Cost and Freight (named port of destination)						
009	**CIF**	Cost, Insurance and Freight (named port of destination)						
016	**DES**	Delivered Ex Ship (named port of destination)						
017	**DEQ**	Delivered Ex Quay (named port of destination)						

Cost headings

Code	Heading	FAS	FOB	CFR	CIF	DES	DEQ
100	Loading at seller's premises	S	S	S	S	S	S
150	Domestic precarriage/Local cartage	S	S	S	S	S	S
200	Contract of carriage and dispatch	S	S	S	S	S	B
250	Trade documentation in country of exportation	S	S	S	S	S	S
300	Customs clearance in country of exportation	S	S	S	S	S	S
350	Export charges	S	S	S	S	S	S
400	Transshipment at carrier's terminal [2]	S	S	S	S	B	B
450	Transportation equipment and accessories	S	S	S	S	B	B
500	Transport (Cargo) insurance				S		
550	International main carriage	S	S	S	S	B	B
600	Transshipment at terminal [2]	S	B	S	S	B	B
650	Trade documentation in country of transit/importation	B	B	B	B	B	B
700	Customs clearance in country of importation	B	B	B	B	B	B
750	Import charges	B	B	B	B	B	B
800	Local cartage/Domestic on-carriage	B	B	B	B	B	B
850	Unloading at buyer's premises	B	B	B	B	B	B
900	Other costs **Cost distribution according to party agreement not regulated in incoterms**						

S=Seller pays **B**=Buyer pays

At certain cost headings there may be divergences to be observed from the cost distribution stated above. See remarks in Combiterms 2000 under the detailed description of each trade term.

Remarks

1 The terms FOB, CFR or CIF should be used only when the distribution of costs and/or risks between seller and buyer has been fixed at such time as the goods have passed the ship's rail in the named port of shipment. In other cases one of the corresponding terms FCA, CPT or CIP is more appropriate to use (see next page).

2 "Terminal" stands for quay wharf/port warehouse.

© Sveriges Transportindustriförbunds Service AB